150 YEARS OF
PHOTO JOURNALISM

THE HULTON DEUTSCH COLLECTION

150 YEARS OF PHOTO JOURNALISM

Volume II

Amanda Hopkinson

Könemann

First published in 1995 by Könemann Verlagsgesellschaft mbH
Bonner Straße 126, D-50968 Köln

© 1995 Könemann Verlagsgesellschaft mbH
© 1995 Hulton Deutsch Collection Ltd

Photographs drawn from the Hulton Deutsch Collection, London

This book was produced by The Hulton Deutsch Collection Ltd
Unique House, 21-31 Woodfield Road, London W9 2BA.

Art director: Peter Feierabend
Production manager: Detlev Schaper
Design: Paul Welti
Picture research: Leon Meyer, Sue Percival
Project editor: Elisabeth Ingles
German translation: Manfred Allié, Euskirchen
French translation: Sylvie Adam-Kuenen, Cologne;
Michèle Schreyer, Cologne
Typesetting: Peter Howard
Colour separation: Imago
Printed and bound by Neue Stalling, Germany
Printed in Germany

ISBN 3-89508-102-7

Contents

Inhalt

Sommaire

Introduction

WITHIN the span of fifty years this century, Europe was in the eye of two world wars. Thereafter, western powers were increasingly accused of exporting wars overseas, ostensibly on ideological grounds but in reality to protect economic and neo-colonial interests. Whilst the causes of the First World War remain debatably obscure, the Second World War united the Allied against the Axis countries in a battle increasingly portrayed as one against evil. The allegiance forged between Churchill, de Gaulle, Eisenhower and Stalin was soon to falter. The Korean and Vietnam Wars were joined by US forces sent on the pretext of halting the 'tumbling dice' of world Communism.

The Kremlin's determination to maintain control of the satellite states of the Soviet Union led to its much-decried military interventions in Hungary (1956) and Czechoslovakia (1968). Here the crushing was of largely spontaneous populist uprisings. In other countries, politically organized national liberation movements engaged in an armed struggle against the old imperial foreign powers. Erstwhile Commonwealth countries such as Canada won their autonomy without a struggle, although there is still a frustrated secessionist movement among the French-speaking Québecquois. India had blazed an independence trail through Gandhi's massively successful campaign of civil disobedience, only to find itself faced with partition, granting its substantial Moslem minority the northern territories that became known as Pakistan.

It became a hallmark of this allegedly godless century that religious wars were endemic once more. The increasing militance of Islam and the recourse to *jihad* (or holy war against the infidel) divided many countries against themselves, particularly in Balkan Europe and the Middle East. Here, too, the foundation of the state of Israel in 1948 appeared to Palestinians as another way in which Europe sought to displace its own problems. Civil wars erupted in countries overthrowing the ancient systems of oppression, most particularly in China where in 1949 Mao Tse-Tung inaugurated the People's Republic, the world's largest and one of the few continuing Communist countries.

Yet, curiously, the twentieth century has also been characterized by a popular desire and demand for peace. From small organisms of conscientious objectors during the First World War to worldwide Campaigns for Nuclear Disarmament, groups of individuals have grown into mass movements that have insisted on putting the human race first. Partly this is because wars increasingly affect civilians as much as or more than armies: according to Red Cross statistics, while 85 per cent of First World War casualties were military, the percentage was inverted (15 per cent military: 85 per cent civilian) during the Gulf War of 1988. While no one would advocate a return to the decimating trench warfare of the former, technological advances also rendered redundant the lining-up of armies for the battlefield slaughter. New technologies brought other sorts of advances too. In medicine, the spread of vaccines brought the eradication of smallpox, scarlet fever and leprosy worldwide; that of polio, yellow fever and hepatitis in many countries. Life expectancy virtually doubled in 'developed' countries with many living into their eighties and nineties, twice as long as a century earlier. Yet poorer regions remained plagued by avoidable diseases such as cholera and malaria.

Technological advances could also bring many of us culturally closer. Television soap serials have achieved mass popularity. A whole new art form, cinema, advanced to a peak in the Thirties and Forties. Realistic imaging came further within the popular remit through the widespread availability of cheap photo and video cameras. North American films and video games in particular were widely blamed for the promotion of impersonal violence, especially among the young, among whom sophisticated weaponry and a 'drug culture' were pervasive.

Fashions in music and clothes became complementary, with many regions abandoning traditional customs. Cheap travel on charter aircraft led to exotic tourist resorts producing interchangeable T-shirts and carrier bags worldwide. In turn, western centres of fashion sought inspiration in natural fibres and traditional patterns, particularly with the emergence of Japan on the fashion scene. Other clothes styles mimicked other technological advances: the first moonwalkers of the 1960s generated a rash of space outfits on the catwalks of Paris and Milan. Overall the move was towards more comfortable, wearable clothes and less formality, particularly in women's wear.

The fashionable emaciated look from the 1960s onwards also conflicted with what people increasingly knew about 'slimmer's diseases' such as anorexia and bulimia, and with the extent of world starvation. Wars that the cynical claimed were promoted more by arms manufacturers than ideological causes led to the number of migrants doubling in the 1980s alone. Whole peoples moved, fleeing wars and natural catastrophes, but also increasingly as 'economic refugees', seeking to escape living conditions under which they could not survive. While the global shift was from south to north and east to west, a continent such as Australasia became a whole new regional melting pot.

Despite flickering support for a revival of Italian fascism under Mussolini's granddaughter; the neo-Nazis in Germany and Austria; the racist policies of Le Pen's National Party in France and the British Movement, Europe at the close of this century is consolidating its union, finally incorporating the 'guest' populations it invited to immigrate at a time of rising employment following the Second World War. If the nineteenth century saw a net emigration of Europeans to overseas colonies, then the twentieth has witnessed a shift in the reverse direction. South Africa has finally (and relatively peacefully) transferred to majority rule, as has the last outpost of British imperialism, Northern Ireland. A belated consideration for the situation of indigenous peoples – from Amazon to Africa to Australia – goes hand-in-hand with a respect for their common understanding of the delicate interrelationship between the species of our planet.

For many of today's young generation, the overriding concern is for the sustainable future of the world as a whole, regardless of boundaries and nationalities. A scientifically raised awareness of the five species that every hour become extinct in this unrenewable world has galvanized the ecological impetus to render the destruction of the jungles of Borneo or Brazil of immediate impact in industrialized North America or Western Europe. The European Union, the Congress of Non-Aligned States, and the Organization of African or American States, are all phenomena that could not have been foreseen at this century's start. It remains for the next to reveal where present-day global concerns will lead, if the pursuit of harmony will outweigh that of war.

Einführung

IN einem Zeitraum von nur fünfzig Jahren haben in unserem Jahrhundert in Europa zwei Weltkriege getobt. Und seit Ende des letzten wird immer häufiger der Vorwurf laut, daß der Westen Kriege in andere Länder exportiere, unter ideologischem Vorwand, doch in Wirklichkeit aus ökonomischen und neo-kolonialistischen Motiven. Wie es zum Ersten Weltkrieg kam, ist bis heute umstritten; im Zweiten galt der Krieg der Alliierten gegen die Achsenmächte zusehends als der Kampf gegen das Böse schlechthin. Die Solidarität zwischen Churchill, de Gaulle, Eisenhower und Stalin sollte nicht lange halten — schon bald griffen amerikanische Truppen in den Korea- und den Vietnamkrieg ein, um, wie es hieß, dem Vormarsch des Weltkommunismus Einhalt zu gebieten.

Der Kreml war fest entschlossen, die Satellitenstaaten der Sowjetunion an der kurzen Leine zu halten, daher die militärischen Interventionen in Ungarn (1956) und der Tschechoslowakei (1968), die dem Ansehen der Sowjets sehr schadeten. Wurden hier weitgehend spontane Volksaufstände niedergeschlagen, so kämpften in anderen Ländern politisch organisierte nationale Befreiungsbewegungen mit Waffengewalt gegen die alten Kolonialmächte. Einstige Commonwealth-Staaten wie zum Beispiel Kanada erlangten ihre Unabhängigkeit kampflos, auch wenn im französischsprachigen Québec bis heute eine glücklose Separatistenbewegung tätig ist. In Indien hatte der ungeheure Erfolg von Gandhis Kampagne des zivilen Ungehorsams den Weg zur Unabhängigkeit gebahnt, doch mit ihr kam auch die Zweiteilung des Landes, bei der die große islamische Minderheit die nördlichen Territorien übernahm, die den Namen »Pakistan« erhielten.

Bezeichnend für dieses angeblich so gottlose Jahrhundert war, daß überall wieder Glaubenskriege aufflammten. Die zunehmende Militanz des Islam und die Rückkehr zum Dschihad (dem »heiligen Krieg« gegen die Ungläubigen) spaltete die Bevölkerung vieler Länder, besonders auf dem Balkan und im Mittleren Osten. Hier hatten die Palästinenser die Gründung des Staates Israel von 1948 als einen weiteren Versuch der Europäer empfunden, ihre eigenen Probleme auf die Einheimischen abzuwälzen. Überall, wo Länder das Joch ihrer alten Unterdrücker abschüttelten, kam es zu Bürgerkriegen, besonders heftig in China, wo Mao Tse-tung 1949 die Volksrepublik ausrief, das größte kommunistische Land der Erde und heute einer der letzten Überlebenden des Kommunismus.

Doch kurioserweise läßt sich das 20. Jahrhundert ebenso als ein Jahrhundert des weltweiten Strebens nach Frieden verstehen. Von einzelnen Kriegsdienstverweigerern im Ersten Weltkrieg zu weltweiten Kampagnen für nukleare Abrüstung sind aus Grüppchen und einzelnen Massenbewegungen geworden, für die die Rechte der Menschheit an erster Stelle stehen. Ein Grund dafür ist sicher, daß Kriege in zunehmendem Maße die Zivilbevölkerung treffen und im Verhältnis immer weniger das Militär: Nach Statistiken des Roten Kreuzes waren 85 Prozent der Opfer des Ersten Weltkriegs Soldaten, im Golfkrieg von 1988 war das Verhältnis umgekehrt (15 Prozent Soldaten gegenüber 85 Prozent Zivilisten). Doch niemand wird ernsthaft fordern, zu den verlustreichen Stellungskriegen zurückzukehren, und der technische Fortschritt macht den Aufmarsch der Truppen auf dem Schlachtfeld inzwischen ganz überflüssig. Auch im zivilen Bereich hat die neue Technik viele Schlachten gewonnen. In der Medizin sind durch Fortschritte der Impftechnik Pocken, Scharlach und Lepra weltweit ausgerottet, und Kinderlähmung, Gelbfieber und Hepatitis in vielen Ländern. Die Lebenserwartung in den Industrieländern verdoppelte sich, viele Menschen werden achtzig und neunzig Jahre, doppelt so alt, wie sie vor einem Jahrhundert geworden wären. Doch in den ärmeren Weltgegenden wüten vermeidbare Krankheiten wie Cholera und Malaria nach wie vor.

Technische Fortschritte brachten viele von uns auch kulturell näher zusammen. Fernsehserien erreichen ein gewaltiges Publikum. Eine ganz neue Kunstform, das Kino, kam in den 30er und 40er Jahren zur Blüte. Abbilder der Wirklichkeit wurden mit billigen Photoapparaten und Videokameras für jedermann erschwinglich. Doch andererseits gelten besonders nordamerikanische Filme und Videospiele als eine der Hauptursachen dafür, daß sinnlose Gewalt überall

Zyniker sagten, sie seien eher von den Waffenhändlern als von Ideologien angefacht, sorgten dafür, daß sich allein in den 80er Jahren die Zahl der Flüchtlinge verdoppelte. Ganze Völker waren auf Wanderschaft, flohen vor Kriegen und Naturkatastrophen, waren aber auch in immer stärkerem Maße als »Wirtschaftsflüchtlinge« auf der Flucht vor Verhältnissen, in denen sie nicht überleben konnten. Die globalen Wanderbewegungen verliefen von Süd nach Nord und von Ost nach West, und ein Kontinent wie Australien und Ozeanien wurde zum neuen regionalen Schmelztiegel.

Obwohl noch dann und wann die italienischen Neofaschisten unter Mussolinis Enkelin von sich reden machen, die Neonazis in Deutschland und Österreich, Le Pens Nationalpartei in Frankreich und die britischen Europagegner, steht doch am Ende dieses Jahrhunderts die europäische Einigung bevor, bei der auch die »Gäste« einbezogen werden, die nach dem Zweiten Weltkrieg zu der Zeit, als Arbeitskräftemangel herrschte, in die einzelnen Länder geholt wurden. Im 19. Jahrhundert emigrierten die Europäer in die überseeischen Kolonien, doch im 20. Jahrhundert kehrte sich die Richtung des Stromes um. Südafrika hat nun endlich (und vergleichsweise friedlich) die Regierung der Mehrheit übergeben, und ebenso haben es die Engländer in ihrer letzten Kolonie Nordirland getan. Nun endlich findet auch die Lage der Ureinwohner die Aufmerksamkeit, die sie verdient — vom Amazonas über Afrika bis nach Australien —, und mit dieser Aufmerksamkeit kommt ein Verständnis des ihnen allen gemeinsamen Sinns für das empfindliche Gleichgewicht der Spezies auf unserem Planeten.

Vielen in der heutigen jüngeren Generation kommt es vor allem darauf an, den Fortbestand der Welt als solcher zu sichern, ohne Rücksicht auf Grenzen und Nationalitäten. In jeder Stunde werden fünf Spezies dieses Planeten für immer ausgelöscht, und ein geschärftes ökologisches Bewußtsein hat uns vor Augen geführt, daß die Zerstörung der Regenwälder von Borneo und Brasilien nicht ohne Folgen für die Industrienationen Nordamerikas und Westeuropas bleiben wird. Die Europäische Union, der Kongreß unabhängiger Staaten, die Organisation afrikanischer oder amerikanischer Staaten — das alles sind Dinge, die zu Anfang dieses Jahrhunderts niemand vorausgesehen hätte. Es bleibt dem nächsten Jahrhundert überlassen zu zeigen, wohin die Sorgen der heutigen Welt führen werden und ob das Streben nach Harmonie den Drang zum Krieg überwinden wird.

zunimmt, besonders unter Jugendlichen, die leicht den hochtechnisierten Waffen und der »Drogenkultur« verfallen.

Musik- und Kleidungsmoden wurden weltumspannend und verdrängten in vielen Gegenden die einheimischen Traditionen völlig. Billige Charterflüge verbreiteten die immergleichen T-Shirts und Plastiktüten exotischer Reiseziele rund um den Erdball. Im Gegenzug suchten die westlichen Modezentren ihre Inspiration in Naturfasern und traditionellen Mustern, gerade nachdem die Japaner in der Modeszene Furore machten. Anderswo ahmte die Mode andere technische Fortschritte nach: Als die ersten Menschen auf dem Mond spazierten, sah man auf den Laufstegen von Paris und Mailand eine wahre Flut von Raumanzügen. Insgesamt geht die Tendenz hin zu bequemeren, tragbareren Kleidern, und besonders die Damenmode ist weniger formell geworden.

Das Schlankheitsideal der 60er Jahre stand in einem kuriosen Spannungsverhältnis zu dem, was nun über Krankheiten wie Magersucht bekannt wurde, und dem Hunger überall auf der Welt. Kriege, von denen die

Introduction

C'EST à deux reprises, au XXe siècle, qu'en l'espace de cinquante ans l'Europe s'est trouvée au cœur d'un conflit mondial. Par la suite, les puissances occidentales furent très vivement accusées d'exporter les guerres dans les régions d'outre-mer, masquant sous de fausses préoccupations idéologiques une défense évidente de leurs intérêts économiques et coloniaux. Alors que les causes de la guerre de 1914-1918 demeurent contestables et obscures, la Seconde Guerre mondiale unit les Alliés contre les pays de l'Axe dans une confrontation qui prendra de plus en plus l'allure d'une croisade contre le Mal. L'entente entre Churchill, de Gaulle, Eisenhower et Staline fut de courte durée. Les États-Unis engagèrent dans la guerre de Corée puis celle du Viêtnam sous le prétexte de stopper la progression du communisme dans le monde.

Comme par le passé, le Kremlin, qui était décidé à contrôler les États satellites de l'Union soviétique, intervint militairement en Hongrie (1956) et en Tchécoslovaquie (1968). Dans ces pays, le soulèvement populaire était en grande partie spontané. Dans d'autres, au contraire, ce furent des mouvements de libération nationale politiquement organisés qui engagèrent une lutte armée contre les vieilles puissances impérialistes. Pour la première fois, des pays appartenant au Commonwealth comme le Canada, malgré un mouvement indépendantiste frustré qui perdure chez les Québécois, obtinrent pacifiquement leur indépendance. L'Inde fit office de pionnière avec ses campagnes de désobéissance civile prônées par Gandhi. Elles rencontrèrent un écho favorable et montrèrent une réelle efficacité dans la lutte contre les Anglais. Plus tard, ce grand pays devra accorder les territoires du Nord à sa forte minorité musulmane, lesquels formeront ultérieurement le Pakistan.

Ce siècle, que l'on dit sans Dieu, est paradoxalement caractérisé par les guerres à caractère religieux. La montée en puissance de l'islamisme et le recours au Djihad (la Guerre sainte) divisa de nombreux pays en Europe, particulièrement dans la région des Balkans, mais aussi au Moyen-Orient. En 1948, la création de l'État d'Israël apparut aux Palestiniens comme une façon

pour l'Europe de déplacer ses propres problèmes. Des guerres civiles éclatèrent dans des pays qui renversaient les anciens systèmes d'oppression. Ce fut le cas en Chine où, dès 1949, Mao Tsé-Toung inaugura la République populaire, le plus vaste pays communiste du monde.

Paradoxalement, ce XXe siècle s'illustre aussi par une forte aspiration populaire à la paix. Depuis les petits groupes d'objecteurs de conscience contre la Première Guerre mondiale aux campagnes internationales pour le désarmement nucléaire, les individus organisés se sont regroupés au sein de mouvements de masse n'ayant pour autre ambition que de donner à l'être humain une place prépondérante. Il est vrai que, de plus en plus, les guerres modernes affectent tout autant, voire plus, les civils que les militaires. Selon les chiffres fournis par la Croix-Rouge, si 85% des victimes de la Première Guerre mondiale étaient des militaires, le pourcentage s'était exactement inversé en 1988 pendant le conflit du Golfe. Si la guerre meurtrière des tranchées appartient à une époque révolue, les progrès technologiques rendent également caduc l'alignement des armées sur le champ de bataille. Les techniques nouvelles ont généré aussi des progrès d'un autre genre, tout particulièrement dans le domaine médical. En effet, la propagation des vaccins a entraîné la disparition de la variole, de la scarlatine et de la lèpre dans le monde. L'éradication de la poliomyélite, de la fièvre jaune et de l'hépatite virale est en cours dans de nombreux pays. L'espérance de vie dans les nations développées, où l'existence se prolonge souvent entre quatre-vingts et quatre-vingt-dix ans, a doublé par rapport au siècle dernier. Néanmoins, les régions plus pauvres sont encore affligées de maladies, comme le choléra et le typhus, qu'il serait pourtant possible d'éradiquer.

Culturellement, les progrès technologiques seraient aussi susceptibles de rapprocher les populations. Qu'on le salue ou qu'on le déplore, il est incontestable que les séries télévisées populaires ont conquis de larges secteurs du public planétaire. Une toute nouvelle forme d'art, le cinéma, a connu son apogée durant les années 30 et 40. Puis l'image se popularisa irrésistiblement avec l'accession à la photo bon marché et au caméscope.

confortable et moins formelle de la confection, en particulier pour le vêtement féminin.

Dans les seules années 80, le nombre des émigrants doubla. Si la cause est à chercher dans les conflits où les intérêts des marchands d'armes et des usines d'armement l'emportent sur les motifs purement idéologiques, il n'en demeure pas moins qu'un exode de type nouveau est en train d'apparaître : celui des « réfugiés économiques » cherchant à échapper à des conditions difficiles qui ne permettent plus leur survie.

Tandis qu'on assistait à des transformations globales aussi bien du nord au sud que de l'est à l'ouest, un continent, s'affirma de plus en plus comme un tout nouveau creuset de cultures : l'Australie.

À la fin de ces années 80, en dépit de certains mouvements réactionnaires, l'Europe de cette fin de siècle consolide néanmoins son union, et tente tant bien que mal d'intégrer les travailleurs émigrés appelés à y travailler lors du boom de l'emploi consécutif à la Seconde Guerre mondiale.

Si le XIXᵉ siècle a vu les Européens émigrer vers les colonies d'outre-mer, le XXᵉ siècle fut le témoin du phénomène inverse.

L'Afrique du Sud, à l'instar de l'Irlande du Nord, est enfin (presque pacifiquement) passée à un gouvernement digne des nations démocratiques. Une nouvelle considération, bien que tardive, pour les populations autochtones amazonniennes, africaines et australiennes s'accompagne du respect et de la compréhension communes des relations délicates gouvernant les espèces qui peuplent notre planète.

Aujourd'hui, faisant fi des frontières et des nationalités, le souci primordial d'un grand nombre de jeunes concerne notre avenir commun. La prise de conscience, entretenue par les scientifiques, que chaque heure passée voit disparaître inexorablement cinq espèces dans le monde, a galvanisé l'élan écologique. Hormis une aide efficace en direction des jungles de Bornéo ou du Brésil, cet élan a permis d'avoir un impact immédiat dans les pays industrialisés d'Amérique du Nord et d'Europe de l'Ouest. L'Union européenne, le Congrès des États non alignés, l'Organisation des États africains ou américains sont autant de structures qu'il eût été difficile d'imaginer au début du siècle. Ce qu'il reste présentement à faire, c'est avant tout d'anticiper sur les problèmes actuels et de tout mettre en œuvre afin que la recherche de l'harmonie prenne le pas sur celle de la guerre.

Dans cette saga moderne, les films américains et les jeux vidéo furent accusés d'avoir servi la promotion de la violence anonyme, en particulier auprès des jeunes.

Dans le domaine de la musique et de la confection, l'apparition de la mode comme un important phénomène de société obligea de nombreuses régions à se défaire de leurs habitudes traditionnelles. Des charters se mirent à emmener les touristes, à des prix de plus en plus économiques, pour des destinations exotiques. Ceux-ci en ramenèrent tee-shirts et sacs en matière plastique qui, à leur tour, essaimèrent le globe. L'un après l'autre, les centres occidentaux de la confection cherchèrent l'inspiration dans les fibres naturelles et les modèles traditionnels. Ce mouvement fut surtout sensible après l'entrée du Japon sur la scène de la mode. D'autres styles vestimentaires intégrèrent les progrès scientifiques dans leurs créations : en 1968, les premiers hommes à marcher sur la Lune inspirèrent une série de tenues « spatiales » dans les défilés parisiens et milanais. En général, la mode s'orientait vers une conception plus

FIDEL CASTRO

VIRGINIA WOOLF

ALBERT EINSTEIN

INDIRA GANDHI

ALEXANDER FLEMING

QUEEN ELIZABETH II

LE CORBUSIER

EVA PERÓN

CHARLES DE GAULLE

PRINCESS GRACE

NIKITA KHRUSHCHEV

JACQUELINE ONASSIS

SIMONE DE BEAUVOIR

WINSTON CHURCHILL

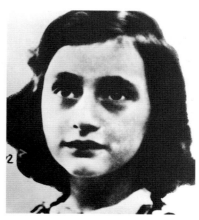

ANNE FRANK

IDI AMIN

MARILYN MONROE

ROBERT OPPENHEIMER

MOTHER TERESA

RICHARD NIXON

THE PRINCESS OF WALES

MAO TSE-TUNG

MARGARET THATCHER

ANDY WARHOL

Images

1918 to the present

Aspects of the 1920s and 1930s

UNTIL the twentieth century, fashion concerned men at least as much as women. Concepts such as 'power dressing' and 'dressing to kill' may not have been so labelled, but clothing as an expression of sex and control was a male province.

Fashion in women's attire developed relatively gradually in the nineteenth century, from the smooth sweep of crepe and chiffon in Empire-line gowns to the fussy bustles and lacy overskirts of the Victorian era. Power and sexuality were not yet linked to the role of women, which in the eighteenth and nineteenth centuries was primarily to be demure and obedient. That, at least, was the behaviour expected of upper-class women, those belonging to the only level of society which could afford to follow fashion anyway. Perhaps one of the greatest changes to take place in women's fashions this century is the factor of economic control. No longer attired merely as a delightful ornament displaying her husband's wealth, the twentieth-century woman can dress to please herself at a price she can afford. This has meant two major differences, both closely linked to women's new purchasing power. One is the growth of a medium-price range, independent of either couturier exclusivity or chain-store mass production; the other is a preference for garments practicable for work and daily living rather than decoration and ostentation.

The first major shift came in the wake of the Great War. With so many men away, women entered the industrial workplace in considerable numbers. Even after the war the male death toll from the trenches and the aftermath of the 'flu epidemic was so high that women never wholly returned to their home-bound role. The 1920s saw an adaptation of styles – bobbed haircuts, suits and trousers – to new living conditions, coloured by the whole mood of the flappers' jazz era.

The 1930s saw the parallel development of the well-dressed

1

woman, with her fitted bodice, stiletto heels and neat hat, and increasingly frenetic leisure designs to match the mood of the times. Fashion moved with the speed of new transport through increasingly racy styles. The rise of cabaret and film stars began to set the more masculine trends that became common currency in the 1940s: tailored trouser suits demonstrated that women were increasingly wearing the pants and even the top hats of the men, with accessories that stretched to copies of their cigarette holders and briefcases.

Gabrielle Chanel, nicknamed 'Coco', became a byword for neat elegance in the 1920s and '30s (2). She liberated women from corsets and heavy dresses, putting them instead into tailored suits and chemises and bobbed hairstyles. From a poor background, she mingled with the richest and most famous, but claimed never to feel truly at home. She never married. Her first perfume (called No.5 after her lucky number) became a world best-seller, and her costume jewellery gave the *nouveaux riches* permission to set aside their pearls. There was also plenty of scope for other unorthodox details – like the metal garters and the clocks on these silk stockings (1).

The elegance of Thirties fashion, as epitomized by the films of Myrna Loy, Ginger Rogers and Marlene Dietrich, was in strong contrast to the hard lives of Mid-West American farmers and their families, or the families of the poor and unemployed in Britain. The Depression following the Wall Street Crash of 1929 was a deeper and more far-reaching recession than any before or since. It led to a world slump, beginning with a drastic drop in wheat prices when over-production in the US and Canada flooded markets, and new competition from Soviet timber caused a further collapse. The despair of the Mid-West farmers was documented in the seminal book by Walker Evans and James Agee, *Let Us Now Praise Famous Men* (1930).

Bis zu unserem Jahrhundert war Mode mindestens ebensosehr eine Sache der Männer wie der Frauen. Zwar hat es Bezeichnungen wie »power dressing« oder »dressed to kill« noch nicht gegeben, doch von jeher kleideten Männer sich, um ihre Überlegenheit und Sexualität zu zeigen.

Die Damenmode des 19. Jahrhunderts entwickelte sich nach und nach vom weichen Fall der Empirekleider aus Crêpe und Chiffon zu den gekünstelten Turnüren und Spitzenüberröcken der viktorianischen Zeit. Macht und Sexualität kamen im Frauenbild dieser Zeit noch nicht vor, denn im 18. und frühen 19. Jahrhundert hatte eine Frau vor allem still und gehorsam zu sein, zumindest eine Frau der Oberschicht, und sie waren die einzigen, die es sich leisten konnten, mit der Mode zu gehen. Darin bestand vielleicht die größte Neuerung der Mode unseres Jahrhunderts — daß sie nun nicht mehr den Wohlhabenden vorbehalten war. Die Frau des 20. Jahrhunderts war nicht mehr nur ein hübsches Zierstück, mit dem ihr Mann seinen Wohlstand demonstrierte, sondern Frauen konnten tragen, was sie wollten, jede nach ihrem Geschmack und ihrem Geldbeutel. Das brachte zwei große Veränderungen mit sich. Zum einen kamen Kleider mittlerer Preislage auf, unabhängig von den exklusiven Modehäusern und den Massenprodukten der Kaufhäuser; zum anderen lag das Schwergewicht nun auf praktischer Kleidung für Alltag und Beruf und nicht mehr auf Prunk und Dekor.

Die ersten grundlegenden Wandlungen kamen im Zuge des Ersten Weltkriegs. Ein Großteil der Männer war im Feld, und ein beträchtlicher Teil der Frauen begann nun in den Fabriken zu arbeiten. Und auf den Schlachtfeldern und anschließend der großen Grippeepidemie kamen so viele Männer um, daß die Frauen nie wieder ganz an ihren alten Platz am heimischen Herd zurückkehrten. In den 20er Jahren paßte sich der Stil den veränderten Lebensumständen an — die Frauen hatten nun kurze Haare, trugen Kostüme und Hosen, und alles war geprägt vom Lebensgefühl des Jazz-Zeitalters.

In den 30er Jahren entwickelten sich nebeneinander das Bild der gut gekleideten Frau mit enger Taille, hohen Absätzen und adrettem Hut und eine immer ausgefallener werdende Freizeitmode, in der die Stimmung der Zeit zum Ausdruck kam. Der Aufstieg von Kabarett- und Filmstars prägte nun den eher maskulin bestimmten Stil der 40er Jahre: Maß-geschneiderte Anzüge zeigten, daß Frauen zusehends die Hosen und sogar die Zylinderhüte der Männer trugen, und zudem schmückten sie sich mit typisch männlichen Accessoires, mit Zigarettenspitzen und Aktentaschen.

MODEFOTOGRAFIE FÜR DAS HAUS SEEBERGER FRÈRES.

Gabrielle Chanel, genannt »Coco«, wurde in den 20er und 30er Jahren zum Inbegriff gepflegter Eleganz (2). Sie befreite die Frauen von Korsetts und schweren Stoffen und steckte sie statt dessen in Schneiderkostüme und Hemden.

Nirgends kommt die Eleganz der Mode der 30er Jahre besser zum Ausdruck als in den Filmen mit Stars wie Myrna Loy, Ginger Rogers und Marlene Dietrich, und der Kontrast zum anstrengenden Leben amerikanischer Farmer im Mittelwesten oder den Armen und Arbeitslosen in England hätte nicht größer sein können. Die Wirtschaftskrise nach dem Schwarzen Freitag 1929 brachte tiefgreifendere Veränderungen mit sich als jede andere Krise zuvor oder danach. Die ganze Welt wurde in den Strudel gerissen; die Weizenpreise fielen drastisch, als die Überproduktion aus den Vereinigten Staaten und Kanada die Märkte überschwemmte, und die neue Konkurrenz sowjetischer Holzhändler brachte einen weiteren Markt zum Zusammenbruch. Walker Evans und James Agee hielten das Elend der Farmer des Mittelwestens 1930 in einem einflußreichen Buch fest, *Let Us Now Praise Famous Men*.

PHOTOGRAPHIE DE MODE POUR
LA MAISON DE SEEBERGER FRÈRES.

Jusqu'au XXᵉ siècle la mode était une affaire d'hommes autant que de femmes. Même si l'habit en tant qu'arme de « puissance » et de « séduction » était encore un concept inexistant, il n'en demeurait pas moins à l'usage exclusif des hommes comme l'expression du pouvoir sexuel et de la domination.

La mode s'imposa dans le vêtement féminin plutôt petit à petit au cours du XIXᵉ siècle, évoluant du drapé lisse du crêpe et du chiffon de la ligne Empire jusqu'aux tournures maniérées et aux tabliers en dentelle de l'ère victorienne. Ni le pouvoir ni la sexualité n'étaient encore rattachés au rôle de la femme, qui se devait avant tout, aux XVIIIᵉ et XIXᵉ siècles, d'être grave et obéissante. Tel était du moins le comportement attendu des femmes de la bourgeoisie, seules à pouvoir se permettre le luxe de suivre la mode. La maîtrise du pouvoir économique permettra à la femme du XXᵉ siècle de s'habiller selon ses moyens et ses propres goûts. Deux grands phénomènes sont étroitement liés au nouveau pouvoir d'achat de la femme. L'un est l'apparition d'une gamme de prix moyens indépendants des couturiers exclusifs et des productions en série des grands magasins. L'autre est la préférence donnée aux vêtements de travail ou de tous les jours pour lesquels on privilégie le côté pratique au détriment de la décoration et de l'ostentation.

Le premier grand changement se produisit dans le sillage de la Grande Guerre. À cause du nombre élevé d'hommes absents, les femmes s'engouffrèrent en masse dans l'industrie. Même après la fin de la guerre, où tant d'hommes avaient trouvé la mort dans les tranchées tandis que d'autres avaient été décimés par l'épidémie de grippe, les femmes ne se cantonnèrent plus jamais entièrement à un rôle exclusif de ménagère. Dans les années 20, les styles s'adaptent – coiffures à la Jeanne d'Arc, ensembles et pantalons – aux nouvelles conditions de vie et aux couleurs d'une époque jazzy à l'humeur « garçonne ».

Au cours des années 30, on assiste à une évolution vers la femme bien habillée, au corsage ajusté, aux talons aiguilles et au chapeau coquet, à l'apparition de lignes toujours plus frénétiquement décontractées pour répondre à l'humeur du jour. Le succès grandissant des cabarets et des vedettes de cinéma participe au lancement des tendances plus masculines qui devaient se généraliser durant les années 40 : les femmes portent de plus en plus le pantalon et même le chapeau haut-de-forme agrémentés d'accessoires inspirés de leurs fume-cigarettes et leurs serviettes. Gabrielle Chanel, surnommée « Coco », devint synonyme d'élégance dans les années 20 et 30 (2). Elle débarrassa la femme de ses corsets et de ses lourdes robes qu'elle remplaça par des ensembles sur mesure, des robes-chemisiers et des coiffures courtes. Issue d'un milieu modeste, elle fréquenta les plus riches et les plus célèbres, mais affirma toujours ne pas se sentir vraiment à l'aise en leur compagnie. Elle ne se maria jamais. Son premier parfum (baptisé Nᵒ 5, d'après son chiffre porte-bonheur) remporta un succès commercial mondial, tandis que ses bijoux, en toc, donnaient aux nouveaux riches la permission de laisser leurs perles à la maison. D'autres détails aussi peu orthodoxes étaient admis, telles ces jarretières métalliques et les broderies sur le côté de ces bas en soie (1). L'élégance de la mode des années 30 dont les films de Myrna Loy, Ginger Rogers et Marlène Dietrich se faisaient les ambassadeurs contrastait violemment avec l'existence difficile des pauvres et des chômeurs en Grande-Bretagne. L'effondrement de la bourse de Wall Street en 1929 entraîna une récession d'une ampleur et d'une gravité sans précédent. Elle fut suivie d'un marasme mondial qui commença par la chute brutale des prix du blé. Le désespoir des fermiers du Middle West est décrit dans un ouvrage, écrit par Walker Evans et James Agee, intitulé *Let Us Now Praise Famous Men* (1930).

© MACK SENNETT COMEDIES
5110 B.

THE cult of the body beautiful, 1925. Suntanned legs might just be coming into fashion but shoes must be worn on the beach at all costs. These bathing belles sport costumes as artificial as their smiles, and what happens to this kind of 'skating skirt' in the salt water doesn't bear thinking about. But perhaps swimming is not too high up on the agenda.

DER Kult des schönen Körpers, 1925. Sonnengebräunte Beine kamen gerade in Mode, doch niemand ging ohne Schuhe an den Strand. Diese Badenixen führen Kleider vor, die genauso unnatürlich sind wie ihr Lächeln, und was aus einem solchen Röckchen, das eher an ein Eislaufkostüm erinnert, wird, wenn es ins Salzwasser kommt, ist gar nicht auszudenken. Doch hatte Badevergnügen wahrscheinlich ohnehin keine Priorität.

LE culte du beau corps, 1925. Les jambes bronzées devenaient peut-être à la mode, mais les chaussures n'en restaient pas moins, quoi qu'il en coûtât, indispensables sur la plage. Ces jolies baigneuses paradent dans des tenues aussi artificielles que leurs sourires. En outre, on frémit à la pensée de ce qui pouvait arriver dans l'eau salée avec ce genre de « jupe de patinage ». Mais la nage ne figurait pas forcément au programme.

2

THEATRE had a part to play in a model's training. This German model is dramatically posed and lit to make a back view as alluring as a front one, the head tossed to one side like a cabaret singer's (1). Elsa Schiaparelli (2), remarkable for her unexpected plainness in one devoted to beauty, and primarily known for her fashion choice of a shocking pink that came to be called after her, here puts down a further marker. Arriving in London in 1935, she announced 'Trousers for Women' in the same crusading tone as 'Votes for Women'. And to demonstrate that she, too, is on to a winner, she wears them herself, albeit in more restrained form as culottes.

DAS Theater spielte einen wichtigen Part bei der Ausbildung eines Models. Dieses deutsche Mannequin nimmt eine dramatische Pose ein und ist so beleuchtet, daß die Rückenansicht genauso anziehend wirkt wie ein Frontalporträt; den Kopf hat sie zur Seite geworfen wie eine Sängerin im Kabarett (1). Elsa Schiaparelli (2), die sich für eine Modeschöpferin immer betont einfach kleidete, und die vor allem durch den nach ihr benannten schockierenden Rosaton im Gedächtnis geblieben ist, macht hier ein weiteres Mal Geschichte. Bei ihrer Ankunft in London im Jahre 1935 forderte sie »Hosen für die Frau« mit den gleichen flammenden Worten, mit denen zuvor »Wahlrecht für die Frau« gefordert worden war. Und um zu zeigen, daß sie ebenso siegesgewiß ist, trägt sie sie gleich selbst, wenn auch in der gemäßigten Form der Culotte.

L'ART dramatique faisait partie de la formation des mannequins. On a fait prendre à ce mannequin allemand une pose théâtrale sous un éclairage destiné à la rendre aussi aguichante de dos que de face, la tête inclinée sur le côté à la manière d'une chanteuse de cabaret (1). Elsa Schiaparelli (2), remarquable de simplicité, ce qui est inattendu chez quelqu'un qui se consacre à la beauté, était avant tout connue en raison du rose flamboyant, qui reçut son nom, et qu'elle choisit de mettre à la mode. On la voit poser ici un nouveau jalon. Arrivée à Londres en 1935, elle proclama « les femmes en pantalon » sur le même ton revendicatif que « le vote aux femmes ». Elle-même le portait pour se montrer dans le coup, bien que dans sa variante plus modeste de jupe-culotte.

1   2

THERE is something self-consciously out-to-shock about the contemporary captions to these beach beauty pictures. Though it is evidently *risqué* to show her legs in a public place, this model's daring has to be infantilized: she is dressed like a child in 'a yellow linen sunsuit [which] makes a charming background for the quaint shell bead necklace, the latest in country jewellery' (1). In 1932, the outsized Japanese butterflies beneath their parasols remind us: 'Women smokers number almost as many as the men these days, and it was natural for these bathers to produce cigarettes and matches as they enjoyed a laze in the sun on the diving board at Cliftonville' (2).

DIE Texte, mit denen seinerzeit diese Bilder von Strandschönheiten präsentiert wurden, haben etwas bemüht Kokettes. Bei dem linken zum Beispiel wird das Mannequin, obwohl es ja damals gewagt war, soviel Bein in der Öffentlichkeit zu zeigen, beschrieben wie ein kleines Mädchen: »Sonnenanzug aus gelbem Leinen, genau das Richtige, um das putzige Muschelkollier zu zeigen, der letzte Schrei in Spielzeugschmuck« (1).

1932 geben uns diese Mesdames Butterfly unter ihren Sonnenschirmen zu verstehen: »Es gibt heute fast ebenso viele Raucherinnen wie Raucher, und diese drei, die auf einem Sprungbrett in Cliftonville die Sonne genießen, finden überhaupt nichts dabei, ihre Zigarettenpäckchen und Streichhölzer hervorzuholen.« (2)

LES légendes rédigées par les contemporains sur ces photographies de beautés posant sur la plage ont décidément un petit quelque chose de délibérément choquant ! Même s'il était manifestement risqué de montrer ses jambes dans un lieu public, l'audace de ce mannequin se doit d'être infantilisée : elle est habillée de manière enfantine, sa « tenue de plage en lin jaune faisant ressortir de façon charmante un bien joli collier de coquillages, dernier cri en matière de bijou de plein air » (1). En 1932, ces papillons japonais plus grands que nature sous leurs parasols nous rappellent que « les femmes sont presque aussi nombreuses à fumer que les hommes aujourd'hui, et [que] c'était un geste naturel pour ces baigneuses de sortir des cigarettes et des allumettes tout en prenant le soleil sur leur plongeoir à Cliftonville » (2).

DANCERS take a break from Manhattan's *Merry Whirl* show, sporting their 'Koko Kooler' headgear to protect themselves less from the New York sun than from its refraction off the water's surface (1). Meanwhile in Britain in 1932, the craze for sailor flares allowed copious display of back and behind at Thorpe Bay's 'pyjama parade', worthy of the West End hit musical *The Pajama Game* (2).

EINE Pause für die Tänzerinnen der *Merry Whirl*-Show in Manhattan. Die »Koko Kooler«–Hüte schützen sie weniger vor der New Yorker Sonne als vor den Reflexionen des Lichts im Wasser (1). In

England waren 1932 nach dem großen Erfolg des West-End-Musicals *The Pajama Game* Seglerhosen in Mode, und hier auf der »Seemannsparade« in Thorpe Bay wurden Rücken und Po gezeigt (2).

L ES danseuses pendant une pause du spectacle de Manhattan, *Merry Whirl*, paradent avec leur couvre-chef « Koko Kooler », moins destiné à les protéger du soleil new-yorkais que de sa réfraction à la surface de l'eau (1). Pendant qu'en

Grande-Bretagne, à Thorpe Bay, en 1932, l'engouement pour les lignes évasées des vêtements de marin permettait de dénuder généreusement le dos et les reins à la « pyjama parade », digne du spectacle de variétés en vogue à West End, *The Pajama Game* (2).

PHYSICAL studies, often linked to eurythmics and Isadora Duncan-style 'Greek' dancing, was a part of a whole back-to-nature programme current in the 1920s. In Germany this had a more sinister dimension, working on an assumption of human perfectability that chimed in with Hitlerian notions of higher beings derived from the combination of female spirituality and male superiority.

LEIBESÜBUNGEN, oft verbunden mit Eurhythmie und »griechischen« Tänzen in der Art Isadora Duncans, waren ein wichtiger Teil der Zurück-zur-Natur-Bewegung der 20er Jahre. In Deutschland hatte dies eine unheilvolle Seite, weil dort die Vervollkommnung des Körpers mit der Nazi-Ideologie einherging, nach der die Verbindung weiblicher Spiritualität mit männlicher Überlegenheit Übermenschen hervorbringen sollte.

L'ÉTUDE du corps, souvent liée à la gymnastique rythmique et à la danse d'inspiration « grecque » telle que celle d'Isadora Duncan, faisait partie de tout un programme de retour à la nature alors en vogue dans les années 20. En Allemagne elle avait pris des contours plus sinistres, développant l'affirmation de la perfectibilité de l'homme et popularisant les notions hitlériennes d'êtres supérieurs nés de la combinaison de la spiritualité féminine et de la supériorité masculine aryennes.

THE theories behind the cult of physical education had something in common with present-day 'New Age' philosophies, communing with nature, attuning to the elements and 'alpha-waving' the brain into harmony with the spheres. American girls took it up enthusiastically, whether singly (2) or in groups like Ida Schnall's Daily Dozen girls, forming a starfish on Brighton Beach, New York (1).

DIE Weltanschauung, die hinter solchen Leibesübungen stand, hatte vieles mit unseren heutigen New-Age-Philosophien gemeinsam — Einklang mit der Natur, »Alphawellen« des Hirns, die im Rhythmus

der Sphärenharmonien schwingen. Amerikanerinnen machten begeistert mit, ob allein (2) oder in Gruppen wie Ida Schnalls Daily Dozen Girls, die hier einen Seestern am New Yorker Brighton Beach bilden (1).

Les théories inspirant le culte de la culture physique présentent des traits communs avec les philosophies actuelles du « Nouvel Âge » : communier avec la nature, être à l'unisson des éléments et amener le cerveau en harmonie avec les sphères par le « flux alpha ». Elles furent reprises avec enthousiasme par les Américaines, en solitaire (2) ou en groupe ; ainsi les « Daily Dozen Girls » de Ida Schnall dessinant sur la plage de Brighton, à New York, une étoile de mer (1).

HOUSEWIVES in 1930s Germany were
encouraged to accompany domestic
virtue with body-toning gymnastics, high
heels notwithstanding: how to make the bed
healthily! (3). Filmstar Joan Crawford (1),
formerly a dancer, gave the high kick her all
– and an international seal of marketability.
At the English Scandinavian Summer School
of Physical Education in Kent, 130 pupils
from 14 countries demonstrated their lessons
in balance and poise on the parallel bars (2).

DEUTSCHE Hausfrauen der 30er Jahre
sollten auch bei der Hausarbeit ihren
Körper mit Gymnastik stählen: So wird
athletisch das Bett gemacht, und noch dazu
in Stöckelschuhen! (3) Als ehemalige
Tänzerin wußte Filmstar Joan Crawford die
Beine zu schwingen (1) und kam damit
überall auf der Welt an. An der Englisch-
Skandinavischen Sommerschule für
Sporterziehung in Kent demonstrierten 130
Schülerinnen aus 14 Ländern ihr Können
am Barren (2).

DANS les années 30, les ménagères
allemandes étaient encouragées à ne pas
oublier, outre leurs vertus domestiques, de
travailler leurs corps par la gymnastique :
comment faire le lit de façon efficace avec
de hauts talons ! (3). La vedette de cinéma,
Joan Crawford (1), avait été danseuse : elle
donna ici son maximum ; ce qui lui valut de
connaître une réussite commerciale
internationale importante. À l'école d'été
d'éducation physique anglo-scandinave, dans
le Kent, 130 élèves venues de 14 pays font
une démonstration de ce qu'elles ont appris
en restant en équilibre sur des poutres (2).

2

3

IN 1932, office workers from the City of London took to the rooftops. With Tower Bridge in the background and Adelaide House beneath their feet, 40 secretaries spent their lunch-hour skipping (1). A decade later, the great outdoors was a suitable background for some rather strained and unusual ballet exercises, demonstrated by dancers for the average housewife to follow (3). In 1935, contingents of The Women's League of Health and Beauty, an organization which had adopted some of the ideals then current in Germany, proclaimed 'AIM: RACIAL HEALTH' on their banners as they arrived in London's Hyde Park to give a display (2).

I<small>M</small> Jahre 1932 stiegen Londoner Büroangestellte auf die Dächer. Vierzig Sekretärinnen verbringen ihre Mittagspause mit Seilspringen, im Hintergrund die Tower Bridge, unter sich das Adelaide House (1). Zehn Jahre später gab die freie Natur den passenden Hintergrund für diese merkwürdigen und nicht ganz einfach aussehenden Ballettübungen ab; Tänzerinnen führten sie vor, und Hausfrauen sollten sie nachturnen (3). 1935 marschierte die Women's League of Health and Beauty (Frauenliga für Schönheit und Gesundheit), die einige der damals in Deutschland herrschenden Ideale übernommen hatte, unter dem Banner »UNSER ZIEL: GESUNDHEIT DER RASSE« im Londoner Hyde Park auf (2).

E<small>N</small> 1932, des employées de la City de Londres montent sur les toits. Le pont de la Tour dans le dos, l'Adelaïde House sous les pieds, 40 secrétaires font du saut à la corde pendant leur pause-déjeuner (1).

Dix ans plus tard, les grands espaces se prêteront tout à fait à des exercices de ballet passablement éprouvants et inhabituels à l'intention de la ménagère ordinaire (3). En 1935, des détachements de la Ligue féminine de la santé et de la beauté, organisation qui avait adopté certains des idéaux en vogue en Allemagne, déployaient des bannières proclamant « OBJECTIF : SANTÉ RACIALE » en arrivant à Hyde Park, à Londres, pour s'y livrer à une démonstration(2).

DEVICES for those loath to undertake serious exercise but prepared to submit to slimming devices. One woman greets the 'first appearance in England of New Gymnastic Apparatus' designed for a confined space by simultaneously somersaulting and cartwheeling (1). Another demonstrates the 'spring leg' which comes with the aim of 'perfecting the limbs' as a 'developing treatment for our athletic ladies' (2). Rosemary Andree straps her high heels and, rather bravely, her neck into a 'slimming exerciser' whose exact function remains a mystery (3).

GERÄTE für alle, die zwar nichts für Sport übrighatten, aber um der Schlankheit willen turnen wollten. Eine Frau begrüßt »das erste Exemplar eines neuartigen Gymnastikapparates in England«, mit dem man auf engem Raum gleichzeitig einen Purzelbaum schlagen und eine Rolle drehen konnte (1). Eine andere führt die »Beinfeder« vor, die »perfekte Waden« versprach, eine »Trainingshilfe für unsere Athletinnen« (2). Rosemary Andree hat keine Furcht, Stöckelschuhe und Hals in diesen »Schlankheitstrimmer« zu stecken, dessen genaue Funktion rätselhaft bleibt (3).

DES installations étaient à la disposition de celles qui, peu enclines à éxécuter des exercices sérieux, étaient prêtes néammoins à se soumettre à l'action des appareils « amincissants ». Une dame se réjouit de la « première apparition en Angleterre d'un nouvel appareillage de gymnastique », conçu pour les petits espaces, permettant tout à la fois les sauts périlleux et les roues (1). Une autre fait la démonstration de la « jambe à ressort », qui avait pour objectif de « perfectionner les membres » par un « traitement extensif à l'intention de nos dames athlétiques » (2). Rosemary Andree passe ses hauts talons et – fort courageusement – son cou dans les courroies d'un « appareil amincissant » dont le fonctionnement exact demeure un mystère (3).

2

1

3

FROM January 1920 until December 1933 'the manufacure, sale or carriage' of alcoholic drink was forbidden by the 18th Amendment to the US Constitution. Kegs (2) were destroyed by federal police. 'Bootlegging' (illicit distilling and distribution) fell under the control of criminal gangs who went to war with each other to secure profits. Seven members of the O'Banion-Moran gang were lined up against a Chicago warehouse wall in 1929 and machine-gunned in what became known as the St Valentine's Day Massacre (1). The Depression that followed the Wall Street Crash of 1929 led to a world slump. The US bread-basket turned rapidly into a dustbowl, forcing families to tramp off in search of work (5). Some joined the breadlines in the major cities (3). The photographer Dorothea Lange documented some of the resulting desolation (4).

VOM Januar 1920 bis zum Dezember 1933 waren »Herstellung, Verkauf oder Besitz« von Alkohol in den Vereinigten Staaten per Gesetz verboten (18. Amendment der Verfassung, die Prohibition). Bundespolizisten zerschlugen die Fässer (2). Das Schwarzbrennen (bootlegging) wurde von Verbrecherbanden gesteuert, die sich gegenseitig bekämpften, um sich möglichst hohe Profite zu sichern.

Im sogenannten Massaker am Valentinstag wurden 1929 in Chicago sieben Mitglieder der O'Banion-Moran-Gang in einem Lagerhaus an die Wand gestellt und mit dem Maschinengewehr erschossen (1). Die große Wirtschaftskrise, die auf den Schwarzen Freitag an der Wall Street (1929) folgte, zog die ganze Welt mit hinab. Die Kornkammer Amerikas verwandelte sich im Handumdrehen in eine Staubwüste, die Farmerfamilien mußten fortziehen und anderswo Arbeit suchen (5). Manche standen bald bei den Suppenküchen der Großstädte an (3). Die Photographin Dorothea Lange gehörte zu denen, die das Elend dokumentierten (4).

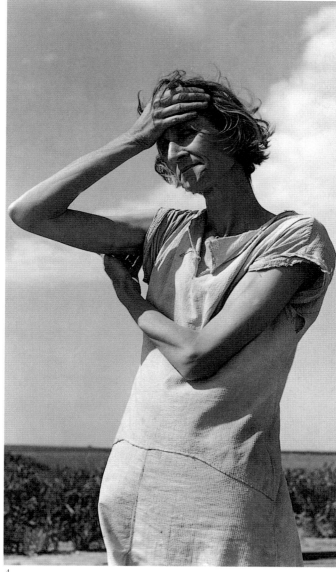

De janvier 1920 à décembre 1933, « la fabrication, la vente ou le transport » de boissons alcoolisées sont interdits en vertu du dix-huitième amendement de la Constitution des États-Unis. Les barils (2) étaient détruits par la police fédérale. La distillation et la distribution illégales sont réglées par les gangs de malfaiteurs qui se font la guerre afin d'en contrôler les bénéfices. Sept membres du gang O'Banion-Moran furent alignés et mitraillés contre le mur d'un entrepôt à Chicago en 1929 au cours de ce qui fut appelé le massacre de la Saint-Valentin (1). La dépression, qui suivit l'effondrement de la bourse de Wall Street en 1929, entraîna le marasme mondial. L'Eldorado américain s'assécha très vite, contraignant des familles entières à partir sur les routes à la recherche d'un travail (5). Certaines vinrent gonfler les queues devant les centres de ravitaillement des principales villes (3). La photographe Dorothea Lange exécuta tout un dossier sur les ravages ainsi produits (4).

UNEMPLOYMENT in the 1930s: sit-ins at a Welsh colliery (1); the Jarrow Crusade, a march by the jobless from the North (2); riots in Bristol (3); the Prince of Wales visits miners' homes on a tour of the coalfields (4).

ARBEITSLOSIGKEIT in den 30er Jahren: Proteste walisischer Bergarbeiter (1); der »Jarrow-Kreuzzug«, ein Hungermarsch der Arbeitslosen aus dem englischen Norden (2); Aufstände in Bristol (3); der Prince of Wales besucht Bergarbeiterhäuser auf seiner Rundfahrt durch die Bergwerksgebiete (4).

CHÔMAGE dans les années 30 : occupation d'une houillère dans le Pays de Galles (1) ; la croisade de Jarrow, marche des chômeurs descendus du Nord (2) ; émeutes à Bristol (3) ; le Prince de Galles rendant visite à des familles de mineurs au cours d'une tournée dans les bassins houillers (4).

2

CHILDREN'S street games include any number of domestic improvisations: washing lines for swings (1) and skipping-ropes; chalked pavements for hopscotch and football; old furniture goalposts and a particular kind of leapfrog (2) to cries of 'Jimmy Jimmy Knacker 1-2-3!' These pictures of East End slums were published in *Picture Post* in 1950, at the height of Labour Party reforming welfare legislation. The magazine had been a longtime campaigner for the Beveridge Report, written by the Master of University College, Oxford, and published in 1942. It proposed a comprehensive scheme of social insurance 'from the cradle to the grave' as checks against poverty and mass unemployment. It was the Churchill government's refusal to take its implementation seriously that helped the Labour Party's victorious landslide in the 1945 elections on a platform of 'free welfare, healthcare and education for all'.

DIE Kinder auf der Straße konnten aus allem ein Spiel machen: Aus Wäscheleinen wurden Schaukeln (1) oder Springseile; auf das Pflaster wurden mit Kreide Fußballfelder oder Felder für Himmel und Hölle gezeichnet; Torpfosten bestanden aus alten Möbeln, und es gab eine bestimmte Art von Froschhüpfen (2), zu dem man »Jimmy Jimmy Knacker 1-2-3!« brüllte. Diese Aufnahmen aus den Slums des Londoner East End erschienen 1950 in der *Picture Post*, zu der Zeit, als die Labour-Regierung die Wohlfahrtsgesetze reformierte. Die Illustrierte hatte sich schon seit längerem für den Beveridge Report eingesetzt, ein vom Master des University College, Oxford, 1942 veröffentlichtes Papier, in dem dieser sich für eine umfassende Sozialversicherung »von der Wiege bis zum Grabe« als dem besten Mittel gegen Verelendung und Massenarbeitslosigkeit aussprach. Die Regierung Churchill nahm diese Vorschläge nicht ernst, und dadurch erklärt sich der überwältigende Erfolg der Labour Party bei den Wahlen von 1945.

LES enfants jouaient dans la rue avec toutes sortes d'articles ménagers : des cordes à linge en guise de balançoires (1) et cordes à sauter ; de la craie pour la marelle et le football ; du vieux mobilier comme poteaux de but et pour un saute-mouton particulier (2) aux cris de « Jimmy Jimmy Knacker 1-2-3 ! » Ces photographies des bidonvilles de East End parurent dans le *Picture Post* en 1950, au plus fort de la mise en place par le parti travailliste d'une législation réformant la protection sociale. La revue faisait depuis longtemps campagne en faveur du rapport Beveridge, paru en 1942, dont l'auteur n'était autre que le principal du University College à Oxford. Il proposait un plan exhaustif d'assurance sociale pour parer « du berceau jusqu'à la tombe » à la pauvreté et au chômage généralisé. C'est le refus du gouvernement de Churchill de le mettre sérieusement en œuvre qui valut au parti travailliste sa victoire éclatante aux élections de 1945 sur la plate-forme de la « gratuité pour tous des services sociaux, des soins de santé et de l'instruction ».

THESE back-to-backs had changed little since they were first built at the height of the Industrial Revolution. Insanitary, with their outdoor privies, their lack of a bathroom or safe kitchens, they nevertheless fostered a sense of community missing in the post-war high-rise blocks. In 1920, a visitor from Dr Barnardo's inspects the unhygienic conditions of the slums (1). In 1945, a teenage daughter cleans shoes for a family of sixteen crammed into a typical 'two-up two-down' lebt (2). In Liverpool in 1954, a summer dawn sees a row of housewives out scrubbing their front steps and pavement areas (3).

DIESE Reihenhäuser waren seit ihrer Errichtung in der Blütezeit der industriellen Revolution kaum verändert worden. Sie hatten unhygienische Toiletten im Garten, kein Bad, keine feuersichere Küche. 1920 inspiziert ein Repräsentant der Dr.-Barnardo-

Kinderheime die ungesunden Verhältnisse in den Slums (1). 1945 putzt dieses junge Mädchen die Schuhe einer sechzehnköpfigen Familie, die in einem typischen Häuschen mit vier Zimmern lebt (2). An einem Sommermorgen 1954 in Liverpool reinigen die Frauen dieser Straße ihre Treppenstufen und den Bürgersteig (3).

CES maisons dos à dos construites au plus fort de la révolution industrielle n'ont guère changé. Malgré leur insalubrité (sans commodités, salle de bains et cuisine), elles favorisaient une vie communautaire. En 1920, un visiteur est envoyé par le docteur Barnardo examiner les conditions d'hygiène désastreuses des bidonvilles (1). 1945, une adolescente nettoyant les chaussures des seize personnes de sa famille entassées dans un « deux pièces en haut – deux pièces en bas » typique (2). Liverpool en 1954 : des ménagères frottent les marches devant leur porte (3).

3

The Rise of Fascism

Perhaps the most damning feature to emerge from all the books, lectures and opinions about European fascism is that the reasons for its rise were so predominantly negative. Economically, Europe was reeling from crash, depression and slump. To counter the ignominy as well as the poverty wrought by mass unemployment by guaranteeing not only wages and housing but uniforms and status through military conscription was an offer to which there seemed little alternative. Rearmament was also attractive to a Germany that felt herself humiliated by the terms of the Treaty of Versailles at the conclusion of the Great War; one result was a witch-hunt for the 'enemies within' that could be blamed for defeat.

Political enemies at first took precedence over racial ones, in Germany as in Italy. The smashing of the Spartacists and the killing of Rosa Luxemburg and Karl Liebknecht in 1919 failed to unseat a nascent but entrenched Socialist and Communist movement. Fears that the recent Russian Revolution would spread through Europe were in no way allayed by the vacillations of the Weimar régime, apparently as incapable of pursuing a political as an economic programme. If democracy could not deal with the problems, it was argued, then maybe democracy should make way.

The term 'Fascism' originated in Milan in 1919 with the formation of the *Fascio di Combattimento*, an anti-Socialist militia called after the bundle of rods that was the symbol of ancient Roman legislature. It took an authoritarian form under Mussolini in the decade from 1922. Rome in 1932 saw 40,000 Junior Fascists aged between 14 and 18 gather for a rally addressed by him. This very junior Junior Fascist served as a mascot, and is seen here saluting Il Duce (2). A former Socialist himself, Mussolini confusingly boasted: 'We allow ourselves the luxury of being aristocratic and democratic, reactionary and revolutionary'. Unlike Hitler, Mussolini primarily vaunted his pride in the glories of a real imperial past; a wish to destroy both the 'putrefying corpse' of parliamentary democracy and to strangle at birth any attempt at creating a Marxist state. His anti-internationalism extended to an insistence that Fascism was an Italian creed 'not for export'. It took until July 1938 and the formation of the Axis alliance for him to renege and become overtly anti-Semitic and to issue a *Manifesto della Razza* in imitation of his German ally.

Meanwhile in Spain, between 1936 and 1939, Franco's Falangist Party fought with German support to unseat the elected Republican government. Civil war erupted when the army rose against the government in July 1936: here, a Republican soldier throws a hand grenade at enemy trenches (1). General Franco, the future dictator who would rule Spain repressively for 35 years, stationed his headquarters in Spanish Morocco. From there he had to ferry insurgents across the Straits of Gibraltar and would have been unable to attain victory without the assistance of Fascist forces from Germany and Italy.

The postwar English historian A. J. P. Taylor has sought to diminish Hitler's role, considering that 'in principle and in doctrine, Hitler was no more wicked and unscrupulous than many other contemporary statesmen'. Few, however, would rush to concur. One has only to take, almost at random, a passage from *Mein Kampf* (My Struggle, 1923) to establish the histrionic fanaticism that swept so much before it, determining the fate of nations and the deaths of 55 millions:

'The adulteration of the blood and racial deterioration conditioned thereby are the only causes that account for the decline of ancient civilizations; for it is never by war that nations are ruined but by the loss of their powers of resistance, which are exclusively a characteristic of pure racial blood. In this world everything that is not of sound stock is like chaff.'

That this reads today as nonsensical rhetoric more appropriate to a stock-breeders' manual than a political manifesto is a measure of the discredit into which the term 'Fascism' has finally fallen.

1

DIE Quintessenz all der Bücher, Vorträge und Meinungen über den europäischen Faschismus ist die Erkenntnis, daß er so große Macht gewinnen konnte, weil die Zeiten so schlecht waren. Europa lag nach der Weltwirtschaftskrise am Boden, und hier wurden nicht nur Arbeit und Unterkunft versprochen, durch die man mit der Schande und Armut der Massenarbeitslosigkeit fertigwerden konnte, sondern dazu noch Uniformen und das Ansehen eines militärischen Dienstranges — dazu schien es keine Alternative zu geben. Für die Deutschen, die sich von den Bedingungen des Versailler Vertrages gedemütigt fühlten, war die Aussicht auf Wiederaufrüstung verlockend, und nun konnten sie die Feinde im eigenen Lande gnadenlos verfolgen.

Zunächst stand in Deutschland wie in Italien eher politische Feindschaft im Vordergrund und nicht die Rassenzugehörigkeit. Die Niederwerfung des Spartakistenaufstandes und die Ermordung Rosa Luxemburgs und Karl Liebknechts 1919 konnte die noch junge, aber schon verwurzelte sozialistische und kommunistische Bewegung nicht vernichten. Die Ängste, daß die Russische Revolution auf ganz Europa übergreifen könnte, wurden durch die Schwäche der Weimarer Regierung noch geschürt, die in politischer Hinsicht ebenso orientierungslos wirkte wie in wirtschaftlicher. Wenn die Demokratie nicht mit den Schwierigkeiten fertigwerden konnte, sagten sich die Leute, dann sollte die Demokratie einer anderen Staatsform Platz machen.

Die Bezeichnung »Faschismus« kam 1919 in Mailand auf, wo der *Fascio di Combattimento* gegründet wurde, eine antikommunistische Miliz, die sich nach dem Rutenbündel benannte, das im alten Rom das Symbol der Legislative gewesen war. Seit 1922 nahm er unter Mussolini autoritäre Züge an. 1932 versammelten sich in Rom 40.000 Jungfaschisten zwischen 14 und 18 Jahren, um ihn sprechen zu hören. Dieser sehr junge Juniorfaschist (2) war als Maskottchen dabei, und man sieht, wie eifrig er den Duce begrüßt. Mussolini, der früher selbst Sozialist gewesen war, rühmte sich in Paradoxen: »Wir erlauben uns den Luxus, aristokratisch und demokratisch, reaktionär und revolutionär zugleich zu sein.« Anders als Hitler konnte Mussolini stolz auf die Tradition eines Weltreichs zurückblicken, und er wollte den »stinkenden Leichnam« der Demokratie beiseite räumen und jeglichen Versuch, einen marxistischen Staat zu errichten, im Keime ersticken. Sein Nationalismus ging so weit, daß er sogar verlauten ließ, der Faschismus sei eine italienische Weltanschauung, die »nicht für den Export bestimmt« sei. Erst 1938, als der Bund der Achsenmächte geschlossen war, gab er sich offen antisemitisch und veröffentlichte ein *Manifesto della Razza* nach dem Vorbild seiner deutschen Verbündeten.

In Spanien bekämpfte derweil 1936 bis 1939 Francos Falangistenpartei mit deutscher Unterstützung die gewählte republikanische Regierung. Als die Armee sich im Juli 1936 gegen die Regierung erhob, hatte der Bürgerkrieg begonnen: Hier (1) wirft ein republikanischer Soldat eine Handgranate auf feindliche Schützengräben. General Franco, der künftige Diktator, der 35 Jahre lang über Spanien herrschen sollte, errichtete sein Hauptquartier im spanischen Marokko. Von dort mußte er seine Aufständischen per Schiff über die Straße von Gibraltar bringen und hätte sich niemals durchsetzen können, wenn faschistische Truppen aus Deutschland und Italien ihm nicht geholfen hätten.

Der englische Historiker A. J. P. Taylor schrieb später, man solle Hitlers Rolle nicht überbewerten: »In seinen Prinzipien und Ansichten war Hitler nicht schlechter und gewissenloser als viele andere Politiker seiner Zeit.« Doch nur wenige pflichteten ihm bei. Man muß sich nur eine willkürlich ausgewählte Passage aus *Mein Kampf* von 1923 ansehen, dann begreift man, daß hier ein größenwahnsinniger Fanatiker das Schicksal ganzer Nationen und den Tod von mehr als 55 Millionen Menschen besiegelte: »Die Blutsvermischung und das dadurch bedingte Senken des Rassenniveaus ist die alleinige Ursache des Absterbens aller Kulturen; denn die Menschen gehen nicht an verlorenen Kriegen zugrunde, sondern am Verlust jener Widerstandskraft, die nur dem reinen Blute zu eigen ist. Was nicht gute Rasse ist auf dieser Welt, ist Spreu.« Daß sich das heute als hohle Rhetorik liest, die eher in ein Handbuch für Viehzüchter paßt als in ein politisches Manifest, zeigt uns, welcher Verachtung der Begriff »Faschismus« anheimgefallen ist.

Des ouvrages, conférences et opinions qu'inspirèrent le fascisme européen, on retiendra le souci constant de mettre en valeur un contexte essentiellement négatif propice à son essor. Économiquement, l'Europe se trouvait dans un état d'effondrement, de dépression et de marasme. Tant pour échapper à l'angoisse qu'à la pauvreté causées par un chômage massif, il n'y avait guère d'autre choix possible que d'accepter non seulement le salaire et le logement, mais aussi l'uniforme et le statut que garantissait un engagement dans l'armée. Le réarmement séduisait aussi une Allemagne humiliée par les clauses du traité de Versailles qui avait conclu la Grande Guerre. Il en résulta notamment une chasse aux sorcières contre les « ennemis de l'intérieur » rendus responsables de la défaite.

L'Allemagne, à l'instar de l'Italie, s'en prit d'abord aux ennemis politiques avant de s'occuper de la question raciale. L'écrasement des spartakistes, suivi de l'assassinat de Rosa Luxemburg et de Karl Liebknecht en 1919 ne parvinrent pas à déstabiliser un mouvement ouvrier où les communistes jouaient déjà un grand rôle. La crainte de voir la jeune révolution russe se propager en Europe ne se trouvait guère dissipée devant les hésitations du régime de Weimar apparemment incapable de mettre en œuvre un programme économique et politique. Si la démocratie n'était pas en mesure d'affronter les problèmes, disait-on, c'est peut-être qu'elle devait céder la place.

Le terme « Fascisme » prit naissance à Milan en 1919 avec la formation du *Fascio di Combattimento*, milice antisocialiste qui tenait son nom du faisceau de verges servant de symbole à la magistrature romaine dans l'Antiquité. Il incarna dès 1922 le régime autoritaire de Mussolini, et cela pendant dix ans. À Rome, en 1932, ce sont 40 000 jeunes fascistes âgés de 14 à 18 ans qui sont ici rassemblés pour écouter Mussolini. Ce tout petit fasciste servait de mascotte ; on le voit ici saluant *Il Duce* (2). Ancien socialiste lui-même, Mussolini aimait à répéter ces paroles qui rendent perplexes : « Nous nous offrons le luxe d'être aristocratiques et démocratiques, réactionnaires et révolutionnaires ». Contrairement à Hitler, il était animé d'une fierté qui puisait dans un véritable passé impérial : du désir tout à la fois de

détruire la « carcasse pourrissante » de la démocratie parlementaire et d'étouffer dans l'œuf toute tentative de créer un état marxiste. Son anti-internationalisme allait jusqu'à souligner que le fascisme était une croyance italienne « non destinée à l'exportation ». Il faut attendre juillet 1938 et la constitution de l'alliance de l'Axe pour qu'il se dédise, se déclare ouvertement antisémite et fasse publier son *Manifesto della Razza* à l'instar de son alliée allemande.

Pendant ce temps, en Espagne, de 1936 à 1939, le parti phalangiste de Franco était soutenu par l'Allemagne dans sa lutte qui visait à confisquer la République. La guerre civile éclata lorsque l'armée entra en Juillet 1936 en rébellion contre le gouvernement : un soldat républicain lance ici une grenade à main vers une tranchée ennemie (1). Le général Franco, candillo d'un régime qui durera trente-cinq ans, établit son quartier général au Maroc espagnol. De là il lui fallut faire traverser aux insurgés le détroit de Gibraltar en bateau: c'est aux forces fascistes venues d'Allemagne et d'Italie qu'il devra en partie la victoire.

L'historien anglais de l'après-guerre, A.J.P. Taylor, s'emploie à minimiser le rôle de Hitler, estimant que « s'agissant du principe et de la doctrine, Hitler ne fut ni plus mauvais ni moins dénué de scrupules que beaucoup d'autres de nos hommes d'État contemporains ». Peu s'empresseront cependant de lui donner raison. Il suffit de prendre, presque au hasard, un passage de *Mein Kampf* (1923), pour se convaincre qu'il s'agit bien là d'un fanatisme orchestré et dévastateur qui devait tracer la destinée de nations entières et décider de la mort de 55 millions de personnes :

« L'adultération du sang et la dégénérescence raciale qui en a résulté sont là les seules causes du déclin des civilisations antérieures ; car ce n'est jamais la guerre qui cause la ruine des nations mais bien la perte de leurs pouvoirs de résistance, qui sont une caractéristique exclusive d'un sang de race pure. Dans ce monde, tout ce qui n'est pas de souche saine est de l'ivraie ».

Aujourd'hui, cette ineptie ampoulée résonne plus comme un manuel destiné aux éleveurs que comme un manifeste politique, à la mesure du discrédit attaché au terme « fascisme ».

1

2

3

4

ON 7 January 1919 the Spartacists –
their name derived from the slaves
who led the last revolt to overthrow
Roman rule – took to the streets of Berlin,
which they then barricaded. For over a
week the battle raged. Fighting deeds and
speeches (1) followed; rallies and
allegiances blurred – the hammer and sickle
(3) v. 'Down with the Spartacists'
Dictatorship of Blood!' (4). On 16 January
the popular revolutionary leaders 'Red
Rosa' Luxemburg (2) and former
Reichstag deputy Karl Liebknecht were
murdered by officers of the Garde Kallerie
Schutzen Division, an irregular right-wing
force officered by professionals from the
dissolved army, sent to arrest them. Instead
the leaders were tortured, shot and their
bodies thrown into a canal. The officers
were never brought to trial.

AM 7. Januar 1919 gingen die
Spartakisten — die sich nach dem
Anführer des letzten Sklavenaufstands
gegen die Römer benannt hatten — in
Berlin auf die Straße und errichteten ihre
Barrikaden. Über eine Woche dauerten die
Straßenkämpfe. Kämpfe in Taten und
Worten folgten (1); Zugehörigkeit
verwischte sich — Hammer und Sichel (3)
kontra »Nieder mit der Blutdiktatur des
Spartakus!« (4) Am 16. Januar wurden die
populäre Revolutionsführerin Rosa
Luxemburg (die »Rote Rosa«) (2) und der
ehemalige Reichstagsabgeordnete Karl
Liebknecht von Mitgliedern der
Gardekavallerie-Schützendivision, eines
inoffiziellen rechtsgerichteten Freikorps,
dessen Offiziere Berufssoldaten aus der
aufgelösten Armee waren, ermordet. Die
Männer hatten die beiden Anführer
verhaften sollen, doch statt dessen folterten
und erschossen sie sie und warfen ihre
Leichen in einen Kanal. Die Offiziere
wurden nie vor Gericht gestellt.

LE 7 janvier 1919, les spartakistes, du
nom des esclaves qui organisèrent la
dernière révolte contre la domination
romaine, – entreprirent de barricader les
rues de Berlin. Pendant plus d'une semaine
la bataille fit rage. Les accords tactiques et
les discours suivirent (1) ; les
rassemblements et les allégeances se
déroulèrent dans la confusion. Ici, la
faucille et le marteau (3). « À bas la
dictature sanguinaire et spartakiste » (4). Le
16 janvier, les chefs de file de la révolution
populaire « Rosa la rouge » Luxemburg (2)
et l'ancien député au Reichstag, Karl
Liebknecht, sont blessés par des officiers en
mission commandée de la Garde Kallerie
Schutzen Division, une force irrégulière
rassemblant des éléments de droite et
encadrée par des professionnels issus de
l'armée dissoute. En fait de cela, ils furent
torturés avant d'être abattus, et leurs
cadavres furent jetés dans un canal. Les
officiers ne furent jamais traduits en justice.

1

JANUARY 1919 was a time of elections to the National Assembly, which had before it the task of drawing up a new constitution. Because of the disturbances on the streets of Munich and Berlin, much of the business had to be moved to Weimar. In Berlin this quaint-looking government armoured car bears a warning skull and placard: 'Beware! Stay in your homes! Coming onto the streets can put your life at risk: you will be shot!' (1). As though bearing this out, Berlin civilians flee the machine-gun fire from Chancellor Ebert's government troops (2).

IM Januar 1919 wurde die Nationalversammlung gewählt, die eine neue Verfassung ausarbeiten sollte. Wegen der Unruhen in den Straßen von München und Berlin wurden die Amtsgeschäfte größtenteils nach Weimar verlegt. In Berlin warnt dieser kuriose offizielle Panzerwagen unter dem Totenschädel: »Achtung! In den Häusern bleiben! Auf der Straße Lebensgefahr, da scharf geschossen wird!« (1) Wie um dies zu beweisen, fliehen Berliner vor den Maschinengewehren von Reichspräsident Eberts Regierungstruppen (2).

JANVIER 1919 fut l'époque des élections à l'Assemblée nationale, laquelle avait pour tâche d'élaborer une nouvelle Constitution. En raison des troubles qui avaient éclaté dans les rues de Munich et de Berlin, on transféra presque tout à Weimar. À Berlin, ce véhicule blindé des autorités publiques offre un bien curieux spectacle avec sa tête de mort et son inscription en guise d'avertissement : « Attention ! Restez chez vous ! Sortir dans la rue peut vous coûter la vie : vous risquez d'être abattus ! » (1). Comme pour lui donner raison, des civils s'enfuient à Berlin sous les rafales des mitraillettes gouvernementales du chancelier Ebert (2).

THE confusion caused by circumstances at the war's end led women (1) and even children (2) to fraternize with the military. While the Spartacists looked to nascent workers' soviets to create a 'free socialist republic of Germany', there were rapid and increasing signs that the Socialist People's Militia and Freikorps would not fight with the newly created city soviets. The revolution collapsed when the militias threw in their lot with the police and armed forces.

IN den Wirren der ersten Nachkriegszeit sympathisierten Frauen (1) und sogar Kinder (2) mit den Militärs. Die Spartakisten hofften, daß Arbeiterräte »eine freie sozialistische Republik in Deutschland« schaffen würden, doch bald war offensichtlich, daß die sozialistischen Volksmilizen und Freikorps nicht gegen die neugeschaffenen Stadträte kämpfen würden. Die Revolution war zu Ende, als die Milizen sich auf die Seite der Polizei und der Armee schlugen.

LA confusion qui règne à la fin de la guerre conduisit des femmes (1), voire des enfants (2) à fraterniser avec les militaires. Tandis que les spartakistes comptaient sur les comités ouvriers naissants pour créer la base d'une « République socialiste libre d'Allemagne », il apparut bientôt de plus en plus clairement que la milice du peuple socialiste et les *Freikorps* (volontaires) ne combattraient pas aux côtés des comités tout juste créés dans les villes. La fin de la révolution était scellée lorsque les milices décidèrent de lier leur sort à celui de la police et des forces armées.

TROTSKY, here at Petrograd (St Petersburg) in 1921 (1), was supposedly 'in the vanguard of the Revolution, while Lenin was in the guard's van'. As erstwhile War Minister and Head of the Red Army, he paid a visit to the Red Commanders of the Russian Military Academy at Moscow (2). From 1917 to 1922, Lenin was undisputed leader, but from 1922 until his death in 1924, he suffered three serious heart attacks and was obliged to retire to the country (3). His meeting there with Stalin in the summer of 1922 was a prophetic one (4). While Trotsky described Stalin as 'the Party's most eminent mediocrity', Lenin concluded: 'I am not always sure that he knows how to use power with caution.' In 1923, he recommended Stalin's dismissal.

TROTZKI, hier 1921 in Petrograd (St. Petersburg) (1), galt als »der Schaffner der Revolution, und Lenin war der Bremser«. Als damaliger Kriegsminister und Oberbefehlshaber der Roten Armee stattet er hier (2) den Roten Kommandeuren der Russischen Militärakademie in Moskau einen Besuch ab. Von 1917 bis 1922 war Lenin der unangefochtene Führer der

2

3

4

Revolution, doch von 1922 bis zu seinem
Tode 1924 erlitt er drei schwere Herzanfälle
und mußte sich zurückziehen (3). Sein
Treffen dort mit Stalin im Sommer 1922
sollte zukunftsweisend sein (4). Lenin kam
zu dem Schluß: »Ich bin mir nicht immer
sicher, ob er beim Umgang mit der Macht
das rechte Maß kennt.« 1923 empfahl er,
Stalin zu entlassen.

Trotski, ici à Petrograd (Saint-
Pétersbourg) en 1921 (1) était supposé
« à l'avant-garde de la Révolution et
Lénine sous la garde de celle-ci ». Ancien
ministre de la Guerre et de chef de l'Armée
rouge, il rendit visite aux commandants
communistes à Moscou (2). Lénine régna
de 1917 à 1922. Mais, dès 1922 et jusqu'à
sa mort en 1924, trois graves attaques

cardiaques le contraignirent à se retirer à la
campagne (3), où il eut une entrevue avec
Staline au cours de l'été 1922 (4). Alors
que Trotski qualifiait Staline de
« médiocrité la plus éminente du Parti »,
Lénine concluait : « Je ne suis pas toujours
sûr qu'il sache faire un bon usage du
pouvoir. » En 1923, il recommanda le
limogeage de Staline.

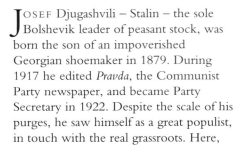

JOSEF Djugashvili – Stalin – the sole Bolshevik leader of peasant stock, was born the son of an impoverished Georgian shoemaker in 1879. During 1917 he edited *Pravda*, the Communist Party newspaper, and became Party Secretary in 1922. Despite the scale of his purges, he saw himself as a great populist, in touch with the real grassroots. Here,

in his Marshal's uniform, he visits Schelkovo aerodrome (4), and is presented with flowers by young Pioneers (3). Eleven-year-old Mamlakat Nakhengova travels from Tajhikistan to present a Tajik translation of his book *Stalin about Lenin* (2). Children were also commandeered to sell certificates for government construction loans (1).

JOSEF Dschugaschwili, genannt Stalin, der einzige Bolschewikenführer aus niederem Stand, kam 1879 in Georgien zur Welt. 1917 war er leitender Redakteur der Parteizeitung *Prawda*, und 1922 wurde er Generalsekretär der Partei. Trotz der Grausamkeit seiner Säuberungen verstand er sich als populistischer Politiker, der wußte, was das Volk wirklich wollte. Hier

4

besucht er, in seiner Marschallsuniform, den Flugplatz Schelkovo (4) und bekommt von jungen Pionieren Blumen überreicht (3). Die elfjährige Mamlakat Nakhengova ist aus Tadschikistan gekommen, um eine tadschikische Ausgabe von Stalins Buch *Stalin über Lenin* zu präsentieren (2). Kinder wurden auch dazu verpflichtet, staatliche Bauanleihen zu verkaufen (1).

JOSEPH Djougachvili – Staline – le seul chef bolchevique d'origine paysanne, naquit en 1879 dans la famille d'un bottier géorgien tombé dans la misère. Pendant l'année 1917, il fut rédacteur à la *Pravda*, le journal du Parti, avant de devenir son secrétaire général en 1922. Malgré l'ampleur des purges qu'il ordonna, il s'estimait toujours proche de la base. On le

voit ici en uniforme de maréchal visitant l'aéroport de Schelkovo (4) et recevant des fleurs des mains de jeunes pionniers (3). Mamlakat Nakhengova, âgée de onze ans, a fait le voyage du Tadjikistan pour lui remettre la traduction de son ouvrage *Staline à propos de Lénine* (2). On réquisitionnait aussi des enfants chargés de vendre des bons d'emprunt pour financer la construction (1).

IN the Spanish Civil War, over half a million people died and millions more were made refugees (1). Children were pushed to the front of the bread queue at Le Perthus on the French border (3). At Irun, a French journalist, Raymond Vanker, discovered a baby alone in a house under intense fire. He escaped to France over the Hendaye bridge, the child in his arms (2).

IM Spanischen Bürgerkrieg kam über eine halbe Million Menschen um, und Millionen waren auf der Flucht (1). Hier in Le Perthus an der französischen Grenze werden die Kinder zur Essensausgabe vorgeschickt (3). In Irún fand der französische Journalist Raymond Vanker in einem Haus, das unter schwerem Beschuß stand, ein zurückgelassenes Baby. Er floh mit dem Kind in den Armen über die Brücke von Hendaye nach Frankreich (2).

LA guerre civile espagnole coûta la vie à plus d'un demi-million de personnes et transforma des millions d'autres en réfugiés (1). Au Perthus, à la frontière française, on poussait les enfants au premier rang des queues de ravitaillement (3). À Irún, le journaliste français Raymond Vanker trouva un bébé resté seul dans une maison soumise à des tirs nourris. Il s'enfuit en direction de la France par le pont Hendaye avec l'enfant dans les bras (2).

1

LOYAL Republican Spanish troops at ease in 1936 (1) contrast with jack-booted Foreign Legionaries on a 'hunt the Reds' mission in Mérida, rifles raised (2).

LOYALE Truppen der spanischen Republik während einer Pause, 1936 (1), und im Kontrast dazu die fremden Legionäre in Mérida, wie sie in ihren Springerstiefeln mit erhobenen Gewehren »die Roten jagen«. (2)

LA décontraction des troupes espagnoles républicaines loyalistes en 1936 (1) contraste avec la « chasse aux rouges » dans laquelle se sont lancés les hommes de la légion étrangère, bottes montantes et fusils brandis à Mérida (2)

ON 29 August 1936, this group of Republicans was forced to surrender by the Nationalist rebels (1). In their ill-assorted uniforms and weapons, they look more like a ragtag than a national army, suggesting how many of the regular troops were anti-Republican. A 17-year-old lies dead from a bullet in the head (2). A vivid account of one man's experience is offered by George Orwell's *Homage to Catalonia*. Words were enormously important to the ideological battle: after all, Franco's Falangists adopted the Foreign Legionaries' war cry 'Death to Intellectuals! Long live death!' The Republicans responded with poster propaganda like this Catalan advertisement post calling women to arms (4). All the unions, particularly female-dominated ones such as the garment-workers, organized women like these militia seated wearily at a roadside (3). Their lack of uniforms, even boots, implies that this was taken late in the war.

AM 29. August 1936 zwangen die nationalistischen Rebellen diesen Trupp Republikaner zur Kapitulation (1). In ihren verschiedenerlei Uniformen und Waffen sehen sie eher wie ein bunt zusammengewürfelter Haufen aus als wie eine Nationalarmee, und man kann ahnen, wie viele reguläre Truppen sich auf die Seite der Gegner geschlagen hatten. Ein siebzehnjähriger Gefallener mit einer Kugel im Kopf (2). George Orwell hat in *Homage to Catalonia* eindrucksvoll seine Kriegserlebnisse in Spanien beschrieben. Ideologische Kriegführung war von großer Bedeutung: Schließlich hatten Francos Falangisten den Kampfruf der Fremdenlegion übernommen, »Tod den Intellektuellen! Lang lebe der Tod!« Die Republikaner antworteten mit Plakaten darauf, wie hier an einer Litfaßsäule in Katalonien, wo Frauen zu den Waffen gerufen werden (4). Gewerkschaften, besonders von Frauen beherrschte wie die

3

4

Näherinnengewerkschaft, organisierten Frauenmilizen; hier (3) sieht man einige Kämpferinnen erschöpft am Straßenrand sitzen. Da sie keine Uniformen tragen, nicht einmal Stiefel, dürfte das Bild gegen Ende des Krieges entstanden sein.

L E 29 août 1936, les insurgés forcent un groupe de républicains à se rendre (1). Leurs uniformes dépareillés et leurs armes leur donnent plus l'allure d'une armée en déroute que d'une armée nationale. Un jeune homme de dix-sept ans tué d'une balle dans la tête (2). George Orwell, dans son *Hommage à la Catalogne*, raconte d'une

manière vivante l'expérience d'un homme. Les mots comptaient énormément : après tout, les phalangistes de Franco n'avaient-ils pas adopté le cri de guerre du *Tercio* (une légion étrangère) : « Vive la mort ! » Les républicains ripostaient par des affiches de propagande pour inviter les femmes à prendre les armes (4). Tous les syndicats, en particulier féminins, comme celui des ouvrières du vêtement, embrigadaient les femmes, comme ces miliciennes assises, épuisées, sur le bord de la route (3). L'absence d'uniforme et de bottes laisse penser que la photographie a été prise vers la fin de la guerre.

Refugees jam the roads into France (1). In January 1939, Franco's victorious troops entered Barcelona supported by General Yague's feared 'Moors', meeting with only sporadic resistance. Here some of the 3000 Czech, Polish and German members of the International Brigade merge with the retreating Republican army and the mass of refugees fleeing north (2).

Flüchtlinge drängen sich an den Straßen nach Frankreich (1). Im Januar 1939 marschierten Francos siegreiche Truppen, verstärkt durch die gefürchteten »Moros« (Marokkaner), in Barcelona ein und trafen nur noch auf vereinzelten Widerstand. Auf diesem Bild (2) schließen sich einige der 3.000 Tschechen, Polen und Deutschen, die mit der Internationalen Brigade ins Land gekommen waren, der geschlagenen republikanischen Armee und den zahllosen Flüchtlingen im Strom nach Norden an.

Les réfugiés s'amassaient sur les routes en direction de la France (1). En janvier 1939, les troupes victorieuses de Franco entraient dans Madrid appuyées par les redoutés « Maures » du général Yague, où elles ne rencontrèrent qu'une résistance sporadique. Ici quelques-uns des 3 000 Tchèques, Polonais et Allemands, membres des brigades internationales, se mêlent à l'armée républicaine battant en retraite et aux flots de réfugiés qui font route vers le Nord (2).

2

THE March on Rome has been called
'the Fascist-inspired myth of the way
in which Mussolini came to power in
Italy'. In 1922, civil war appeared
imminent and the ex-socialist Mussolini
demanded the formation of a Fascist
government to save the country from
socialism. On 29 October, King Victor
Emmanuel III invited him to come from
Milan to Rome, and Mussolini did so on
the overnight express. On 30 October
Mussolini formed the government and on
the 31st some 25,000 blackshirts were
imported, also by train, for a ceremonial
parade (1). The 'March on Rome' was as
histrionic an exaggeration as the
expressions on Il Duce's face as he
addresses his 'marchers', the
'Representatives of National Strengths',
from the Palazzio Venezia (2).

DEN Marsch auf Rom hat man den
»faschistischen Mythos von Mussolinis
Machtergreifung in Italien« genannt. 1922
schien ein Bürgerkrieg unvermeidlich, und
der ehemalige Sozialist Mussolini forderte
die Bildung einer faschistischen Regierung,
um das Land vor dem Sozialismus zu
bewahren. Am 29. Oktober lud König
Viktor Emmanuel III. ihn ein, von Mailand
nach Rom zu kommen, woraufhin
Mussolini schon den Nachtexpress nahm.
Am 30. Oktober bildete er seine
Regierung, und am 31. kamen, ebenfalls
per Zug, etwa 25.000 Schwarzhemden zur
feierlichen Parade (1). Der »Marsch auf
Rom« war eine genauso lächerliche
Übertreibung wie der Gesichtsausdruck des
Duce, mit dem er die Eintreffenden, die
»Vertreter nationaler Stärke«, vom Palazzo
Venezia aus begrüßt (2).

LA marche sur Rome a été appelée
« l'arrivée au pouvoir de Mussolini en
Italie mythifiée par les fascistes ». En 1922,
alors que la guerre civile semble
imminente, l'ex-socialiste Mussolini
réclame la constitution d'un gouvernement
fasciste pour sauver le pays du socialisme.
Le 29 octobre, le roi Victor Emmanuel III
convie à Rome Mussolini, qui se trouvait
alors à Milan. Celui-ci arrive par l'express
de nuit. Le 30 octobre, il constitue son
gouvernement ; le 31 il fait venir quelque
25 000 chemises noires, également par le
train, pour participer à une parade
solennelle (1). La « marche sur Rome » est
une affabulation, tout comme sont
volontairement exagérées les mimiques du
Duce s'adressant du Palazzio Venezia à ses
« marcheurs », aux « représentants des
forces nationales » (2).

1

2

3

4

Mussolini in mufti between (left to right) Generals Balbo, de Bono, de Vecchi and Bianchi (1). Napoleonic theories about small men with big ambitions and complexes seemed exemplified by Franco, Hitler and – especially – Mussolini. This applied even more so to the Austrian Chancellor Dolfuss (at left), known as Millimetternich or

Mickey Mouse for being under 5 feet tall, here fraternizing with his fellow-dictator shortly before his assassination in 1934 (2). Mussolini brought the Führer to gaze at the hefty white marble nymph Pauline Borghese, Napoleon's sister, at the Villa Borghese (4). He then led the Fascist officials off in a disorderly goose-step during the Roman Parade (3).

Mussolini in Zivil zwischen den Generalen Balbo, de Bono, de Vecchi und Bianchi (1, von links nach rechts). Die Idee vom »Napoleonkomplex« — daß kleinwüchsige Männer einen ganz besonderen Ehrgeiz entwickeln — scheint durch Franco, Hitler und ganz besonders durch Mussolini bestätigt zu werden. Noch mehr traf das auf den österreichischen Kanzler Dollfuß zu (links), den man wegen

seiner knappen ein Meter fünfzig den »Millimetternich« nannte; hier sieht man ihn in bestem Einvernehmen mit seinem Diktatorkollegen, kurz vor seiner Ermordung 1934 (2). Dem Führer zeigte Mussolini in der Villa Borghese die Marmorstatue Venus (4). Er führte die faschistische Prominenz in einem etwas aus dem Takt gekommenen Gänsemarsch zur Römischen Parade (3).

MUSSOLINI en civil entre (de gauche à droite) les généraux Balbo, de Bono, de Vecchi et Bianchi (1). Les théories à propos de Napoléon et des hommes de petite taille dotés de grandes ambitions et de gros complexes semblent se vérifier à travers Franco, Hitler et Mussolini. Elles sont encore plus vraies dans le cas du chancelier autrichien Dollfuss (à gauche) surnommé

« Mickey la souris », fraternisant avec un de ses homologues dictateurs peu de temps avant d'être assassiné en 1934 (2). À la Villa Borghese, Mussolini conduisit le Führer contempler la nymphe qui représente Pauline Borghese, sœur de Napoléon (4). Il entraîna ensuite la délégation fasciste dans un pas de l'oie désordonné à la Parade romaine (3).

1

FASCIST march-pasts were intended to unite the nations and the generations. In 1936 the Marine branch of the *Figli della Lupa* (Sons of the She-wolf – presumably a reference to Romulus, Remus and the glories of ancient Rome) marched beneath Mussolini's raised salute (1). In 1945 in Tripoli Fascist women were organized in militias, possibly as advance warning of fresh neo-imperialist intentions in the region, only months before the invasion of Abyssinia (2). And secondary schoolboys underwent military training even when it was too hot to wear much beyond plimsolls and sunhats (3).

DIE Faschistenaufmärsche sollten die Nationen und Generationen zusammenbringen. 1936 zog die Marineabteilung der *Figli della Lupa* (Söhne der Wölfin — eine Anspielung auf Romulus und Remus und den Ruhm des alten Rom) an Mussolini vorüber, der die Hand zum Gruß erhoben hat (1). 1945 werden die Faschistenfrauen in Tripolis zu Milizen organisiert, möglicherweise ein Vorzeichen, daß sich neoimperialistische Ambitionen in der Gegend zu regen begannen, nur Monate vor der Invasion Abessiniens (2). Und Schuljungen mußten ihre soldatische Ausbildung auch dann absolvieren, wenn es so heiß war, daß man außer Sonnenhut und Turnschuhen nicht viel tragen konnte (3).

L'IDÉE des défilés fascistes était de réunir les nations et les générations. En 1936, la section marine des *Figli della Lupa* (les fils de la louve ; probable référence à Romulus, Remus et aux gloires de la Rome antique) défilent au-dessous de Mussolini qui salue debout (1). En 1945, à Tripoli, les femmes fascistes sont organisées en milices, probablement afin de prévenir les velléités néo-impérialistes qui se font jour dans la région, à quelques mois seulement de l'invasion de l'Abyssinie (2). Ailleurs, des écoliers du secondaire suivent un entraînement militaire en dépit d'une chaleur n'autorisant guère que les tennis et le chapeau de soleil (3).

2

3

Nazism

ADOLF Hitler was on the face of it perhaps the least likely of Fascist dictators. Non-German and erratically educated, a professional failure in everything he had tried before entering politics, at first he neither looked nor acted the part. Instead of the statuesque physique of a Nordic god, he was small and black-haired and dark-eyed, a vegetarian in a decidedly carnivorous country. Yet his own mixed psychology succeeded in touching a chord that played on both Germans' fears and their pride. By creating an enemy 'other' of mythic dimensions, he could unite the German-speaking peoples in pursuit of his goal, the foundation of the 1000-year Third Reich.

If the enemy did not actually exist, then it would have to be invented. In Central Europe, Ashkenazi Jews had been largely assimilated during their 500-year-long sojourn, many having been known as 'Court Jews' for their sought-after pre-eminence in the arts that sent them from one principality to the next to perform as musicians and artists. Many of these described themselves by nationality rather than religion and thought of themselves as Germans or Austrians before Jews. Ironically, by defining Jews not by their religion but by being even one-eighth of Jewish blood, Hitler was including himself in, by dint of one grandparent. If the stereotype of the grasping miser didn't exist, it would be promoted by scurrilous graffiti and wild accusations. When, after Kristallnacht, Propaganda Minister Goebbels surveyed the mess of shattered glass on the streets of Berlin, he groaned: 'They [the SA/Stormtroopers' mob] should have broken fewer Jewish windows and taken more Jewish lives.'

When the Communists failed to carry out the awaited revolutionary putsch, the burning of the Reichstag was staged as a pretext to clamp down in their suppression. Much blame has been attached to the policy of appeasement pursued by both French and British governments through the 1920s and 30s, though Churchill was the sole politician in favour of a military response when Hitler annexed the Rhineland in 1936. The truth was probably that too much of Europe was preoccupied with licking its own wounds from the Great War and with the shortage of manpower and political will to wish for any further warmongering.

ADOLF Hitler war unter den faschistischen Diktatoren vielleicht derjenige, dem man es am wenigsten zutraute. Als Österreicher mit nur unvollständiger Schulbildung, der in allem, was er versucht hatte, bevor er in die Politik ging, glorreich gescheitert war, sah er nicht nur nicht danach aus, sondern benahm sich auch anfangs nicht wie ein Führer. Er hatte nicht die Statur eines nordischen Gottes, sondern war klein und schwarzhaarig mit dunklen Augen, ein Vegetarier im Land der Fleischesser. Und doch rührte er mit seiner konfusen Psyche eine Saite an, die sowohl die Ängste als auch den Stolz der Deutschen erklingen ließ. Er beschwor ein Feindbild von geradezu mythischen Ausmaßen herauf, und damit konnte er die deutschsprachigen Völker vereint für sein großes Ziel gewinnen, die Gründung eines »tausendjährigen Dritten Reichs«.

Wenn es keine Feinde gab, dann mußte man welche erfinden. In Mitteleuropa hatten sich im Laufe ihrer fünfhundertjährigen Wanderschaft zahlreiche Ostjuden niedergelassen, viele davon »Hofjuden«, die als gefragte Musiker oder Miniaturmaler von einem Fürstenhof zum anderen zogen. Viele davon fühlten sich eher einer Nation zugehörig als einer Religionsgemeinschaft und verstanden sich zuerst als Deutsche oder Österreicher und erst dann als Juden. Für Hitler war es nicht die Religion, sondern das Blut, das zählte, und ironischerweise hätte er sich, da auch jemand mit einem Achtel Judenblut noch als Jude galt, selbst dazurechnen müssen, denn dem Vernehmen nach hatte er einen jüdischen Großvater. Wenn die Leute nicht von sich aus das Vorurteil vom »raffgierigen Geizkragen« hatten, bekamen sie es durch verleumderische Wandsprüche und aus der Luft gegriffene Anschuldigungen eingetrichtert. Als nach der »Reichskristallnacht« der Propagandaminister Goebbels das zerschmetterte Schaufensterglas auf den Berliner Straßen musterte, seufzte er: »Ich wünschte nur, [die SA-Männer] hätten weniger jüdische Scheiben und mehr jüdische Schädel eingeschlagen.«

Als der vorausgesagte Kommunistenaufstand auf sich warten ließ, wurde der Brandanschlag auf den Reichstag inszeniert, damit man einen Vorwand für ihre Verfolgung hatte. Vieles ist später der zu nachgiebigen

ADOLF Hitler était peut-être le plus paradoxal de tous les dictateurs fascistes. Non Allemand, ayant bénéficié d'une éducation disparate et échoué à tous les métiers auxquels il s'était essayé avant de se lancer dans la politique, il n'avait a priori ni le parcours ni le physique de l'emploi. Au lieu d'avoir la stature et l'apparence d'un dieu nordique, sa chevelure était noire et ses yeux foncés. Enfin, il était végétarien dans un pays résolument carnivore. Pourtant, sa psychologie composite sut jouer des peurs et de l'orgueil des Allemands. En créant un ennemi « différent », aux dimensions mythiques, il réussit à unir les peuples de langue allemande derrière lui à la poursuite de son objectif : fonder le Troisième Reich millénaire.

Puisque l'ennemi n'existait pas vraiment, il serait inventé. En Europe centrale, les Juifs ashkénazes étaient largement assimilés depuis leur arrivée, cinq siècles plus tôt. Beaucoup étaient appelés les « Juifs de cour » parce qu'ils excellaient dans les métiers artistiques. Ils étaient de ce fait très recherchés, voyageant d'une principauté à l'autre en tant que musiciens ou portraitistes. Ils se définissaient davantage par rapport à leur nationalité qu'en fonction de leur religion, et se considéraient d'abord allemands ou autrichiens avant d'être juifs. L'ironie voulut qu'en ne définissant pas le Juif par sa religion mais par le fait d'avoir un huitième de sang juif, Hitler s'incluait lui-même. En effet, l'un de ses grands-parents était juif. Le stéréotype du Juif âpre au gain sera accentué par des graffiti injurieux et des accusations insensées. Quand, après la Nuit de cristal, Goebbels, ministre de la Propagande, se rendit sur les lieux, devant le triste état des rues de Berlin jonchées de débris de verre, il gémit : « Ils [les sbires des troupes d'assaut] auraient mieux fait de briser un peu moins de vitres juives et de supprimer plus de Juifs. »

Après l'échec du putsch révolutionnaire tant attendu, l'incendie du Reichstag fut monté de toutes pièces et utilisé comme un prétexte pour réclamer la suppression des activités communistes. On a beaucoup reproché, tant au gouvernement français que britannique, la politique d'apaisement qui fut la leur tout au long des années 20 et 30. C'est oublier que Churchill fut le seul homme politique favorable à une riposte militaire en 1936 après l'annexion de la Rhénanie par Hitler. La vérité était probablement que l'Europe, trop préoccupée de panser ses propres blessures au lendemain de la Grande Guerre, manquait de ressources humaines et de volonté politique pour risquer de s'engager dans une autre guerre.

Haltung der französischen und britischen Regierungen der 20er und 30er Jahre angelastet worden, doch immerhin war Churchill der einzige Politiker, der sich für einen militärischen Gegenschlag einsetzte, als Hitler 1936 das Rheinland besetzte. In Wahrheit war wohl ganz Europa zu sehr damit beschäftigt, die Wunden des Ersten Weltkriegs zu lecken, mit Massenarbeitslosigkeit und politischer Orientierungslosigkeit, als daß man sich auf einen neuen Krieg hätte einlassen können.

2

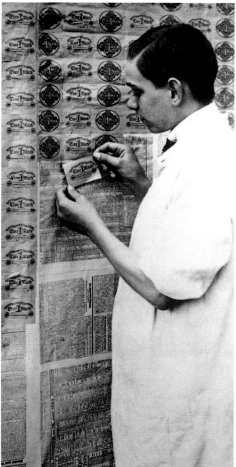

INFLATION turned to hyperflation in the wake of the Great War. In 1923, one US dollar became worth Reichsmark 4.2m; five years later it had doubled its decline. Banknotes became cheaper than toys (1) or wallpaper (3), and this shopkeeper abandoned his till for tea-chests to store the wads (2). Politically, the Reichstag proved itself likewise bankrupt. In the September elections, the Nazi Party increased its own vote from 810,000 to a staggering 6,409,600. Parliamentary democracy was now suspended and parliament became paralysed by the rot within and the threat from without.

DIE Inflation nahm nach dem Ersten Weltkrieg bis dahin ungekannte Ausmaße an. 1923 war ein US-Dollar 4,2 Millionen Reichsmark wert; fünf Jahre darauf war der Wert der Mark auf die Hälfte gesunken. Banknoten waren weniger wert als Bauklötze (1) oder Tapete (3), und hier hat ein Ladenbesitzer es aufgegeben, die Bündel noch in die Kasse zu stopfen, und nimmt statt dessen Teekisten (2). Und der Reichstag erwies sich in politischer Hinsicht als ebenso

bankrott. Bei den Wahlen im September 1930 konnten die Nationalsozialisten ihre Stimmen von 810.000 auf unglaubliche 6.409.600 erhöhen. Damit war die parlamentarische Demokratie am Ende, und das Parlament gelähmt von der Zersetzung im Inneren und der Bedrohung von außen.

L'INFLATION se changea en hyperinflation au lendemain de la Grande Guerre. En 1923, un dollar des États-Unis valait 4,2 millions de Reichsmark, et perdait le double de sa valeur cinq ans plus tard. Les billets de banque valaient moins cher que les jouets (1) ou le papier peint (3). Ce commerçant a délaissé sa caisse pour entreposer ses rouleaux de billets dans des caisses à thé (2). Politiquement le Reichstag s'avérait tout aussi en faillite. Au cours des élections de septembre, le parti nazi augmenta son score, lequel passa de 810 000 voix au chiffre inquiétant de 6 409 600. La démocratie parlementaire se trouva alors suspendue, le Parlement paralysé sous le coup de sa propre déliquescence et de la menace extérieure.

3

1

2

3

IN the Warsaw ghetto, where this man and boy are pictured (1), Orthodox Jewish boys attend Sabbath *schule* (3). The diversity of Jewish occupations included serving as market porters (2). Signs from Schwedt-am-Oder in 1935 read 'Jews are not wanted in this place!' (5), while a Jewish tailor's shop in Vienna (6) is defaced with graffiti saying, 'If you wash this off, you can holiday in Dachau!' – this in 1938. Even after the war the legacy of race-hatred can still be read. This bench says it is 'Not for Jews' (4).

IM Warschauer Ghetto, wo diese Aufnahme von einem Mann und einem Jungen entstand (1), gingen die orthodoxen jüdischen Jungen am Sabbatabend zur Schule (3). Juden waren in den verschiedensten Berufen tätig, hier als Träger auf dem Markt (2). Schwedt an der Oder zeigte 1935 deutlich, wo es politisch stand (5), und einem jüdischen Schneider in Wien (6) wird Urlaub in Dachau versprochen, wenn er die Schmierereien übertüncht — und das schon 1938. Selbst nach dem Krieg blieben die Zeichen des Rassenhasses noch sichtbar: Diese Bank ist »nicht für Juden« (4).

4

5

6

DANS le ghetto de Varsovie, où fut prise la photographie de cet homme et de cet enfant (1), les garçonnets juifs orthodoxes allaient à la *Schule* (école) sabbatique (3). Parmi les divers emplois exercés par les Juifs, on trouve celui de porteur sur le marché (2). Les panneaux à Schwedt-an-der-Oder signalaient en 1935 : « Ici on ne veut pas de Juifs ! » (5). Ailleurs, la boutique d'un tailleur juif à Vienne (6) est barbouillée de graffiti prévenant : « Si tu effaces cette inscription, tu es bon pour un petit voyage à Dachau ! » Cela en 1938 ! Même après la guerre, la haine raciste pouvait encore s'affiches dans des inscriptions à l'image de celle figurant sur ce banc : « Pas pour les Juifs » (4).

1

THE aftermath and humiliation of the Great War took time to dispel. In July 1922 the Rathenau Youth Organization assembled before the castle on a 'No More War' demonstration (1). During the so-called 'Kapp Revolution' of the same year, named after an obscure provincial official, right-wingers attempted a *coup d'état* and a proclamation of a new government led by Kapp but were swiftly routed by a general strike of Berlin workers. The rising was noted, however, for the early use of the swastika (however amateurishly painted onto helmets) and for revealing an embryonic Nazi Party (3). Among a group of Hitler's stormtroopers who participated in the Munich putsch of 9 November 1923 is Heinrich Himmler (holding the flag), later Nazi Gestapo chief (2).

ES dauerte seine Zeit, bis Schrecken und Erniedrigung des Ersten Weltkriegs vorüber waren. Im Juli 1922 versammelte sich der Jugendbund Rathenau zu einer Demonstration unter dem Motto »Nie wieder Krieg« (1). Beim sogenannten Kapp-Putsch von 1920, nach einem obskuren Provinzbeamten benannt, versuchten rechtsgerichtete Kräfte einen Staatsstreich und proklamierten eine neue, von Kapp geführte Regierung, die aber nach einem Generalstreik der Berliner Arbeiter bald wieder aufgeben mußte. Bemerkenswert ist dieser Putsch für den frühen Einsatz von Hakenkreuzen, wenn auch recht amateurhaft auf die Stahlhelme gemalt, der erste größere Auftritt der eben erst gegründeten NSDAP (3). Zu den SA-Männern, die an Hitlers Münchner Putsch vom 9. November 1923 beteiligt waren, gehörte auch Heinrich Himmler (mit Flagge), der spätere Gestapochef (2).

LES conséquences de la Grande Guerre et l'humiliation qui s'ensuivit mirent du temps à disparaître. En juillet 1922, l'organisation Rathenau de la jeunesse manifestait devant le château pour qu'il n'y ait « jamais plus de guerre » (1). La même année, au cours de ce qu'on appela la « révolution Kapp », du nom d'un obscur responsable provincial, des éléments de droite tentaient de proclamer par un coup d'État un nouveau gouvernement dirigé pas Kapp. Ils furent promptement mis en déroute grâce à la grève générale déclenchée par les ouvriers berlinois. L'émeute retint cependant l'attention parce qu'à cette occasion la croix gammée apparut pour la première fois (même si son dessin laisse à désirer), révélant ainsi l'existence d'un parti nazi à l'état embryonnaire (3). Au milieu de l'un des groupes formés par les troupes d'assaut d'Hitler, qui participa au putsch de Munich le 9 novembre 1923, on aperçoit Heinrich Himmler (tenant le drapeau), qui devint plus tard le responsable de la Gestapo (2).

2

3

Not since Savonarola had Europe seen such pyres of books. As part of the 1933 bonfire of 'anti-German literature' many of Europe's greatest writers were consigned to the flames in Berlin's Opernplatz (1). Another bonfire in 1933 was that of the Reichstag (2). Goering reached the scene, already proclaiming: 'The Communist Party is the culprit… We will show no mercy. Every Communist must be shot on the spot.'

Seit Savonarola hatte es in Europa keine solche Bücherverbrennung mehr gegeben. Als 1933 auf dem Berliner Opernplatz »undeutsches Schrifttum« in Flammen aufging, waren die Werke vieler der bedeutendsten Schriftsteller Europas dabei (1). Ein anderer großer

1   2

Scheiterhaufen des Jahres 1933 war der Reichstag (2). Als Göring am Ort des Geschehens eintraf, brüllte er unverzüglich: »Das ist das Werk der kommunistischen Partei … Wir werden keinerlei Gnade walten lassen. Jeder Kommunist muß auf der Stelle erschossen werden.«

DEPUIS Savonarole, l'Europe n'avait plus jamais connu de tels autodafés. Un grand nombre d'immenses écrivains européens comptèrent parmi ceux dont les livres brûlèrent sur la Opernplatz à Berlin, en 1933 (1), dans le feu de joie de la « littérature anti-allemande ». L'autre feu de joie fut celui du Reichstag en 1933 également (2). Goering, en arrivant sur les lieux, clama tout de suite : « C'est le parti communiste le coupable...nous ne ferons pas de quartier. Tout communiste doit être abattu sur place.

YOUNG Nazis, dressed remarkably like their Italian counterparts, at the 1932 Reich Youth Convention of the Nazi Party held at Potsdam in the presence of the Führer (1). Adolf Hitler, here ascending the steps of Bückeberg (3), called the destruction of the Reichstag 'a God-given signal', meaning that 'There is nothing that shall now stop us from crushing out this murderous pest with an iron fist.' Others deduced that it was perhaps the country's short-lived democracy that had just gone up in smoke, particularly when Interior Minister Frick added that whatever the outcome of impending elections: 'A state of emergency will exist which will authorize the government to remain in office.' In March 1933, this was followed up with mass police raids particularly aimed at artists, journalists, students and intellectuals – presumably anyone who read books. Trucks were loaded with 'banned material' and residents from the Berlin artists' quarter of Südwestkorso (2).

JUNGE Nazis, deren Uniformen auffallend denjenigen ihrer italienischen Brüder ähneln, beim Reichsjugendtag der nationalsozialistischen Partei, der 1933 in Potsdam im Beisein des Führers stattfand (1). Adolf Hitler, der hier zum ersten nationalsozialistischen Erntedankfest den Bückeberg hinaufschreitet (3), nannte den Brand des Reichstags ein »Geschenk des Himmels«, denn: »Nun gibt es nichts mehr, was uns daran hindern wird, dies

mörderische Ungeziefer mit eiserner Faust auszumerzen.« Andere fanden eher, daß es die junge Demokratie des Landes war, die da in Flammen aufging. Im März 1933 folgte eine Welle von Polizeirazzien, die besonders Künstler, Journalisten, Studenten und Intellektuelle traf — alle, die Bücher lasen. Lastwagenweise wurde »verbotenes Schrifttum« aus dem Berliner Künstlerviertel um den Südwestkorso abgefahren (2).

JEUNES nazis, à la Convention de la jeunesse du Parti, qui se déroula en 1932 à Potsdam en présence du Führer (1). On notera la similitude avec les uniformes de leurs homologues italiens. Adolf Hitler, qu'on voit ici gravir les marches de Bückeberg (3), qualifia de « signe divin » la destruction du Reichstag, parce que « rien ne pourra maintenant nous empêcher d'écraser cette engeance d'assassins sous un poing d'airain. » D'autres, peut-être, y virent la fin d'une brève démocratie, notamment

lorsque le ministre de l'intérieur, Frick, ajouta que quels que soient les résultats des élections à venir, « l'état d'urgence sera décrété pour permettre au gouvernement de rester en place. » En mars 1933, il se vit confirmé par les rafles de police visant tout particulièrement les artistes, les journalistes, les étudiants et les intellectuels. Le « matériel interdit » et les habitants du quartier Südwestkorso, où vivaient les artistes berlinois, furent embarqués dans des camions (2).

2

On 12 November 1933 Berlin streets were packed with flag-waving, megaphone-bearing Nazis, calling out voters for the plebiscite (1). Stormtroopers dispatched to the polling booth anyone who had failed to vote (2). The 1936 anniversary of the 1923 March on Munich was restaged by Hitler and his cohorts from the beer hall where the original putsch was plotted to the Königsplatz (3).

Am 12. November 1933 waren die Berliner Straßen voll von Nazis, die Wähler zu den Urnen nötigten (1). SA-Männer halfen nach, wenn jemand sich der Wahl entziehen wollte (2). 1936 fand zum Jahrestag des Münchner Aufstandes von 1923 eine Parade statt, bei der Hitler und seine Kohorten vom Bürgerbräukeller, in dem sie den Putsch geplant hatten, zum Königsplatz zogen (3).

Le 12 novembre 1933, les nazis envahirent les rues de Berlin pour appeler les électeurs à participer au plébiscite (1). Les troupes d'assaut expédiaient à l'isoloir tous ceux qui n'avaient pas voté (2). L'anniversaire de la marche sur Munich de 1923, célébré en 1936 par Hitler et ses troupes, est organisé depuis la brasserie où le putsch avait été conçu jusqu'à la Koenigsplatz (3).

3

IN 1935 Hitler inspected the guard of
honour before receiving the new
Spanish Ambassador at the presidential
palace (1). Hermann Goering displays an
unusually ambiguous response to the
attention he and his medals are receiving
from his pet lioness, oddly named 'Caesar'
(2). Some say this is Hitler's only
worthwhile legacy – the Volkswagen, a car
tough and reliable as a tank, designed in
1938 and still running (4). This one-theme
postcard vendor (3) is clearly a Hitler fan,
having adopted his moustache and adapted
his clock to suit.

IM Jahre 1935 inspiziert Hitler die
Ehrengarde vor dem Empfang des neuen
spanischen Botschafters im Präsidenten-
palast (1). Hermann Göring ist ausnahms-
weise einmal die Aufmerksamkeit, die ihm
und seinen Orden entgegengebracht wird,
zuviel — von seiner zahmen Löwin, die
auf den Namen »Cäsar« hörte (2). Nach
Meinung vieler die einzig positive
Hinterlassenschaft Hitlers — der Volkswagen, ein Auto so robust wie ein Panzer,
1938 entworfen und noch heute gebaut
(4). Dieser Postkartenverkäufer hat nur ein
einziges Bildmotiv für seine Karten und ist
offenbar ein Verehrer des Führers, denn er
hat nicht nur sein Bärtchen übernommen,
sondern besitzt sogar eine passende
Wanduhr (3).

3

4

HITLER inspectant en 1935 la garde d'honneur avant d'accueillir le nouvel ambassadeur d'Espagne au palais présidentiel (1). Hermann Goering a un comportement singulièrement ambigu face aux attentions prodiguées sur sa personne et ses médailles par sa lionne apprivoisée répondant au nom de « Caesar » (2). Certains estiment que c'est la seule chose valable léguée sous Hitler: la Volkswagen, une voiture fiable comme un char d'assaut, conçue en 1938 et encore aujourd'hui sur les routes (4). Ce vendeur de cartes postales (3) au thème unique est manifestement un admirateur d'Hitler auquel il emprunte la moustache et en l'honneur duquel il a adapté son horloge.

1

2   3

In 1935 Hitler's army entered the Saarland (3), in 1936 the Rhineland (1); in 1938 it was the Egerland. Female adoration seems to have increased over the period, with 50,000 young women of Carlsbad sporting their best scarves and *dirndln*, their brightest smiles (2). Each step nearer France proved more of a pushover than the Germans anticipated, it being

against the terms of the treaties of Versailles and Locarno. When in 1935 Britain also signed a treaty permitting Germany to rebuld its naval strength, the French press fumed: 'Does London imagine that Hitler has renounced any of the projects indicated in his book *Mein Kampf*? If so, the illusion of our friends across the Channel is complete'.

1935 marschierten Hitlers Armeen im Saarland ein (3), 1936 im Rheinland (1), und 1938 im Egerland. Offenbar flogen den Soldaten zusehends die Herzen des schönen Geschlechts zu, denn hier in Karlsbad sind schon 50.000 Frauen gekommen und zeigen ihr schönstes Lächeln (2). Der Vormarsch in Richtung Frankreich war für die Deutschen ein Kinderspiel, obwohl jeder Schritt ein Verstoß gegen die Verträge von Versailles

und Locarno war. Als 1935 die Engländer einen Vertrag mitunterzeichneten, der den Deutschen gestattete, ihre Marine wiederaufzubauen, empörte sich die französische Presse: »Glaubt denn die Regierung in London, Hitler habe die Ziele aufgegeben, die er in seinem Buch *Mein Kampf* beschreibt? Wenn ja, dann könnten unsere Freunde jenseits des Ärmelkanals sich nicht schwerer täuschen.«

EN 1935 l'armée d'Hitler pénètre en Sarre (3) et en 1936 en Rhénanie (1) avant d'arriver dans l'Egerland (la Bohême) en 1938. 50 000 jeunes femmes à Carlsbad arborent leurs plus beaux fichus et leur sourire le plus éclatant (2). Au fur et à mesure qu'ils se rapprochaient de la France, sa conquête apparaissait aux Allemands de plus en plus facile, bien qu'elle allât ainsi à l'encontre des clauses

stipulées sur les traités de Versailles et de Locarno. Lorsqu'en 1935 la Grande-Bretagne signa à son tour le traité permettant à l'Allemagne de reconstituer sa puissance navale, la presse française fulmina : « Londres s'imagine t-elle qu'Hitler ait renoncé à un seul de ses projets mentionnés dans son livre *Mein Kampf* ? Si oui, nos amis d'Outre-Manche se font bel et bien des illusions ».

CHAMBERLAIN's policy of appeasing Hitler pleased some, not least, of course, the Führer himself, who fêted him at no fewer than three conferences in September 1938 (1, 2); or the Ludgate Circus florist (4) honouring the British Prime Minister who wanted 'peace at any price'. Unfortunately, appeasement went too far: the Czechs and French felt betrayed by it; many English politicians and commentators mistrusted it; and finally even Hitler turned out to have been keener on invading the Sudetenland than accepting the Czech surrender brokered for him by Chamberlain. On 1 October Hitler occupied the Sudetenland anyway, and Chamberlain waved his famous scrap of white paper (3), announcing that the terms of the Munich agreement spelt the intention of the British and German nations 'never to go to war with one another again'.

CHAMBERLAINS versöhnlicher Kurs gefiel manchem, nicht zuletzt natürlich dem Führer selbst, der ihn auf gleich drei Konferenzen im September 1938 feierte (1, 2), oder auch der Floristin in Ludgate, die ihr Fenster zu Ehren des britischen Premiers dekorierte, der »Frieden um jeden Preis« wollte (4). Leider ging die Appeasement-Politik zu weit: Die Tschechen und Franzosen fühlten sich betrogen davon; viele englische Politiker und Kolumnisten trauten ihr nicht; und am Ende stellte sich heraus, daß Hitler es eher auf das Sudetenland abgesehen hatte als auf die tschechische Kapitulation, die Chamberlain für ihn aushandelte. Am 1. Oktober marschierten die deutschen Truppen im Sudetenland ein, und Chamberlain zeigte sein berühmtes Blatt Papier und verkündete, daß gemäß den Münchner Verträgen die britischen und deutschen Nationen »nie wieder gegeneinander Krieg führen werden« (3).

3

WE ARE PROUD OF YOU

GOD BLESS YOU

4

La politique menée par Chamberlain en vue d'apaiser Hitler plaisait à certains, en premier au Führer, qui le fêta à l'occasion de trois conférences qui se déroulèrent en septembre 1938 (1, 2) ; mais aussi à la fleuriste du cirque Ludgate (4) qui rend hommage au Premier ministre britannique désireux de présenter « la paix à tout prix ». Malheureusement il alla trop loin dans l'apaisement, donnant aux Tchèques et aux Français le sentiment d'être trahis, suscitant la méfiance de bien des hommes politiques et observateurs anglais. Hitler lui-même préféra l'invasion des Sudètes à une capitulation tchèque que Chamberlain lui offrait. Le 1er octobre, Hitler occupait tout de même les Sudètes tandis que Chamberlain annonçait en agitant son célèbre chiffon de papier blanc (3) que les clauses de l'accord de Munich énonçaient l'intention des nations britannique et allemande de « ne plus jamais se livrer la guerre ».

War in Europe: The Blitz

HITLER'S 'secret weapon' – in Goering's words the 'miracle weapon' – was intended to bomb the British into submission. It came out of the Occupied Pas de Calais as a jet-propelled bomber flying at 400 mph and carrying a ton of explosives. The beauty for the Germans was that it required no pilot and was capable of scoring two hits in one: steered by a gyroscope it left a characteristic trail of orange smoke and exploded within fifteen seconds of impact; it also scored a major propaganda coup by being the first of its kind and remaining immune to anti-aircraft fire from the 'ack-ack' units deployed on Britain's south coast.

The onslaught became known as London's 'second blitz' and the aircraft themselves as 'doodlebugs' or 'buzz bombs' from the noise they made, flying at low altitudes. Colin Perry, an eighteen-year-old living with his family in Tooting, kept a diary. One night he recorded: 'Two incendiary bombs fell in the next road to us, but the wardens speedily put out the small fires. Bombs fell everywhere. Midnight and we were all indoors, undressed… As I lay asleep, rather half-and-half, I listened to the roar of hundreds of 'planes. Three or four bombs fell just near us with deafening explosions, like a firework – Bang! and the shsssing and hissing of sparks… This was Hitler's big attempt, and I knew that the 'planes I had seen in the afternoon, was hearing now, constituted part of the greatest air-battle of mankind. I went back to bed, guns, guns, guns, thud, thud, thud… I listened to three screamers, meooowwwwheeelll – they went. About a mile away I think. I preferred the screaming bomb, it at least gave, however brief, a warning. How those outside the shelters dived for cover. Not a word said but one, impulsive, automatic dive. The screech certainly was rather ghostly.'

400 people were killed and at least 1400 seriously injured, thousands more fleeing their shattered East End as refugees. London's Dockland was on fire, the gasworks also burning; some blazes lasted up to a week. 86 of the Luftwaffe's 500 were shot down to 22 of the RAF, but they returned the following night to hit every borough of Metropolitan London. On 11 September, Churchill made a morale-raising broadcast: 'These cruel, wanton indiscriminate bombings of London are, of course, a part of Hitler's invasion plans. He hopes, by killing large numbers of civilians, and women and children, he will terrorize and cow the people of this mighty imperial city… What he has done is to kindle a fire in British hearts, here and all over the world, which will glow after all traces of the conflagration he has caused in London have been removed.' When, of course, Churchill determined to bomb the civilian populations of historic Dresden, Leipzig and Berlin, 'cruel', 'wanton' and 'indiscriminate' were not the adjectives employed in his propaganda.

The Civil Defence volunteers, with those conscripted into the Firefighters and the Home Guard, took on the firing and flattening of unsafe buildings; the re-laying of gas and water mains and telephone lines; the rebuilding of roads and bridges. They had also to help dig out the dead, rescue the wounded, bring in supplies of gasmasks or milk and attempt to deliver news and letters to houses that no longer existed. Masks were issued in 1939 to the British population, including the youngest: Neville Mooney was the first baby born in London after the declaration of war and arrived home from hospital in a new designer model (1). During one of Hitler's last forays in 1944, little Barbara James is being carried from the shell of her home (2).

Hitlers »Geheimwaffe« — oder, wie Göring sie nannte, die »Wunderwaffe« — sollte England in die Knie zwingen. Die raketengetriebenen Flugbomben wurden im okkupierten Pas-de-Calais gestartet und brachten ihre Tonne Sprengstoff mit 600 Stundenkilometern über den Kanal. Aus deutscher Sicht war das Beste an den V-Waffen, daß sie keine Piloten brauchten, und zudem wirkten sie gleich zweifach: Die durch einen Kreiselkompaß gesteuerten Raketen, die einen orangeroten Rauchstreifen hinterließen, explodierten binnen fünfzehn Sekunden nach dem Aufschlag, und sie waren als erste Geschosse ihrer Art, die noch dazu immun gegen die Flakstellungen entlang der britischen Südküste waren, ein gelungener Propagandacoup.

In London wurde die Kampagne als »zweiter Blitz« bekannt, die Raketen hießen *doodlebugs* oder *buzz bombs*, nach dem typischen Geräusch, das sie kurz vor dem Aufschlag machten. Der achtzehnjährige Colin Perry, der mit seiner Familie im Londoner Stadtteil Tooting wohnte, führte Tagebuch. In jener Nacht schrieb er: »Zwei Brandbomben gingen draußen auf der Straße nieder, aber die Wachposten hatten die kleinen Brände schnell gelöscht. Überall regnete es Bomben. Mitternacht, wir waren alle im Haus, im Nachtzeug... Ich lag im Bett, schlief aber nur halb und hörte dem Dröhnen der Flugzeuge zu, Hunderte davon. Ein paar Bomben schlugen direkt bei unserem Haus ein, mit ohrenbetäubendem Knall, wie Feuerwerkskörper — Womm! Und dann das Zischen und Fauchen der Funken... Das war Hitlers Großangriff, und ich wußte, daß die Flugzeuge, die ich am Nachmittag gesehen hatte, deren Motoren ich nun hörte, in der größten Luftschlacht flogen, die die Menschheit je gesehen hatte. Ich zog mir die Decke über den Kopf, überall die Flaks, tack-tack-tack... drei Heuler hintereinander hörte ich, miiiiiauuuuwiiiie — dann waren sie vorbei. Vielleicht eine Meile weit fort. Mir waren die Heuler lieber, weil sie einen warnten, wenigstens ein paar Sekunden vorher. Was rannten die Leute draußen, die nicht in einen Schutzraum gekommen waren, und suchten nach Deckung! Kein einziges Wort fiel, doch wie auf Kommando, automatisch, warfen sich alle nieder. Das Heulen ging einem wirklich durch Mark und Bein.«

400 Menschen kamen um, und mindestens 1.400 wurden schwer verwundet; Tausende flohen aus ihren zerbombten Wohnungen im East End. Die Docks standen in Flammen, die Gasanstalt brannte, manche Feuer konnten erst nach einer Woche gelöscht werden. 86 der 500 Luftwaffenbomber wurden abgeschossen, die RAF verlor 22, doch in der folgenden Nacht waren die Deutschen wieder da, und kein Viertel der Londoner Innenstadt blieb verschont. Am 11. September hielt Churchill zur Stärkung der Moral eine Rundfunkansprache: »Diese grausamen, gewissenlosen, willkürlichen Bombenangriffe auf London sind natürlich Teil von Hitlers Invasionsplänen. Er hofft, wenn er Zivilisten in großer Zahl tötet, Frauen und Kinder, könne er die Menschen dieser gewaltigen Hauptstadt in Angst und Schrecken versetzen... Doch statt dessen hat er ein Feuer in den britischen Herzen entfacht, hier zu Hause und überall auf der Welt, das noch wärmen wird, wenn die Brände in London längst gelöscht sind.« Als Churchill sich entschloß, Bomben auf die Bewohner der Städte Dresden, Leipzig und Berlin zu werfen, war freilich in den offiziellen Verlautbarungen von »grausam«, »gewissenlos« und »willkürlich« nicht die Rede.

Die Helfer der Civil Defence Services mußten sich auch um die Opfer kümmern: die verschütteten Leichen bergen, die Verletzten retten, Gasmasken und Milch bringen, Zeitungen und Briefe zustellen, wo die Häuser gar nicht mehr existierten. Jeder bekam eine Gasmaske, selbst die Jüngsten: Neville Mooney war das erste Kind, das nach der Kriegserklärung in London zur Welt kam, und verließ das Krankenhaus mit einem maßgeschneiderten Exemplar (1). Die kleine Barbara James wird 1944 nach einem der letzten Nazi-Angriffe aus ihrem ausgebombten Heim getragen (2).

L'ARME secrète de Hitler, ou plutôt l'« arme miracle », pour reprendre les termes de Goering, devait finir par soumettre les Britanniques à force bombardements. Elle apparut dans le Pas-de-Calais occupé sous l'aspect d'une fusée propulsée par des réacteurs, qui volait à la vitesse d'environ 644 km/h avec une tonne d'explosif à son bord. Pour les Allemands, son intérêt résidait dans le fait qu'elle n'avait nul besoin de pilote et qu'elle pouvait frapper simultanément deux cibles. À pilotage gyroscopique, après avoir laissé dans son sillage une traînée de fumée orange caractéristique, elle explosait moins de quinze secondes dès l'objectif atteint. Première de son genre invulnérable aux tirs antiaériens des unités de DCA déployées sur le littoral sud de la Grande-Bretagne, elle servit grandement la propagande.

Les Anglais baptisèrent l'offensive sur Londres le « deuxième éclair », quant aux aéroneufs eux-mêmes, ils furent surnommés « punaises » ou encore « bombes bourdonnante » en raison du bruit qu'ils faisaient à basse altitude. Colin Perry, un jeune homme de dix-huit ans, qui vivait à Tooting avec sa famille, tenait un journal. Il y nota cette nuit-là : « Deux bombes incendiaires ont touché la rue voisine, mais les *wardens* (civils chargés de la défense passive) sont rapidement parvenus à éteindre les débuts d'incendie. Des bombes sont tombées partout. Il était minuit, nous étions tous rentrés, tous habillés… Je m'étais allongé pour dormir, plutôt d'un œil, tout en écoutant le rugissement de centaines d'avions. Trois ou quatre bombes explosèrent tout près de là, dans un vacarme assourdissant, tel un feu d'artifice. Les éclairs fusaient… Ce fut un formidable coup d'essai de la part de Hitler. Je savais bien que les avions aperçus dans l'après-midi et qui maintenant menaient la danse livraient la plus grande bataille aérienne de tous les temps. Je retournai alors au lit tandis que les canons bégayaient. J'écoutai trois bombes dites « hurlantes » passer au loin en miaulant. À environ un kilomètre et demi d'ici, pensai-je. Je préférais les bombes hurlantes qui, même si ce n'était qu'un cours instant avant, prévenaient avant d'exploser. Les gens hors des abris plongeaient alors à couvert. Tandis que se faisaient ces plongeons impulsifs et automatiques, le hurlement semblait sorti tout droit de la gorge d'un spectre. »

400 personnes périrent tandis que 1400 autres furent gravement blessées, sans oublier les milliers de réfugiés qui avaient fui East End après que leurs foyers furent dévastés. La zone autour du port de Londres était en flammes, de même que l'usine à gaz. Certains incendies mirent une semaine avant de s'éteindre. Sur les 500 appareils alignés par la Luftwaffe, 86 furent abattus contre 22 appareils pour l'aviation britannique ; mais cela n'empêcha pas les pilotes allemands de revenir la nuit suivante pilonner chaque arrondissement de la métropole londonienne. Le 11 septembre, Churchill délivra sur les ondes un discours réconfortant : « Ces bombardements cruels, aveugles et sauvages de Londres font, bien entendu, partie du plan d'invasion de Hitler. Ce dernier espère, en massacrant massivement les populations civiles, femmes et enfants compris, soumettre par la terreur le peuple de cette puissante cité impériale… Il a en fait allumé un brasier dans le cœur des Britanniques, ici et partout à travers le monde, qui brûlera bien après que toutes traces des dévastations qu'il a infligées à Londres auront été supprimées. » Il va de soi que lorsque Churchill prit la décision de faire bombarder les populations civiles des villes historiques qu'étaient Dresde, Leipzig et Berlin, son vocabulaire fut moins virulent.

Les membres de la Défense passive, les pompiers et l'armée affectée à la défense du territoire (*Home Guard*), tous volontaires, se chargeaient d'incendier et de démolir les bâtiments représentant un danger pour la sécurité, de remplacer les principales canalisations d'eau et de gaz, ainsi que les lignes téléphoniques, et de reconstruire les routes et les ponts. Ils devaient aussi aider à déterrer les morts, secourir les blessés, ravitailler en lait ou en masques à gaz, et s'efforcer de délivrer les nouvelles et les lettres à des adresses qui n'existaient plus. Des masques furent fournis en 1939 à la population britannique, y compris aux plus jeunes : Neville Mooney fut le premier bébé à naître à Londres après la déclaration de la guerre. Il fit le trajet de l'hôpital jusqu'à chez lui équipé d'un modèle de masque de conception nouvelle (1). En 1944, pendant l'un des derniers raids hitlériens, la petite Barbara James est transportée hors de sa maison dont il ne reste plus que la carcasse (2).

THE Great War had seen an estimated million gas casualties, a figure clearly deliberately reduced for propaganda purposes by each of the combatant nations. Gas warfare had been introduced by the Germans and the assumption was that in

the next war it was to become a weapon of choice in bombing campaigns. All children in state schools were given 'gas instruction lessons' (1) while housewives practised wearing them as they carried on their daily pursuits (2).

DER Erste Weltkrieg forderte nach Schätzungen eine Million Gas-Tote, wobei die Zahlen auf beiden Seiten aus Gründen der Propaganda zu niedrig angesetzt sein dürften. Der Gaskrieg war eine deutsche Erfindung, und alle gingen

davon aus, daß Gasbomben im nächsten Krieg eine Hauptwaffe sein würden. In den staatlichen Schulen bekamen sämtliche Kinder »Gasunterricht« (1), und Hausfrauen trugen Gasmasken bei der täglichen Arbeit (2).

LES victimes du gaz se comptèrent par millions durant la Grande Guerre. Pour des raisons évidentes, ce chiffre était volontairement minimisé dans chaque camp pour les besoins de la propagande. Utilisé pour la première fois dans le conflit par les Allemands, on était persuadé que le gaz deviendrait l'arme préférée au cours des bombardements de la prochaine guerre. Tous les élèves des écoles publiques recevaient des « cours d'initiation au gaz » (1) pendant que les ménagères s'exerçaient à exécuter leurs tâches quotidiennes affublées d'un masque (2).

FROM 1939, upwards of three million children, including infants and babes-in-arms with their mothers, were evacuated from the major city centres to the countryside to avoid the bombing (1). Some 'sea evacuees' were even sent as far afield as Canada and the United States, where many languished, though some thrived apart from their families (3), keeping up to date with newspapers. These children (2), along with their boxed gas-masks, are returning via Waterloo Station after taking the risk of spending Christmas 1939 in their London homes.

VON 1939 an wurden drei Millionen Kinder, darunter Säuglinge und Kleinkinder mit ihren Müttern, aus den Zentren der Großstädte aufs Land evakuiert, wo ihnen weniger Gefahr durch Bomben drohte (1). Einige wurden »nach Übersee verschickt« und kamen bis in die USA und nach Kanada, wo viele todunglücklich wurden; andere genossen das Leben fernab ihrer Familie, und Zeitungen halfen ihnen, auf dem laufenden zu bleiben (3). Hier (2) kehren Kinder, jedes mit seiner Gasmaske im Täschchen, von der Waterloo Station zu ihren Evakuierungsorten zurück, nachdem sie riskiert hatten, das Weihnachtsfest 1939 zu Hause in London zu verbringen.

À PARTIR de 1939, on évalue à plus de trois millions le nombre des enfants, y compris les tout-petits, les nourrissons et leurs mères, à être évacués des grandes villes pour être amenés dans les campagnes (1). Certains « évacués par mer » partaient pour le Canada ou les États-Unis. Si beaucoup d'entre eux languissaient, d'autres s'épanouissaient loin de leurs familles (3) en suivant l'actualité dans les journaux. Ces enfants (2) qui transportent leur masque à gaz dans une boîte repartent par la gare de Waterloo, après avoir pris le risque de passer l'hiver 1939 dans leur foyer londonien.

2

3

PERHAPS the most famous British picture of the War (overleaf). New Year's Eve 1940 and, two days after the raid, London's East End still burns around St Paul's Cathedral. The cathedral, however, remained standing, a symbol of resistance.

DIES (folgende Seite) ist vielleicht das berühmteste Kriegsbild aus England überhaupt. Silvester 1940, und zwei Tage nach dem Luftangriff brennt das Londoner East End rund um die St.-Pauls-Kathedrale noch immer. Doch die Kathedrale blieb bestehen, ein Symbol des Widerstands.

VOICI peut-être la photographie la plus célèbre de la guerre en Grande-Bretagne (au verso). Il l'agit du réveillon de 1940, tandis que depuis deux jours, l'incendie d'East End continue de faire rage. La cathédrale Saint Paul demeura toutefois debout, comme le symbole de la résistance.

A IR raids also struck other cities: these show some of the devastation meted out to Liverpool and Canterbury. With many women requisitioned for war work once the men were conscripted, it was the grandparents (and the foster parents of evacuee children) who took responsibility for the young (2, 3). London's old Roman Wall with its outer ring of city churches and dwellings was severely damaged: here, in May 1941, a postman attempts to deliver in historic Watling Street (1); a fruit stall does good business in 1940 under the slogan 'Hitler's bombs can't beat us' (5); and in Kensington, the library of the famous Holland House (built in 1607 by Sir Walter Cope, Gentleman of the Bedchamber to James I) was virtually destroyed by a Molotov 'breadbasket' (4). The east wing was somehow saved, and now houses the King George Memorial Youth Hostel.

AUCH andere Großstädte hatten unter den Luftangriffen zu leiden — diese Bilder geben einen Eindruck von den Zerstörungen in Liverpool und Canterbury. Viele Frauen wurden zur Arbeit in den Fabriken verpflichtet, nachdem die Männer eingerückt waren, und die Großeltern (und Pflegeeltern der evakuierten Kinder) übernahmen nun die Verantwortung für die Kleinen (2, 3). Die römischen Stadtmauern Londons und der Ring von Stadtkirchen und Siedlungen, der sie umgab, nahmen schweren Schaden; hier versucht ein Postbote im Mai 1941, in der historischen Watling Street zuzustellen (1); ein Obstkarren macht 1940 gute Geschäfte mit dem Slogan »Wir lassen uns von Hitlers Bomben nicht unterkriegen« (5); und in Kensington sieht man die Trümmer der Bibliothek von Holland House (1607 erbaut von Sir Walter Cope, dem Kammerjunker Jakobs I.), das eine Brandbombe fast völlig zerstörte (4). Nur der Ostflügel wurde verschont und dient heute als Jugendherberge, das King George Memorial Youth Hostel.

D'AUTRES grandes villes firent également les frais des attaques aériennes : ici les dévastations infligées à Liverpool et à Canterbury.Parce que nombre de femmes avaient été réquisitionnées pour les travaux de guerre, tandis que les hommes étaient mobilisés, les grands-parents (et les parents nourriciers des enfants évacués) se retrouvèrent chargés de prendre soin des enfants (2 et 3). Le vieux mur romain de Londres, avec sa ceinture extérieure d'églises et de logements, fut sérieusement endommagé : ici en mai 1941, le facteur s'efforce d'assurer la distribution postale dans la rue historique de Watling Street (1) ; un vendeur de fruits fait de bonnes affaires en 1940, fort du slogan : « Les bombes de Hitler ne peuvent pas nous abattre » (5) ; tandis qu'à Kensington, la bibliothèque de la célèbre Holland House (construite en 1607 par Sir Walter Cope, gentilhomme attaché au service de la chambre de Jacques 1er) fut pratiquement détruite par une « corbeille à pain » molotov (4). L'aile orientale, qui en réchappa par miracle, abrite aujourd'hui l'auberge de jeunesse du mémorial du roi George.

3

4

5

1

2

EVERYTHING that could afford shelter was invoked for those who stayed in the cities. Anderson shelters that served to resist all but a direct hit were useless to houses without garden space in which to erect them. That included all of the tenement blocks and back-to-backs of the poorer areas in every town. Street shelters were found to suffer from weak mortar; houses could not withstand blast. Everything was utilized, from railway arches, cellars, schools and civic buildings, train and underground stations, right down to day-nursery cupboards (2) for the young and staircases for the rest (1).

In 1940 the government appeal for aluminium and iron led to this aircraft production dump (3), at which the whole population could contribute to the war effort. From the wealthy of Chelsea who removed their garden railings to this young lad who, possibly with a degree of relief, brought in the family bathtub from a house clearly off the mains (4), everyone could contribute at least a pot or a pan to be smelted into aluminium for the aircraft assembly presses across the country.

DIEJENIGEN, die in den Städten blieben, suchten Luftschutz, wo sie ihn fanden. Die sogenannten Anderson-Shelter aus Stahlblech, die alles mit Ausnahme eines direkten Treffers aushielten, konnte man nur im Garten aufstellen, und bei den Miets- und Reihenhäusern der ärmeren Stadtviertel war oft kein Platz dafür. Der Mörtel der Schutzhütten an den Straßen erwies sich als zu schwach, und Häuser hielten dem Druck nicht stand. Man nutzte alles, von Eisenbahnbrücken über Keller, Schulen und Verwaltungsgebäude, von Bahnhöfen und U-Bahn-Stationen bis hin zu Schränken in den Kindergärten (2), und wer nichts anderes fand, mußte sich mit einer Treppe begnügen (1).

1940 appellierte die Regierung an die Bevölkerung, Aluminium und Eisen für die Waffenproduktion zu spenden, und dieser Schrotthaufen bei einer Flugzeugfabrik zeigt, daß alle mithalfen (3). Von den Reichen aus Chelsea, die ihre Gartenzäune hergaben, bis hin zu diesem Jungen (4), der — offenbar aus einem Haus, das keinen Wasseranschluß mehr hat, und vielleicht nicht ganz ohne Erleichterung — die Badewanne der Familie bringt, konnte jeder zumindest einen Topf oder eine Pfanne erübrigen, die eingeschmolzen wurden, um Aluminium für die über das ganze Land verteilte Flugzeugproduktion zu gewinnen.

TOUT ce qui pouvait servir d'abri était bon à prendre pour ceux qui restaient dans les grandes villes. L'abri Anderson qui résistait à tout, sauf à un impact direct, n'était d'aucune utilité si la maison ne possédait pas de jardin suffisamment grand pour l'y ériger. C'était le lot commun des immeubles construits dos à dos, situés dans les zones les plus défavorisées de chaque ville. Les abris extérieurs s'avérèrent inefficaces contre les tirs de mortier, aussi faibles fussent-ils, et les maisons ne résistaient pas au souffle de l'explosion. On utilisait tout, qu'il s'agît des arches des voies ferrées, des caves, des bâtiments scolaires ou municipaux, des gares ferroviaires ou des stations de métro, jusqu'à employer les armoires des pouponnières (2) pour les plus jeunes et la cage d'escalier (1) pour les autres.

L'appel lancé en 1940 à la population par les autorités nationales pour recueillir de l'aluminium et du fer favorisa l'apparition de ces décharges (3) de matériaux destinés à la production aéronautique. Chacun put y aller de sa contribution à l'effort de guerre. En y voit des gens appartenant aux couches aisées de Chelsea qui apportaient les barreaux entourant leur jardin jusqu'à ce jeune gars qui, peut-être un peu soulagé, apportait la baignoire familiale retirée d'une maison bien évidemment coupée du réseau de distribution (4). Dans tout le pays, chacun put faire au moins le don d'une marmite ou d'une casserole dont l'aluminium serait fondu et pressé aux fins de l'industrie de guerre.

3

4

1

Amerıcan GIs – Overpaid, Over-sexed and Over Here – brought gloom to British men and a sparkle to the women. Children came fresh to Wrigley's gum and Hershey bars (2); women to tipped Virginia tobacco (3); and the GIs themselves demanded big-band Bourbon-fuelled night clubs to remind them of home (4). Even the American Red Cross got involved in running a 'Coney Island' arcade provided by the Amusement Caterers' Association (1).

Die amerikanischen GIs waren den Männern ein Dorn im Auge, doch bei den Frauen hochwillkommen. Die Kinder bekamen ihre ersten Wrigley-Kaugummis (2), die Frauen Virginia-Zigaretten mit Filtern (3). Die GIs selbst waren immer auf der Suche nach Nachtclubs mit Big Bands und Bourbon, damit sie sich wie zu Hause fühlen konnten (4). Selbst das amerikanische Rote Kreuz half mit, den »Coney Island«-Spielsalon zu betreiben (1).

Alors que les femmes britanniques découvraient l'Amérique par le biais de ses soldats, les enfants découvraient la gomme Wrigley et les barres Hershey (2). Si les Anglaises appréciaient les cigarettes de Virginie (3), les GIs, quant à eux, voulaient reconstituer l'atmosphère de la mère patrie (4). La Croix-Rouge américaine elle-même géra la galerie Coney Island, proposée par l'Association des fournisseurs de distractions (1).

4

1   2

1

(Previous pages)
1944 saw the US army advancing through Nazi terrain (1). This tank was knocked out by US engineers (3). The Signal Corps, in Normandy await the Allied landings (2).

(vorige Seiten)
1944 schoben amerikanische Truppen die Front durch das von den Nazis eroberte Terrain zurück (1). Dieser deutsche Panzer wurde von amerikanischen Pionieren kampfunfähig geschossen (3). Die US-Fernmeldetruppe (2) erwartet 1944 die Landung der Alliierten.

(pages précédentes)
DÈS 1944, l'armée américaine repoussait la ligne de front nazie (1). Ce char d'assaut allemand a été mis hors de combat par le génie américain (3). Des radiotélégraphistes américains se reposent en 1944 en Normandie (2), en attendant les Alliés.

2

LANGUAGE is clearly not a necessary means of communication when there is something in common to celebrate. After regaining their country from the German Occupation, French villagers fraternize with GIs of the liberating forces (2, 4), while in the town of St Sauveur Lendelin residents shower armoured personnel carriers with flowers (3). When, close to the end of the war on the continent (27 April 1945), the US and the Ukraine First Armies met at Torgau on the Elbe, reporter Iris Carpenter of the Boston Globe (1) wanted to get her compatriot's first-hand account.

MAN muß nicht unbedingt dieselbe Sprache sprechen, wenn es etwas Gemeinsames zu feiern gibt: Nach der Befreiung von der deutschen Besatzung verbrüdern sich die Bewohner eines französischen Dorfes mit den GIs der Befreiungstruppen (2, 4), und die Mädchen des Städtchens St. Sauveur Lendelin werfen den Soldaten in ihren Panzerwagen Blumen zu (3). Als sich am 27. April 1945, kurz vor Ende des Krieges in Europa, die Erste US-Armee und die Erste Armee der Ukraine in Torgau an der Elbe trafen, war Iris Carpenter, Reporterin des *Boston Globe*, dabei, um von ihren Landsleuten einen Bericht aus erster Hand zu bekommen (1).

IL est manifestement possible de comprendre la langue de l'autre lorsqu'on a quelque chose en commun à célébrer. Après la libération des pays, les villageois français fraternisent avec les soldats américains des forces de libération (2 et 4), tandis que dans la ville de Saint-Sauveur-Lendelin, les habitants font pleuvoir des fleurs sur les véhicules blindés transportant les troupes (3). Quand, vers la fin de la guerre sur le continent (le 27 avril 1945), les premières armées américaine et ukrainienne opérèrent leur jonction à Torgau, sur l'Elbe, la journaliste Iris Carpenter du Boston Globe (1) voulut obtenir d'un de ses compatriotes un compte rendu de première main.

3

4

The end of the German Occupation brought recriminations for many in France (1). Here youthful members of the *maquis* (Resistance fighters) undergo weapons training (2) with an international variety of Sten, Ruby, Mark II and Le Français pistols, Colt and Bulldog revolvers, air-dropped by the London-based Free French, led by General de Gaulle.

NACH dem Ende der deutschen Besatzung hatten viele Franzosen sich wegen Kollaboration zu verantworten (1). Hier sieht man jugendliche Widerstands-kämpfer (*maquis*) bei Übungen mit einer internationalen Mischung an Waffen, mit Sten-, Ruby-, Mark II- und Le Français-Pistolen, Colt- und Bulldog-Revolvern, allesamt von Flugzeugen der Freien Französischen Armee abgeworfen, die von London aus operierte und unter der Führung von General de Gaulle stand (2).

EN France, avec la fin de l'occupation allemande, sonna également l'heure des règlements de comptes (1). Ici, des jeunes du maquis s'entraînent au maniement des armes provenant d'un arsenal international (2) – Sten, Ruby, Mark II, Le Français, Colt et Bulldog –, parachutées par la France libre, l'organisation du général de Gaulle, basée à Londres.

1 2

THE Russian people lost more lives than any other nation during the Second World War: over 20 million are estimated to have died. Like Napoleon, Hitler threw division after division into the war on the eastern front, only to see them driven back or, more humiliatingly still, defeated by the Russian winter, an even fiercer enemy than the Russian troops. The fall of Stalingrad in November 1942 (3) was for many the turning-point of the war, while the siege of Leningrad led to starvation for its beleaguered inhabitants. Even youths joined up to fight, like this boy bidding his mother farewell (1), while Russian villagers who had taken to the woods near Orel to flee the German army here pass the corpses of their soldiers on their return home (2).

DIE Russen waren das Volk im Zweiten Weltkrieg, das die meisten Toten zu beklagen hatte: vermutlich über 20 Millionen Menschen kamen um. Wie Napoleon schickte auch Hitler Division um Division in den Krieg an der Ostfront, und alle wurden sie vom russischen Winter, einem noch erbitterteren Feind als die russische Armee, zurückgetrieben oder ganz geschlagen. Der Fall Stalingrads im November 1942 (3) war für viele die entscheidende Wende des Krieges; in Leningrad verhungerte die belagerte Bevölkerung. Selbst Kinder kamen an die Front, wie dieser Junge, der sich hier von seiner Mutter verabschiedet (1). Russische Bauern, die bei Orel in die Wälder geflohen waren, als die Deutschen kamen, finden bei ihrer Rückkehr ihre gefallenen Soldaten (2).

LE peuple soviétique fut, au cours de la Seconde Guerre mondiale, de toutes les nations, celui qui paya le plus lourd tribut en vies humaines : on l'estime à plus de 20 millions de morts. Comme Napoléon, Hitler lança ses divisions l'une après l'autre à l'assaut du front est avec pour seul résultat de les voir repoussées ou, plus humiliant encore, tenues en échec par l'hiver russe. La chute de Stalingrad, en novembre 1942 (3), signala pour beaucoup un tournant dans la guerre, alors que le siège de Leningrad affamait les habitants de la ville. Même les jeunes s'enrôlèrent pour combattre, tel ce garçon faisant ses adieux à sa mère (1). Ailleurs, des villageois russes, qui s'étaient réfugiés dans les bois non loin d'Orel pour échapper à l'armée allemande, prennent le chemin du retour au milieu des cadavres de leurs soldats (2).

3

EVEN the Soviet army were bogged down in freezing conditions more familiar to them than to the Germans (1). In January 1943 these German prisoners are on a forced march north-west of Stalingrad (2). Red Army instructors take Moscow schoolchildren on 'manoeuvres' in Sokolniky Park, dressed in regulation-issue white snow camouflage (3). They are being taught to build up a 'Front Line' with a gun emplacement.

OBWOHL ihnen die harten Winter vertrauter waren als ihren deutschen Feinden, saßen auch die russischen Truppen fest (1). Im Januar 1943 marschieren deutsche Kriegsgefangene von Stalingrad nordwestwärts (2). Ausbilder der Roten Armee auf »Manöver« mit Moskauer Schulkindern im Sokolniky-Park; die Kinder tragen die standardmäßigen weißen Winter-Tarnanzüge (3). Hier lernen sie, eine »Front« und eine Geschützstellung aufzubauen.

MEME l'armée soviétique, pourtant plus acclimatée que les Allemands se retrouva enlisée dans le froid glacial (1). Janvier 1943 : prisonniers allemands accomplissant une marche forcée au nord-ouest de Stalingrad (2). Des instructeurs de l'Armée rouge font exécuter à des écoliers des « manœuvres » dans le parc Sokol'niki, revêtus de la tenue réglementaire de camouflage, blanc de neige (3). Ils apprennent à édifier une « ligne de front » de canons.

2

3

IN April 1945 Berlin was subjected to street-by-street fighting to gain control of the capital (1). Dimitri Baltermants, famous Russian photographer and war hero, took the victory pictures: the Soviet hammer-and-sickle is raised over the Reichstag (3). May Day 1945: the US Ninth Army meets the Russians on the Elbe. Two soldiers celebrate in a dance, watched by their comrades-in-arms (2).

IM April 1945 kämpften sich in Berlin die einrückenden Armeen Straße um Straße vor (1). Dimitri Baltermants, der berühmte russische Photograph und Kriegsheld, hielt den Sieg in Bildern fest: Die sowjetische Flagge mit Hammer und Sichel wird über dem Reichstag gehißt (3). 1. Mai 1945: Die Neunte US-Armee und die russischen Truppen treffen sich an der Elbe. Zwei Soldaten beim Freudentanz, und ihre Waffenbrüder sehen zu (2).

EN avril 1945, Berlin était le théâtre de combats dont l'enjeu était de conquérir la capitale, rue après rue (1). Dimitri Baltermants, célèbre photographe et héros de guerre russe, prit les photographies de la victoire : le marteau et la faucille soviétiques sont hissés au-dessus du Reichstag (3). 1er mai 1945 : la 9e armée des États-Unis rejoint les Russes sur les bords de l'Elbe. Deux soldats dansent de joie sous le regard de leurs compagnons d'armes (2).

1 2

3

THE War left the problem of ten million displaced persons and refugees. Some cross the Elbe on a damaged bridge (3). A Russian soldier falls asleep at the historic meeting with the Ninth Army (2). He and his horse have travelled over 2000 miles. In Mönchengladbach (1), German residents extend white flags and handkerchiefs in surrender. This Berlin girl fraternizes with British troops (5), while on the balcony of Hitler's Chancellery, Russian, British and US soldiers line up in greeting (4).

AM Ende des Krieges waren zehn Millionen Flüchtlinge unterwegs. Einige überqueren die Elbe auf einer halbzerstörten Brücke (3). Dieser russische Soldat (2) ist beim historischen Treffen mit der 9. Armee eingeschlafen. In Mönchengladbach (1) ergibt sich die deutsche Zivilbevölkerung mit weißen Tüchern. Eine Berlinerin (5) schäkert mit britischen Soldaten und auf dem Balkon von Hitlers Reichskanzlei versammeln sich russische, britische und amerikanische Soldaten (4).

AVEC la fin de la guerre se posa le problème de dix millions de personnes déplacées et réfugiées. Certaines passent l'Elbe sur un pont endommagé (3). Un soldat russe s'endort pendant la jonction historique avec la 9e armée (2). Il a parcouru plus de 3 200 kilomètres. À Mönchengladbach (1), les habitants allemands font signe de reddition. Cette Berlinoise fraternise avec les troupes britanniques (5) Au palais de Hitler, des soldats russes, britanniques et américains alignés saluent la foule (4).

4

5

AMONG the most heartbreaking of situations was that of the internal displacement of refugees who ceased to belong anywhere. Particularly in eastern Europe, borders were so frequently shifted that some no longer knew if they were German-speaking Poles or Polish-speaking Germans. These Germans are unable either to travel on the roads prohibited to all but military transport, or to cross the Elbe with their horses and cattle (1). Neither can they return, so they are condemned to wander endlessly in circles like some kind of an outer Inferno. The other hellish landscape is on the outskirts of Berlin, where this tiny group (2) are the sole survivors of the 150 who left Lodz on what became known as the 'Death March'. Far from finding sanctuary in Berlin, these exiles are now trailing aimlessly along a railroad.

BESONDERS hart war das Los der Flüchtlinge, die nirgendwohin mehr gehörten. Vor allem in Osteuropa veränderten die Grenzen sich so häufig, daß manche nicht mehr wußten, ob sie nun deutsche Polen oder polnische Deutsche waren. Die Deutschen auf diesem Bild (1) dürfen nicht auf der Straße weiterziehen, die den Militärfahrzeugen vorbehalten ist, und auch nicht mit ihren Pferden und dem Vieh die Elbe

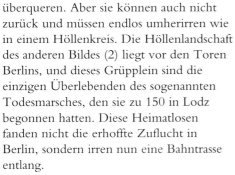

überqueren. Aber sie können auch nicht zurück und müssen endlos umherirren wie in einem Höllenkreis. Die Höllenlandschaft des anderen Bildes (2) liegt vor den Toren Berlins, und dieses Grüpplein sind die einzigen Überlebenden des sogenannten Todesmarsches, den sie zu 150 in Lodz begonnen hatten. Diese Heimatlosen fanden nicht die erhoffte Zuflucht in Berlin, sondern irren nun eine Bahntrasse entlang.

ᴘᴀʀᴍɪ les situations les plus douloureuses figurait celle des gens réfugiés et déplacés. Le cas était surtout classique en Europe de l'Est où le tracé des frontières avait été si souvent modifié que certains ne savaient plus s'ils étaient des Polonais germanophones ou des Allemands d'expression polonaise. Ici ces Allemands ne peuvent ni prendre les routes, interdites à toute circulation civile, ni traverser l'Elbe avec leurs chevaux et leurs bestiaux (1). Ils

ne peuvent pas non plus rentrer, condamnés qu'ils sont à tourner sans fin dans un univers devenu absurde. Cette autre scène infernale se déroule dans la banlieue de Berlin : ce minuscule groupe (2) représente les rescapés des 150 personnes qui avaient quitté Lódz pour entreprendre ce qu'on a appelé la « Marche de la mort ». À défaut de trouver refuge à Berlin, ces exilés cheminent maintenant sans but le long d'une voie ferrée.

1 2

SHORTLY after its foundation in 1948, UNESCO implemented a child healthcare programme intended to combat communicable infections – and infestations. This little refugee from the former Sudetenland (Czechoslovakia) is being deloused (1) while, ten years earlier, these 'Jewish and non-Aryan' refugee children from Vienna are waiting to be transferred by train from Harwich to Dovercourt Bay Camp (2). Since 502 names are too many to remember, each is given a number tagged to their clothes: a final straw in the process of depersonalization brought by the Nazi régime, as the tears here indicate (3).

KURZ nach ihrer Gründung im Jahre 1948 startete die UNESCO ein Gesundheitsprogramm für Kinder, das ansteckende Krankheiten bekämpfen sollte — und Parasiten. Diese kleine Heimatvertriebene aus dem Sudetenland (das nun wieder tschechisch war) wird gerade entlaust (1); zehn Jahre zuvor warteten »jüdische und nicht-arische« Flüchtlingskinder aus Wien auf den Zug, mit dem sie von Harwich in das englische Lager Dovercourt Bay gebracht werden sollten (2). Da keiner sich 502 Namen merken kann, bekommt jedes eine Nummerntafel angesteckt, mit der ihnen das Naziregime, wie die Tränen hier beweisen, auch noch das letzte bißchen Individualität genommen hat (3).

PEU après sa fondation, en 1948, l'Unesco mit en œuvre un programme de soins de santé infantiles en vue de lutter contre les maladies contagieuses et les infections. Cette petite réfugiée, originaire de l'ex-région des Sudètes (Tchécoslovaquie), subit un épouillage (1). Dix ans plus tôt, ces enfants réfugiés « juifs et non aryens », venus de Vienne, attendaient le train qui devait les transférer de Harwich au camp de Dovercourt Bay (2). Parce qu'il est impossible de mémoriser 502 noms, chacun d'eux reçut un numéro attaché à ses vêtements : touche finale dans le processus de dépersonnalisation mis en place par le régime nazi (3).

2

3

1   2

IN wartime Italy, poverty and hunger dogged these Sicilian children. Barefoot infants dressed in sacking watch enviously as their father drains his bowl (1). Polish children evacuated from Russia have somehow ended up tranported to Iran at the end of the war (2); at the height of the Spanish Civil War that preceded World War Two, 4000 Republican children arrive at a camp near Southampton (3) – many had already fled first to France.

DIE sizilianischen Kinder hatten im Krieg in Italien unter Armut und Hunger schwer zu leiden. Die barfüßigen, in Säcke gekleideten Kleinen schauen neidisch zu, wie der Vater seine Schale leert (1). Aus Rußland evakuierte polnische Kinder sind bei Kriegsende im Iran gelandet (2); auf dem Höhepunkt des Spanischen Bürgerkriegs, der dem Zweiten Weltkrieg vorausgegangen war, kommen 4.000 Republikanerkinder, von denen viele zuvor nach Frankreich geflüchtet waren, in Southampton an (3).

PENDANT la guerre, en Italie, ces enfants siciliens étaient pauvres et tenaillés par la faim. Des tout-petits, nu-pieds et habillés dans de la toile à sac, regardent avec envie leur père vider le contenu de son bol (1). Des enfants polonais évacués de Russie se retrouvent inexplicablement transportés en Iran à la fin de la guerre (2). Au plus fort de la guerre civile espagnole, qui précéda la Seconde Guerre mondiale, 4 000 enfants républicains arrivent dans un camp près de Southampton (3). Beaucoup d'entre eux avaient d'abord tenté de se réfugier en France.

3

(Overleaf)

THIS was the true face of Nazism: the face of death. Marked with yellow stars (3), deportees were herded onto trains like cattle, so ignorant of their fate that they brought their pitiful minimum of belongings with them. At Auschwitz, where this cattle-truck was bound (2), 1.5 million were gassed and incinerated. At Buchenwald, liberated by US forces in 1945, these living skeletons (1) were the scant survivors of a further 800,000 who died.

(folgende Seite)

DAS wahre Gesicht des Nazismus: das Antlitz des Todes. Die mit Juden-sternen gekennzeichneten Deportierten (3) wurden in Güterwagen verladen wie Vieh, und sie ahnten so wenig, was ihnen bevorstand, daß sie ihre armselige Habe mitbrachten. In Auschwitz, wohin dieser Viehwagen unterwegs ist (2), wurden 1,5 Millionen Menschen vergast und verbrannt. In Buchenwald, das 1945 von amerikanischen Truppen befreit wurde, kamen weitere 800.000 um, und diese bis aufs Skelett Abgemagerten (1) waren die einzigen Überlebenden.

(Au verso)

LA mort, voilà ce qu'incarnait le nazisme. Marqués de l'étoile jaune (3), les déportés étaient parqués comme du bétail dans les trains, emportant avec eux un minimum d'affaires, ignorant tous du sort qui leur était réservé. À Auschwitz, destination finale de ce fourgon, qui aurait dû servir aux bestiaux (2), un million et demi de personnes furent gazées et précipitées sous terre. À Buchenwald, libéré par les forces américaines en 1945, ces hommes et femmes réduits à l'état de squelettes (1) ont à peine survécu, tandis que 800 000 autres sont morts.

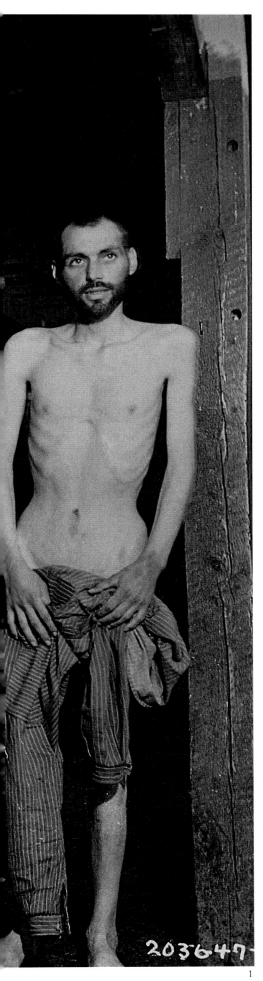

1

2

3

1

4

2

3

The Allies and then the West German government sought to implement a programme of 're-education', through recognition of what had actually taken place. It began at Buchenwald in April 1945, where local civilians were brought in to acknowledge what so many had previously refused to open their eyes to. Some look away before the swinging man (1), and a lorry stacked with corpses, naked and in extreme emaciation (2). Finally, they visit the ovens, whose smoke Weimar townspeople must have witnessed daily (3). A contemporary report noted: 'Many of the witnesses leave the camp in tears. Others appear indifferent and claim they are being subjected to Allied propaganda.'

A few of the sturdiest inmates, brought in as slave-labour from across Europe, survived on minimum rations, working a 12- to 18-hour day. An 11-year-old Czech 'child slave' is reunited with her mother at Kaunitz in 1945 (4). *J'accuse* – a Russian slave labourer singles out a German camp commander notorious for his sadistic brutality (5). At Dachau, some released prisoners rounded on their SS guards in enraged retaliation: soldiers of the US 42nd Division hook out a corpse from the moat round the camp (6).

D IE Alliierten und später die westdeutsche Regierung wollten in einer »Umerziehungskampagne« den Deutschen die Greuel vor Augen führen, die geschehen waren. Sie begann im April 1945 in Buchenwald, wo Einheimische durchs Lager geführt und gezwungen wurden zu sehen, wovor zuvor so viele die Augen verschlossen hatten. Einige wenden den Blick von dem Erhängten (1) und von dem Wagen ab, auf dem die nackten Leichen verhungerter Menschen aufgestapelt liegen (2). Als letztes sehen sie die Verbrennungsöfen, deren aufsteigenden Rauch die Bewohner von Weimar täglich gesehen haben müssen (3). Ein Reporter berichtete seinerzeit: »Viele Zeugen verlassen das Lager mit Tränen in den Augen. Andere machen einen gleichgültigen Eindruck und behaupten, es sei alles alliierte Propaganda.«

Ein paar besonders kräftige Insassen, die als Zwangsarbeiter aus ganz Europa hierher gebracht wurden, überlebten den Hunger und den zwölf- bis achtzehnstündigen Arbeitstag. Ein elfjähriges tschechisches »Sklavenmädchen« findet hier seine Mutter wieder (4). *J'accuse* — ein russischer Zwangsarbeiter klagt einen Lagerkommandanten an, der die Gefangenen besonders brutal und sadistisch behandelte (5). In Dachau nahmen einige befreite Gefangene an ihren SS-Wachen selbst Rache: Soldaten der 42. US-Division holen eine Leiche aus dem Lagergraben (6).

5

LES Alliés et le gouvernement ouest-allemand cherchèrent ensuite à promonvoir un programme de « rééducation » qui impliquait la reconnaissance de la réalité des faits. Il débuta à Buchenwald, en avril 1945, qu'on fit visiter aux populations des alentours pour leur faire reconnaître ce que tant de gens avaient auparavant refusé de voir. Certains détournent les yeux devant le corps qui se balance (1) et le camion où s'empilent les cadavres nus et émaciés (2). La visite se termine devant les fours dont les habitants de la ville de Weimar avaient dû chaque jour apercevoir les fumées (3). Un rapport de l'époque note : « Beaucoup des personnes présentes quittent le camp en larmes. D'autres semblent indifférentes, affirmant subir la propagande des Alliés. »

Un petit nombre de détenus, les plus vigoureux parmi ceux qui furent amenés de toute l'Europe dans les camps de travaux forcés, survécurent aux rations minimales et aux journées de travail de douze à dix-huit heures. Une « enfant des camps », tchèque âgée de onze ans, retrouve sa mère à Kaunitz en 1945 (4). Un prisonnier signale la présence d'un commandant de camp allemand, réputé pour sa brutalité sadique (5). À Dachau, des prisonniers libérés, ivres de revanche, s'en prennent à leurs gardes SS : des soldats de la 42e division américaine repêchent un cadavre dans les douves entourant le camp (6).

6

IN the war at sea, the US Navy suffered in the western Pacific. In December 1944, a wounded US soldier under the auspices of a surgical nurse, his arms raised in agony at the bullet wound to his stomach, lies near the baptismal font of Leyte Cathedral in the Philippines (2). The cathedral alternated as hospital and place of worship. And on 17 May 1945,

the cruiser *Santa Fé* pulls away from the burning carrier USS *Franklin*, victim of a Japanese dive-bombing attack (1). Retreating from the flames of exploding bombs and rockets, the ship's crew cluster on the flight deck. Despite a thousand casualties, the *Franklin* eventually limped thousands of miles home to the Brooklyn Navy Yard.

DIE US-Navy erlitt ihre schwersten Verluste im Westpazifik. Im Dezember 1944 hält eine Krankenschwester in der Kathedrale von Keyte auf den Philippinen Wache bei einem verwundeten Soldaten; er liegt am Taufbecken und wirft wegen der Schmerzen seiner Bauchwunde die Arme in die Luft (2). Die Kathedrale wird für Gottesdienste und gleichzeitig als Lazarett genutzt. Und am 17. Mai 1945 hebt der

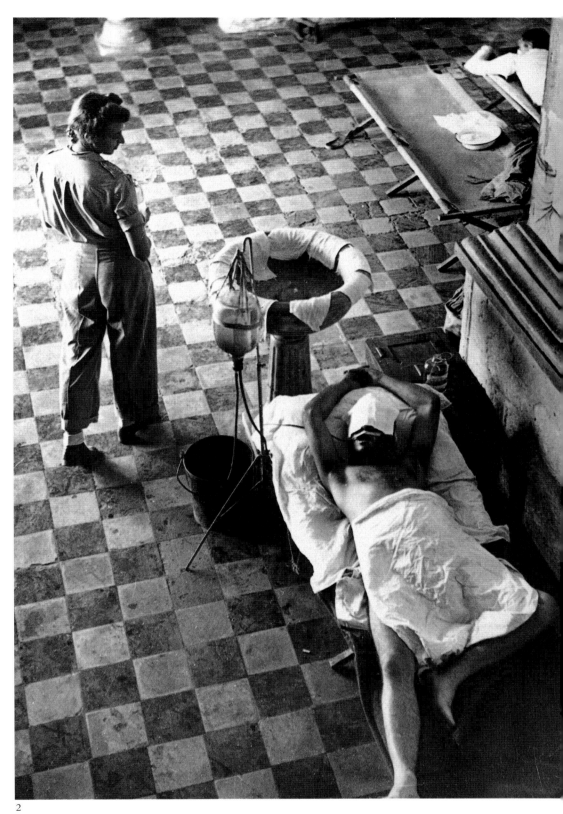

1

2

Aufklärer *Santa Fé* von dem brennenden Flugzeugträger USS *Franklin* ab, der von japanischen Tiefffliegern getroffen ist (1). Die Besatzung flieht vor den explodierenden Bomben und Raketen und drängt sich auf dem Startdeck. Obwohl die *Franklin* tausend Männer verlor, bewältigte sie doch aus eigener Kraft die weite Strecke zurück zum heimischen Brooklyn Navy Yard.

AU cours de la guerre navale, la flotte des États-Unis essuya des pertes dans l'Ouest du Pacifique. Décembre 1944 : un soldat américain blessé est pris en charge par une infirmière de l'équipe chirurgicale ; touché au ventre par une balle, il souffre allongé près des fonts baptismaux de la cathédrale de Leyte aux Philippines (2). La cathédrale sert tour à tour d'hôpital et de lieu de culte. 17 mai 1945 : le croiseur

Santa Fé s'éloigne du navire de transport américain en flammes, le *Franklin*, atteint par les bombardements japonais (1). Battant en retraite devant les incendies provoqués par les explosions, l'équipage du navire s'est rassemblé sur le pont d'envol. Malgré la perte de mille de ses hommes, le *Franklin* parvint à rentrer tant bien que mal, couvrant les milliers de milles qui le séparaient du centre naval de Brooklyn.

JAPANESE kamikaze pilots were famous for their resolve during the Pacific War. While European officers had their cyanide pills to take if captured, Japanese pilots volunteered to fly suicide missions and blow themselves up with their bombers. Here one is helped on with his scarf bearing the Emperor's 'golden sun' (1); another attempts to manoeuvre his 'Zeke' on to the deck of a US warship (2). In the event he crashed into the sea (4), but a neighbouring hospital ship, the USS *Comfort*, was hit; 29 were killed and 33 injured. Luck was allied with the skill of this American pilot, Ensign R. Black: shot up over Palau, he managed to land on an aircraft carrier with his hydraulic system gone and one wing and part of the tailplane shorn off (3).

DIE japanischen Kamikazeflieger waren im Pazifikkrieg berühmt für ihren Mut. Europäische Offiziere hatten ihre Zyanidkapseln, für den Fall, daß sie in Gefangenschaft gerieten, doch die japanischen Piloten meldeten sich freiwillig für Selbstmordflüge. Hier wird einem der Schal umgebunden, den die »goldene Sonne« des Kaisers ziert (1); ein anderer versucht, seine »Zeke« auf dem Deck eines amerikanischen Schlachtschiffs

1

2

3

abzusetzen (2). Dieser verfehlte sein Ziel und stürzte ins Meer (4), doch ein benachbartes Hospitalschiff, die USS *Comfort*, wurde getroffen; es gab 29 Tote und 33 Verwundete. Glück im Unglück und viel Geschick hatte der amerikanische Flieger Ensign R. Black: Er wurde über Palau getroffen, und es gelang ihm, auf einem Flugzeugträger zu landen (3).

LES kamikazes japonais se rendirent célèbres par leur résolution durant la guerre du Pacifique. Tandis que les officiers européens avalaient du cyanure en cas d'interception, les pilotes japonais se portaient volontaires lors des missions suicides à l'aide de leurs avions chargés d'explosifs. On voit ici l'un d'eux se faire nouer son foulard surmonté du « soleil d'or » impérial (1). Un autre tente d'amener son « zeke » sur le pont d'un navire de guerre américain (2). Ce faisant il s'écrase en mer (4), touchant toutefois un navire-hôpital de la marine des États-Unis, le *Comfort* : il y eut 29 morts et 33 blessés. Ce pilote américain réussit à poser son appareil touché au-dessus de Palau sur un navire porte-avions, alors qu'il n'avait plus de système hydraulique, qu'une aile et une partie de la queue de l'avion (3).

4

1

A 'mushroom' or 'cauliflower' cloud and a 'Christmas pudding' were some of the friendly and edible descriptions of the most lethal weapon ever invented. For at least twenty years after the war atomic bomb tests were continued without adequate warnings or precautions. Those at Bikini Atoll by the United States in 1946 show the effects of underwater explosions (aerial view,1); 'crown' of water shooting upwards with the speed of a bullet, (3). Several obsolete ships were sunk (one on the right, (2) and 31 out of 73 were severely damaged. Experts speculated on whether the USS *Arkansas* could have been carried up in the giant waterspout and plunged back as the spout broke. Photos were taken by the US Air Force.

PILZ«, »Blumenkohl« oder »Weihnachtspudding« waren die freundlichen Bezeichnungen, mit denen man die tödlichste Waffe aller Zeiten schmackhaft machte. Mindestens zwanzig Jahre lang wurden nach dem Krieg noch Atomtests ohne ausreichende Vorwarnungen durchgeführt. Auf diesen Bildern zeigen Tests, die die Vereinigten Staaten 1946 im Bikini-Atoll durchführten, die Wirkung von Explosionen unter Wasser (1); eine »Krone« aus Wasser schießt mit der Geschwindigkeit einer Gewehrkugel empor, (3). Mehrere außer Dienst gestellte Schiffe wurden versenkt (eines davon rechts zu sehen, (2). Die Experten spekulierten darüber, ob die USS *Arkansas* von der gewaltigen Fontäne in die Luft geschleudert worden sei und dann wieder aufgesetzt habe. Aufnahmen der US-Air Force.

«CHAMPIGNON », « choux-fleur » ou encore « pudding de Noël » sont quelques-uns des surnoms donnés par les Anglo-Saxons à l'arme la plus mortelle. Après la guerre atomique, on continua pendant au moins vingt ans à faire exploser des bombes expérimentales sans prendre les mesures élémentaires de sécurité. Celles-ci, déclenchées par les États-Unis sur l'atoll de Bikini en 1946, montrent les effets des explosions sous-marines (1). Sur cette prise de vue aérienne, ou distingue bien la couronne d'eau projetée à la vitesse d'une balle (3). Plusieurs navires hors d'usage sombrèrent (droite, 2) et 31 sur 73 furent gravement endommagés. Les spécialistes se demandaient si l'*Arkansas* de la marine américaine serait soulevé dans les airs. Les vues proviennent de l'armée de l'air américaine.

2

3

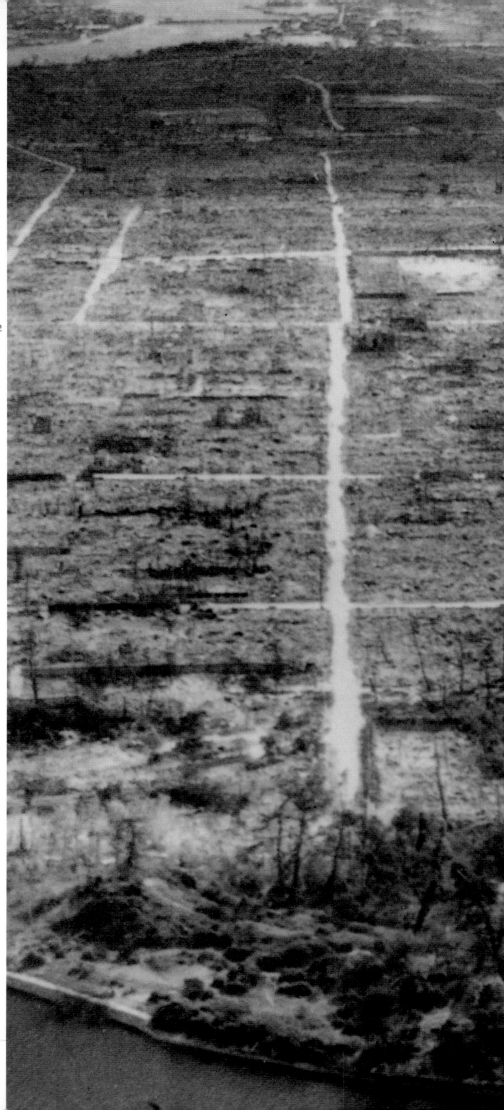

1 2

ON 6 August 1945 a first atomic bomb was unleashed on Hiroshima (2). On 9 August a second landed on Nagasaki (1). The former killed 100,000 outright; another 100,000 were to die in the ensuing months from burns and radiation sickness. The latter killed 75,000 outright. On 10 August, Japan sued for peace – two days after Russia had joined the war against her old enemy. On 14 August President Truman formally declared the end of the Second World War, in which 55 million people died.

AM 6. August 1945 ging die erste Atombombe der Welt auf Hiroshima nieder (2). Am 9. August traf eine zweite Nagasaki (1). In Hiroshima fanden 100.000 Menschen sofort den Tod; weitere 100.000 sollten an den Folgen der Verbrennungen und an Strahlenschäden sterben. Der zweite Abwurf forderte 75.000 unmittelbare Opfer. Am 10. August kapitulierte Japan — zwei Tage nachdem Rußland in den Krieg gegen seinen alten Feind eingetreten war. Am 14. August verkündete der amerikanische Präsident Truman offiziell das Ende des Zweiten Weltkriegs, in dem mehr als 55 Millionen Menschen ihr Leben verloren hatten.

LE 6 août 1945, une première bombe atomique fut lâchée sur Hiroshima (2). Le 9 août, une seconde tomba sur Nagasaki (1). La première tua instantanément 100 000 personnes, tandis que 100 000 autres devaient mourir dans les mois qui suivirent conséquemment aux brûlures et aux radiations. La seconde tua 75 000 personnes sur le coup. Le 10 août, le Japon abdiquait – deux jours après que l'URSS lui eut déclaré la guerre. Le 14 août, le président Truman annonçait officiellement la fin de la Seconde Guerre mondiale qui avait coûté la mort à 55 millions de personnes.

1

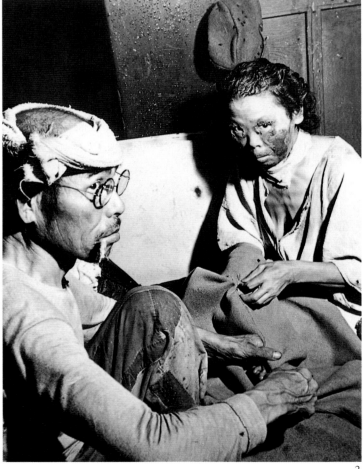

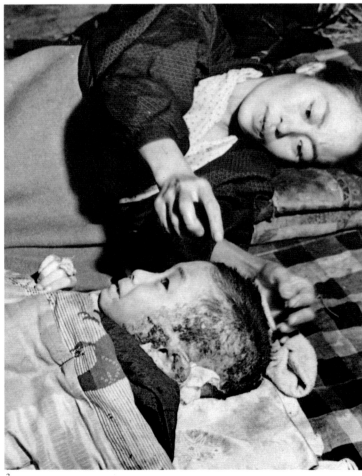

2   3

4

DESPITE the devastation wrought on a civilian population, the bomber crew responsible returned home to a tickertape heroes' welcome at New York's Army Day parade (1). Their jeep boasted of their mission and advertised that 'The Regular Army has a Good Job for you'. In Hiroshima, civilian victims were effectively left to care for themselves in a damaged bank near the blasted town centre (2), where burns and injuries were treated by parents substituting for medical staff (3). Those who survived relatively unscathed wore wartime issue long bloomers and masks against the stench of death within their ruined city (4).

TROTZ der verheerenden Auswirkung auf die Zivilbevölkerung wurde der Bombercrew bei der Militärparade in New York ein rauschender Empfang bereitet (1). Auf ihrem Jeep war ihr Auftrag groß zu lesen, und der Werbespruch lautet: »Die Army hat immer einen guten Job für Dich.« In Hiroshima waren die verwundeten Opfer praktisch sich selbst überlassen; in einem halb eingestürzten Bankgebäude der in Trümmern liegenden Innenstadt (2) richteten sie ein Hospital ein, und Eltern statt Sanitätern kümmerten sich um die Verletzungen ihrer Kinder (3). Diejenigen, die vergleichsweise ungeschoren davonkamen, banden sich Masken um gegen den Todesgeruch in ihrer zerstörten Stadt (4).

MALGRÉ les dévastations infligées aux populations civiles, les équipages des bombardiers furent acclamés à New York à l'occasion de la journée de l'Armée (1). Leurs jeeps portaient des inscriptions vantant leur exploit et prévenait que « dans l'armée de métier vous attend un emploi intéressant ». À Hiroshima, les victimes civiles sont abandonnées à leur sort dans une banque du centre ville dévasté par le souffle de l'explosion (2). Leurs brûlures et leurs blessures sont soignées par des parents, à défaut de personnel médical (3). Ceux qui s'en sortirent portaient les longues culottes bouffantes et les masques distribués pendant la guerre afin de se prémunir contre la puanteur des cadavres (4).

Im Februar 1945 fand im Livadia-Palast in Jalta auf der Krim die Dreimächte-Konferenz zwischen Premierminister Churchill, Präsident Roosevelt und Marschall Stalin statt (2). Roosevelt rang Stalin die Zusage ab, in den Krieg gegen Japan einzutreten und die Gründung der Vereinten Nationen zu unterstützen. Churchill, hier mit Stalin und Zigarren (1), erhielt seine Unterschrift auf dem Vertrag, der die Teilung Deutschlands in französische, britische, russische und amerikanische Besatzungszonen vorsah. Als Gegenleistung erhielt Stalin eine neu festgelegte russisch-polnische Grenze mit polnischer Westgrenze entlang der Oder-Neiße-Linie. Zwar wurde in einer »Erklärung zum befreiten Europa« der Wunsch der drei Staatsmänner nach »freien Wahlen« und »demokratischen Institutionen« in den von Deutschland besetzten Ländern bekräftigt, doch die Vereinbarungen von Jalta erfuhren bittere Kritik auf beiden Seiten. Kommentatoren beschuldigten Roosevelt, er habe »Rußland das Tor zum Fernen Osten geöffnet« und überlasse Stalin Osteuropa, und in England war die Empörung groß, daß Churchill die kosakischen Soldaten verraten habe, die zurück in die UdSSR verbracht wurden, wo der sichere Tod auf sie wartete. Doch die sowjetisch-amerikanischen Beziehungen waren nie herzlicher als damals in Jalta.

1

THE three-power conference held at Livadia Palace, Yalta, in the Crimea, in February 1945, between Prime Minister Churchill, President Roosevelt and Marshal Stalin (2). Roosevelt succeeded in obtaining Stalin's agreement to enter the war against Japan and to cooperate in the founding of the United Nations Organization. Churchill, here with Stalin and cigars (1), further obtained Stalin's signature to the partition of Germany into French, British, Russian and US-controlled zones. Stalin, in return, achieved recognition of a redrawn Russian-Polish border and a western frontier on the Oder-Neisse Line. Despite a 'Declaration on Liberated Europe', affirming the three leaders' desire for 'free elections' and 'democratic institutions' in lands previously controlled by Germany, the Yalta accords were bitterly criticized on both sides. Western commentators accused Roosevelt of 'bringing Russia into the Far East' and 'handing eastern Europe over to Stalin', whilst Britain's part in betraying the Cossack soldiers, forcibly returned to their death in the USSR, caused a row which still resonates. Soviet-US relations were, however, never more cordial than here.

LA conférence des trois grandes puissances se déroula au palais de Livadia, à Yalta, en Crimée, dès février 1945. Elle réunit le Premier ministre Churchill, le président Roosevelt et le maréchal Staline (2). Roosevelt obtint de Staline que celui rentrât en guerre contre le Japon et coopérât à la fondation de l'Organisation des Nations Unies. Churchill que l'on voit ici, cigare à la main, en compagnie de Staline (1), obtint en plus de ce dernier qu'il validât la division de l'Allemagne en zones contrôlées par les Français, les Britanniques, les Soviétiques et les Américains. En contrepartie, Staline fit reconnaître le nouveau tracé des frontières séparant l'URSS et la Pologne ainsi que la frontière occidentale de la ligne Oder-Neisse. Malgré une « Déclaration sur l'Europe libérée », formulant le souhait des trois dirigeants de voir s'instaurer des « élections libres » et des « institutions démocratiques » dans les pays auparavant sous domination allemande, les accords de Yalta furent amèrement critiqués de part et d'autre. Les observateurs occidentaux accusèrent Roosevelt d'avoir « ouvert à la Russie la porte de l'Extrême-Orient » et d'avoir « cédé l'Europe orientale à Staline ». La Grande-Bretagne, quant à elle, en trahissant les soldats cosaques qui furent renvoyés de force en URSS où les attendait une mort certaine, provoqua une vive émotion. Les relations soviéto-américaines, toutefois, ne furent jamais plus cordiales qu'à ce moment-là.

1 2

ON 14 February 1945, the RAF and USAF started a day and a half of relentless bombardment that reduced the eastern German city of Dresden to a smoking ruin. It remained impossible to ascertain how many civilians died, since the population had already doubled to over a million seeking a 'safe haven'. Estimates of the death toll swung from 130,000 to 400,000. In addition to this colossal human cost, Dresden had been compared to Florence for its wealth of Baroque and Rococo art and architecture, its galleries of Dutch and Flemish paintings. Senior Allied military officers were tight-lipped about the diversion of effort away from German centres of communication and oil installations to predominantly civilian and symbolic targets. The Chief of RAF Bomber Command, Air Marshal Arthur Harris, vehemently persisted in his controversial theory that terror bombing was the way to destroy the enemy's will to fight. A year later, these Dresden survivors are still struggling to rebuild their city via a 'human brick chain' (2) while a women's squad starts the first stages of rehabilitating the Zwinger Palace (1). Meanwhile in Berlin's ruined Nollendorf Platz, a Russian-language sign and a knocked-out German tank speak volumes of the city's recent history, in the wake of which these citizens are still searching for a home among the desolation (3).

AM 14. Februar 1945 begannen die Royal Air Force und die US Air Force mit einem anderthalbtägigen Bombardement, das die Stadt Dresden in Schutt und Asche legte. Die Zahl der Zivilisten, die umkamen, ließ sich nie genau bestimmen, denn die Bevölkerung hatte sich durch den Zustrom von Flüchtlingen auf der Suche nach einem »sicheren Hafen« auf über eine Million verdoppelt. Schätzungen der Todesopfer variierten zwischen 130.000 und 400.000. Außerdem wurde eine Stadt zerstört, die wegen ihres Reichtums an Kunst und Architektur als »Florenz des Nordens« galt. Die leitenden Militärs der Alliierten hüllten sich in Schweigen, wenn gefragt wurde, warum sie ihre Aufmerksamkeit von deutschen Verkehrsknotenpunkten und petrochemischen Einrichtungen nun zivilen und letzten Endes symbolischen Zielen zuwandten. Ein Jahr später versuchen diese Überlebenden von Dresden noch immer, ihre Stadt mit einer »menschlichen Backsteinkette« wiederaufzubauen (2), und ein Frauentrupp unternimmt erste Anstrengungen, den Zwinger wieder bewohnbar zu machen (1). Am Nollendorfplatz in Berlin sprechen derweil russische Hinweisschilder und ein zerschossener deutscher Panzer Bände über die jüngste Vergangenheit der Stadt. Heimatlos gewordene Berliner suchen zwischen den Trümmern nach einer neuen Bleibe (3).

LE 14 février 1945, les forces aériennes britannique et américaine entreprirent de bombarder sans répit un jour et demi durant la ville de Dresde, en Allemagne orientale. Il fut impossible d'établir le nombre des civils disparus, car la population, grossie des centaines de milliers de personnes qui cherchaient à « se mettre à l'abri », comptait plus d'un million d'habitants. Les estimations oscillaient entre 130 000 et 400 000. Jadis, on comparait Dresde à Florence pour ses richesses artistiques. La hiérarchie militaire des troupes alliées se montrait avare de commentaires sur le fait que son effort portait moins sur les centres de communications ou les installations pétrochimiques allemandes que sur les objectifs civils et symboliques. Le chef de l'aviation britannique, le général Arthur Harris, s'en tenait énergiquement à sa théorie discutable selon laquelle la terreur provoquée par les bombardements brisait la combativité de l'ennemi. Un an plus tard, ces survivants de Dresde luttent toujours pour reconstruire leur ville, recourant à une « chaîne humaine de briques » (2), et des femmes entreprennent de réhabiliter le palais Zwinger (1). Ailleurs, dans les ruines de la place Nollendorf à Berlin, les panneaux en langue russe et le char d'assaut allemand mis hors de combat expliquent à eux seuls que ces citoyens sont toujours à la recherche d'un refuge (3).

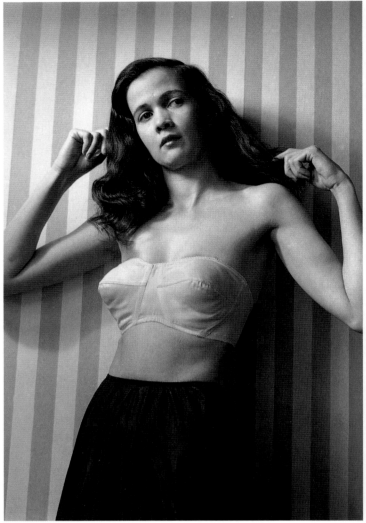

1

2

IN the USA after the war, the Coty Award was instituted for designers who 'have the most significant effect on the American way of dressing'. Despite Christian Dior's much-vaunted New Look that took women out of the regulatory minimum and swathed them in the maximum of pleats, folds and lengths, restrictions were still in place in Europe until the 1950s. A woollen coat could not be wool-lined; no furs were to be employed; no dress could contain over three metres of fabric; only 60 models could take to the catwalk in a single showing.

Postwar undergarments allow a glimpse of what went on beneath Dior's New Look. While, a couple of decades earlier, the most a gel required under her flapper's fringed shift was a bandage to flatten her femininity and a sequinned garter or two, now women were again to be strapped, tied and buckled into undergarments worthy of Scarlett O'Hara. Girdle and corsets (3), suspenders (1) and brassières (2) came with as much seductiveness – and the same range of colouring – as false teeth.

IN den Vereinigten Staaten wurde nach dem Krieg der Coty-Preis gestiftet, für Designer, deren Werk »außerordentlichen Einfluß auf die Art hat, wie Amerikaner sich kleiden«, und Christian Dior machte mit seinem New Look, mit üppigem Überschwang an reich gefälteten Stoffen, Furore; doch in Europa war die Mode noch bis in die 50er Jahre hinein reglementiert. Ein Wollkleid durfte kein wollenes Futter haben, Pelze durften nicht verwendet werden und kein Kleid sollte mehr als drei Meter Stoff verbrauchen.

Ein Blick darauf, wie es unter dem New Look von Dior aussah — Unterwäsche der Nachkriegszeit. Wo noch zwei Jahrzehnte zuvor ein Brustband, um unter dem gefransten Charlestonkleid die weiblichen Rundungen zu verstecken, das Äußerste gewesen war, wurden Frauen nun wieder in Unterwäsche gezwängt, geschnürt und geklammert, die einer Scarlett O'Hara würdig gewesen wären. Hüfthalter und Korsett (3), Strumpf- (1) und Büstenhalter (2) waren ungefähr so verführerisch — und hatten auch dieselbe Farbe — wie ein Satz falscher Zähne.

C'EST au lendemain de la guerre que le *Coty Award* fut institué aux États-Unis pour récompenser les stylistes dont « l'influence est la plus significative sur les habitudes vestimentaires américaines ». Malgré Christian Dior et son « *new look* », tant célébré pour avoir sorti les femmes du minimum obligatoire afin de les envelopper dans un maximum de plissés, de plis et de longueurs, l'Europe resta soumise à des restrictions jusque dans les années 50. Un manteau en lainage ne pouvait pas être doublé de laine ; l'utilisation de la fourrure n'était pas possible ; trois mètres de tissu était le maximum autorisé pour une robe ; enfin, seuls soixante mannequins pouvaient défiler au cours d'une même présentation de mode.

Les sous-vêtements de l'après-guerre permettent de se faire une idée de ce qui se passait sous le « New Look » de Dior. Vingt ans auparavant, le gel obligeait les jeunes femmes à porter un bandage destiné à aplatir leur féminité; elles se retrouvaient maintenant de nouveau sanglées, serrées et bouclées. Gaines et corsets (3), jarretelles (1) et bustiers (2) étaient rarement séduisants.

ON fashion's wilder shores… painting the sky with seaweed (1), hobbling to Ascot on toilet-roll heels (2), polka-dotting and criss-crossing the beach with *piqué* prints (3). By the 1940s, women were clearly confident enough to be their own escorts, rakish enough to bring their own booze, and some were even rich enough to own a camera: altogether smart enough to make their own amusement, whatever appearances might suggest to the contrary with their fashionable but unarguably silly romper suits.

3

AN den stürmischen Ufern der Mode… da werden Bilder mit Seegras in den Himmel gemalt (1), da hoppeln die Damen auf Klopapierrollen nach Ascot (2) und schäkern in tupfen- und streifenbedrucktem Piqué am Strand (3). Es waren die vierziger Jahre, und inzwischen waren Frauen selbstbewußt genug, ohne männliche Begleitung auszugehen, lebenslustig genug, ihre eigene Flasche Wein mitzubringen, und einige waren sogar so reich, daß sie sich eine eigene Kamera leisten konnten — sie hatten Köpfchen genug, daß sie auf ihre Kosten kamen, so albern sie in diesen modischen, aber doch wirklich unmöglichen Spielanzügen auch aussahen.

SUR les plages les plus follement dans le vent, … on peignait le ciel avec des algues (1), on claudiquait jusqu'à Ascot perchées sur des rouleaux de papier hygiénique (2), on transformait les plages en imprimés piqués de pois et de rayures enchevêtrées (3). Dès les années 40, les femmes avaient suffisamment d'assurance pour sortir seules, elles étaient suffisamment débauchées pour arriver avec leurs propres alcools, et certaines étaient même suffisamment riches pour posséder un appareil photographique. Dans l'ensemble, elles se montraient tout à fait capables de pourvoir à leur propre divertissement, malgré ce que laissent suggérer leurs ensembles barboteuses certes à la mode mais incontestablement idiots.

THE 1950s seemed to want to prove
that the years of austerity were forever
behind us. In Britain, Macmillan was
telling the population they had 'never had
it so good', while in Germany Adenauer
promoted economic expansion through
the 'rebuilding' generation. Lashings of
fabric and trimmings spared neither
expense nor fuss – with a certain tongue-
in-cheek mockery in the labels: Jacques
Fath's 'lampshade look' (1) – a bell shape
here (2), a pie frill there.

IN den Fünfzigern wollte offenbar jeder
beweisen, daß die entbehrungsreichen
Jahre für immer vorbei waren. Den Briten
verkündete Macmillan, daß sie es »noch
nie so gut hatten«, und in Deutschland
feuerte Adenauer zum Wiederaufbau an.
Bei der Mode wurde an Stoff und Zierat
und damit an den Kosten nicht gespart —
doch immerhin spricht aus den
Bezeichnungen ein gewisser Humor:
Jacques Faths »Lampenschirm-Look« (1),
hier mit einer Glockenform (2), dort mit
einem Rüschenkragen.

DANS les années 50, on semblait
vouloir prouver que l'époque de
l'austérité était à jamais révolue. En
Grande-Bretagne, MacMillan disait à la
population que « ses conditions n'avaient
jamais été aussi bonnes qu'aujourd'hui »,
pendant qu' en Allemagne Adenauer
encourageait l'expansion économique
portée par la génération de la
« reconstruction ». On n'épargnait ni
argent ni strass dans des modèles où
l'abondance de tissu ne le cédait qu'à celle
de l'ornementation, et auxquels étaient
donnés, non sans un certain humour pince-
sans-rire, des noms de baptême tels que :
« Style abat-jour » (1) de Jacques Fath – ici
une forme de cloche (2), là des fronces.

2

2   3

THE English aristocracy were assumed even by French couturiers to have a certain *je ne sais quoi*. Dior paid his homage to Churchill with *Blenheim*, a wide white satin gown embroidered with flowers (2). Givenchy, a new boy to Paris fashion in 1955, came to Park Lane's grand new Dorchester Hotel to display his 'dazzling white satin dinner dress, slit from calf to ankle, and worn with a crimson velvet stole and pearl and rhinestone bib necklace' (1). And Margaret, Duchess of Argyll (notorious for the slant she gave a favourite good health maxim – 'Go to bed early and often'), here keeps sedate company with her daughter and Norman Hartnell, the Queen's couturier (3).

SELBST französische Couturiers waren überzeugt, daß die englische Aristokratie ein gewisses *je ne sais quoi* hatte. Dior erwies Churchill seine Reverenz, indem er dieses weite, weiße, blumenbestickte Satinkleid *Blenheim* nannte (2). Givenchy, 1955 noch ein junger Spund in der Pariser Modewelt, kam nach London und stellte im exklusiven neuen Dorchester-Hotel in der Park Lane sein »blendend weißes Abendkleid aus Satin« vor, »geschlitzt von der Wade bis zum Knöchel, getragen mit karminroter Samtstola und Kollier aus Perlen und Straß« (1). Und Margaret, die Herzogin von Argyll (berühmt für die neue Wendung, die sie einer altehrwürdigen Gesundheitsregel gab — »Man sollte früh und oft ins Bett gehen«) in friedlicher Eintracht mit ihrer Tochter und dem Hofschneider der Königin, Norman Hartnell (3).

MEME les couturiers français prêtaient à l'aristocratie anglaise un certain je ne sais quoi. Dior présenta ses hommages à Churchill avec *Blenheim*, une robe ample de satin blanc brodée de fleurs (2). Givenchy, qui faisait en 1955 figure de nouvel arrivant sur la scène de la mode parisienne, vint montrer dans le nouvel et magnifique hôtel Dorchester, à Park Lane, son « époustouflante robe de dîner de satin blanc, fendue du mollet à la cheville, portée avec une étole de velours cramoisi et un pectoral de perles et de faux diamants » (1). Margaret, duchesse d'Argyll, célèbre pour son détournement de sens d'une maxime très prisée – « Couchez-vous tôt et souvent » – tient ici sagement compagnie à sa fille et à Norman Hartnell, le couturier de la reine (3).

SPOTS, stripes and floral prints – separately or, where possible, in conjunction. In 1956 the photo-magazine *Picture Post* gave six holiday game prize-winners a tour of popular seaside resorts. And perhaps provided them with their Fifties uniform of cotton waisted frocks?

DRUCKSTOFFE in Pünktchen-, Streifen-, Blumenmustern — einzeln oder, wenn es sich machen ließ, auch zusammen.

Die Illustrierte *Picture Post* schickte 1956 sechs Preisausschreibengewinnerinnen auf eine Reise durch die englischen Seebadeorte. Und vielleicht stiftete sie auch die Uniform der Fünfziger dazu, das taillierte Baumwollkleid?

POINTS, bandes et imprimés floraux. Seuls ou, si possible, combinés. En 1956, le magazine photographique *Picture Post* offrit aux six gagnantes d'un jeu de vacances une tournée dans les stations balnéaires à la mode. Est-ce aussi le magazine qui leur fournit leur uniforme de coton ceintré dans le style des années 50 ?

Feet first… and lasts. The morning queue outside the original Baker Street Marks and Spencer in 1955 is clearly in a mood to promote sensible footwear – and some curious shopping bags (1). Florence has been known for fine leather since the Middle Ages, and

Salvatore Ferragamo made his reputation by keeping the old tradition alive, making lasts for shoes and shoes to last. Each pair was handmade to measure, and the measure of his success was reflected in the roll-call of his famous customers and their named lasts (2).

Schuster, bleib' bei deinen Leisten… wenn man sie sich denn leisten konnte! Die Frauen, die an einem Morgen des Jahres 1955 darauf warten, daß das alte Marks and Spencer in der Londoner Baker Street öffnet, sind wohl eher für vernünftiges Schuhwerk — und stellen auch an Einkaufstaschen keine gehobenen Ansprüche (1). Florentiner Leder ist seit

1 2

dem Mittelalter berühmt, und Salvatore Ferragamo beruft sich auf diese jahrhundertealte Tradition – er wurde selbst berühmt mit Schuhen für Berühmtheiten. Jedes Paar wurde nach Maß handgeschustert, und das Maß seines Erfolges läßt sich an der Kollektion von Leisten der Prominenz ermessen, die er hier stolz präsentiert (2).

EN 1955, la queue matinale qui s'est formée devant le Marks and Spencer, à l'origine dans la rue de Baker Street, a manifestement envie de souliers raisonnables – et de curieux cabas (1). Les cuirs de Florence étaient en effet réputés pour leur beauté depuis le Moyen Âge:

Salvatore Ferragamo bâtit sa réputation en pérennisant cette tradition ancienne, fabriquant des formes pour les chaussures et des chaussures qui gardaient la forme. Chaque paire était fabriquée à la main, sur mesure, tandis que son succès se mesurait à leurs formes (2) et à la liste de ses clients célèbres.

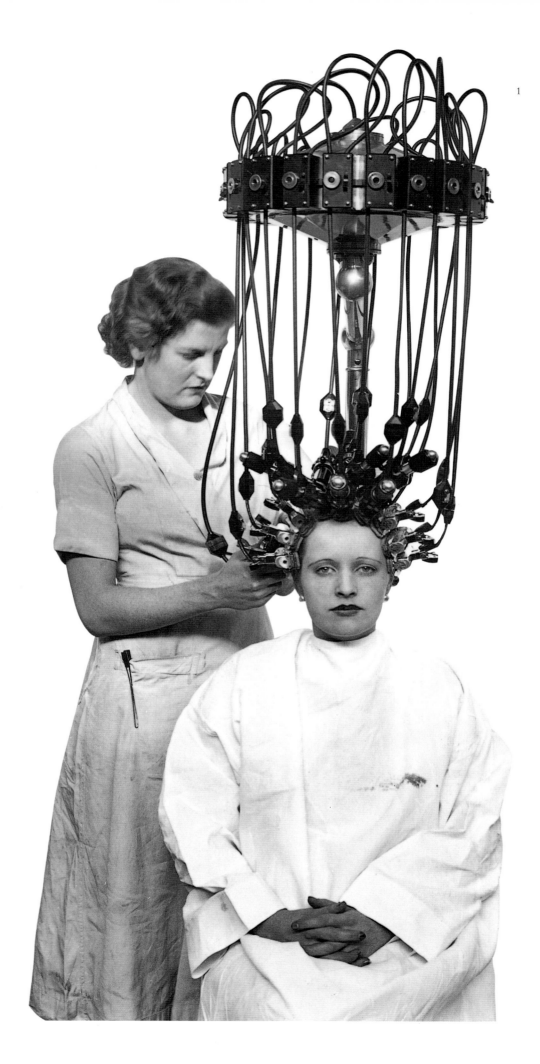

1

MASOCHISM has played its part in hairdressing at least since the ancient Babylonians started slapping heavy layers of mud and wigs on to their heads. This was as nothing compared with the 1935 Gallia machine (1), which resembles a contraption designed by Alice in Wonderland's White Knight, looking all the more dangerous for its approval 'by the Medical Societies as safe and absolutely shock-proof'. The tentacled hair-dryer (2) made its appearance at the Hair and Beauty Fair at London's Olympia Exhibition Centre in 1936. At the White City Fair, a Boadicea helmet mounted on a kind of bellows (3) barely covers the model's plaited earphones in what must be the least practicable and slowest method of drying hair ever invented.

MASOCHISMUS gehört zum Friseurgewerbe, mindestens seit die alten Babylonier sich Lehm und Perücken auf den Kopf klebten. Aber das war nichts im Vergleich zur Gallia-Maschine von 1935 (1), die vom Weißen Ritter aus *Alice im Wunderland* entworfen sein könnte und die noch bedrohlicher wirkt, wenn man bedenkt, daß sie »vom Ärzteverband geprüft und für absolut stromschlagsicher befunden wurde«. Der Haartrockner mit den Tentakeln (2) gab sein Debüt bei der Ausstellung »Haar und Schönheit« im Londoner Olympia Exhibition Centre, 1936. Bei einer anderen Londoner Ausstellung wurde dieser große Fön gezeigt, der in eine Art Ritterhelm bläst (3). Die zu Schnecken geflochtenen Haare der Vorführdame, die aussehen wie Kopfhörer, läßt er frei — wohl der langsamste und unpraktischste Haartrockner, der je gebaut wurde.

LA part de masochisme qui existe dans l'art de la coiffure remonte au moins à l'époque antique, lorsque les Babyloniens entreprirent d'appliquer sur leurs têtes de lourdes couches de boue et des perruques. Mais ce n'était rien en comparaison de la machine Gallia en 1935 (1), qui semblait conçue, tant elle était bizarre, par le cavalier blanc d'*Alice au pays des merveilles*, et d'autant plus dangereuse qu'elle était approuvée « par les sociétés médicales en raison de sa fiabilité et de sa résistance absolue aux chocs ». Ce sèche-cheveux tentaculaire (2) fit son apparition à l'occasion de la Foire de la beauté et de la chevelure qui se déroula en 1936 au centre d'exposition Olympia à Londres. À la foire de White City, un casque à la Boadicée, monté sur une sorte de soufflet (3) et recouvrant à peine les tresses en forme d'écouteurs du modèle, figure ce qui devait être la méthode la moins pratique et la plus lente jamais inventée pour sécher les cheveux.

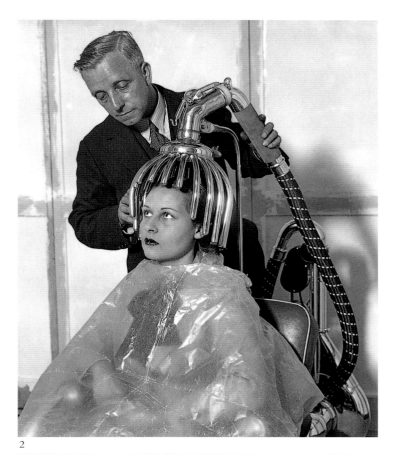

2

3

ALL that glisters is clearly not gold, to judge by this 1932 model surmounted by metallic foil twists torturing her hair into silver curls (1). Messrs Vascos, a London hairdresser's, were responsible for promoting the process which changed a model's hair colour to match her every change of evening dress (including shades of gold, silver and mother-of-pearl): a fashion surely stemming from the Spanish willingness 'to suffer whatever-it-takes – for beauty'. These model girls on a yacht seem rather more inclined to take it easy, cruising down the Côte d'Azur to introduce British-designed polka-dotted bikinis to Cap Ferrat, Cannes and Juan-les-Pins (2).

Es ist nicht alles Gold, was glänzt, jedenfalls nach den Wicklern aus Metallfolie zu urteilen, die hier 1932 silberne Locken produzieren (1). Der Londoner Friseur Vascos warb mit diesem Verfahren, mit dem eine Frau ihre Haarfarbe täglich der Farbe des Abendkleides anpassen konnte (darunter Gold-, Silber- und Perlmutt-Töne) — die Spanier fanden ja schon immer, daß für die Schönheit kein Leid zu groß sei. Da haben es diese Models an der Côte d'Azur schon leichter. Sie sind auf einer Yacht unterwegs und führen in Cap Ferrat, Cannes und Juan-les-Pins britische Pünktchenbikinis vor (2).

TOUT ce qui brille n'est manifestement pas de l'or, à en juger par ce modèle en 1932, dont la tête est surmontée de papillotes métalliques qui lui torturent la chevelure pour la changer en boucles argentées (1). On devait à M. Vascos, coiffeurs à Londres, la promotion du procédé qui modifiait la couleur de la chevelure en l'assortissant à chaque nouvelle tenue de soirée (y compris les nuances d'or, d'argent et de nacre) : une mode qu'on devait certainement au fait que l'Espagnole est prête « à souffrir pour être belle ». Sur ce yacht, ces mannequins semblent plus enclines à prendre du bon temps tandis qu'elles descendent sur la Côte d'Azur pour aller présenter les créations britanniques de bikinis à pois dans les villes de Cap-Ferrat, Cannes et Juan-Les-Pins (2).

1   2

MANDY Rice-Davies, one of the stars of the Profumo scandal that rocked the British establishment in 1963. It reflected most on the journalism of the times that she became known as the 'blonde beehive' (1). The singer Dusty Springfield chose her version of the beehive style to enhance the transistor radio she was presented with at the Ideal Home Exhibition in 1964, a prize for being 'one of the few girls who get into the hit parade' (3). Earlier, in 1954, a customer who has taken a portrait of Marlon Brando into Dominique's Mayfair salon persuades the stylist to give her a cut emulating that of her hero (2).

MANDY Rice-Davies, einer der Stars der Profumo-Affäre, die das britische Establishment 1963 erschütterte. Es sagt viel über den Journalismus jener Tage, daß sie als »blonde beehive« (die Blondine mit der Turmfrisur) bekannt wurde (1). Die Sängerin Dusty Springfield glänzt ebenfalls mit einer solchen Frisur auf der »Ideal Home Exhibition« 1964, wo ein Kofferradiohersteller ihr als »einem der wenigen Mädchen, die in die Hitparade kommen« ein Exemplar präsentierte (3). Zehn Jahre früher, 1954, kam eine Kundin mit einem Bild von Marlon Brando zu Dominique in Mayfair, damit der Haarkünstler ihr eine Frisur nach dem Vorbild ihres Schwarms machen konnte (2).

MANDY Rice-Davies, l'une des vedettes du scandale Profumo qui ébranla la haute société britannique en 1963. Ce n'est guère au crédit du journalisme de l'époque de l'avoir fait connaître comme le « casque blond de Minerve » (1). La chanteuse Dusty Springfield donna sa version du « casque de Minerve », mettant ainsi en valeur le poste récepteur de radio qui lui avait été remis à la Foire du foyer idéal en 1964, prix remporté pour avoir « été l'une des rares filles à figurer au hit-parade » (3). Plus tôt, en 1954, une cliente qui a emporté un portrait de Marlon Brando au salon de Dominique, dans le Mayfair, persuade le styliste de lui faire une coupe valant celle de son héros (2).

3

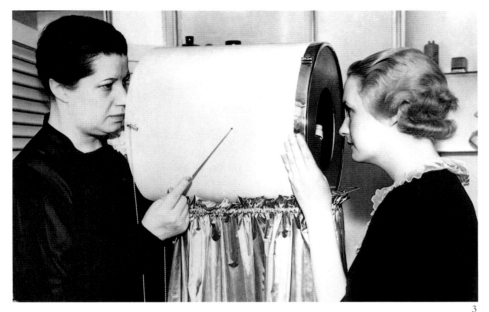

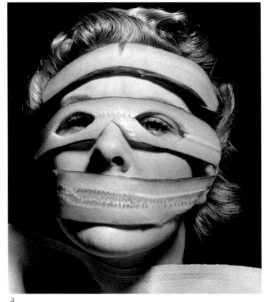

3   4

5   6

MAX Factor shows 1930s Hollywood starlet Renee Adoree how to apply his rouge (1). Helena Rubinstein became a formidable arbiter of women's skin-care and colouring (2). In 1935 she even developed a 'line lie detector' that would show up any crows' feet or giggle wrinkles before the 'patient' was aware of them herself (3). This Norwegian beauty school reverted to *papier mâché* wrapover (5), while others preferred cucumbers (4). The message was plain: 'if you want a peaches and cream complexion, the answer's a lemon'. And wartime exigencies demanded painted 'stockings' (6).

MAX Factor zeigt Renee Adoree, einem Hollywood-Starlet der 30er Jahre, wie Rouge aufgetragen wird (1). Helena Rubinstein wußte ganz genau, welche Pflege und welches Make-up das Gesicht einer Frau brauchte (2). 1935 entwickelte sie sogar einen »Fältchendetektor«, der Krähenfüße und Lachfältchen entdeckte (3). Eine Kosmetikerinnenschule in Norwegen arbeitet mit Gesichtsmasken aus Papiermaché (5), während andere Gurken bevorzugten (4). Als im Krieg keine Strümpfe zu haben waren, wurde die Strumpfnaht einfach aufgemalt (6).

MAX Factor montre à une starlette hollywoodienne dans les années 30, Renee Adoree, comment appliquer son fond de teint (1). Héléna Rubinstein devint l'arbitre redouté en matière de soins de la peau et de teint (2). Elle mit même au point, en 1935, un « détecteur » de rides (3). Cette école de beauté norvégienne est revenue au masque de papier mâché (5), tandis que d'autres préféraient le concombre (4). Le message était simple : « Si vous voulez un teint de pêche à la crème, la solution est le citron ». D'autre part, vu les temps difficiles, il fallait bien recourir aux « bas » peints (6).

THE 1976 Miss World contest provoked a storm when it was won by Miss Jamaica, Cindy Breakespeare, the problem being that Jamaica is over 90 per cent black, while Ms Breakespeare (not to mention her lady-in-waiting, Miss Ghana) was very definitely white (1). Feminist protesters from the British Women's Liberation Movement deplored the exploitation of women's bodies by a system that simply sought to promote them as marketable commodities, while marginalizing others who did not conform to the slender, youthful white stereotype (2).

DIE 1976er Wahlen zur »Miß Welt« sorgten für Aufruhr. Die Siegerin war Cindy Breakespeare, Miß Jamaika, doch obwohl über neunzig Prozent der jamaikanischen Bevölkerung schwarz sind, war Ms. Breakespeare (von der Zweitplazierten, Miß Ghana, gar nicht zu

2

reden) eindeutig eine Weiße (1). Britische Feministinnen demonstrierten gegen ein System, bei dem Frauenkörper als vermarktbare Waren ausgebeutet und alle diskriminiert werden, die nicht dem Stereotyp der schlanken, jungen Weißen entsprechen (2).

EN 1976, l'élection de Cindy Breakespeare, Miss Jamaica, au titre de Miss World, déclencha une tempête. En effet la Jamaïque est peuplée à plus de 90% de Noirs, or Mademoiselle Breakespeare (et ne parlons pas de sa dame d'honneur, Miss Ghana) est incontestablement blanche (1). Les

militantes féministes du Mouvement de libération des femmes britanniques déplorèrent l'exploitation faite du corps féminin par un système qui ne cherchait qu'à le promouvoir en tant que marchandise, marginalisant toutes celles qui n'étaient pas conformes au stéréotype de la femme mince, jeune et blanche (2).

Cinema

CINEMA is essentially a twentieth-century pheno-menon, and although silent films are regarded nostalgically by buffs, the real heyday of the movies did not begin until the first 'talkie', Al Jolson's *The Jazz Singer*, came out in 1927. The Thirties saw a peak of activity, with the first colour films and the development of the Hollywood star system. Among the most luminous of the stars was Charlie Chaplin (1889-1977), reckoned the most popular film personality in the world for the best part of 25 years. Although he achieved great things as a writer, director, producer, musician and actor, it was as the last that he excelled. He created a character that was both entirely of its period and entirely his own: the tramp. For this he borrowed Fatty Arbuckle's voluminous trousers, one of Mack Swain's bushy moustaches (drastically trimmed), Ford Sterling's boatsized shoes (on the wrong feet), a tight jacket and a tiny derby, and the little tramp emerged, forever down-at-heel, out of luck and on a collision course with the unwieldy world around him. This still from 1928 (1) shows Chaplin as he epitomized silent cinema, intro-ducing pathos and humour to an adoring audience.

The decades of the Thirties and Forties could boast such highly stylized screen goddesses as Marlene Dietrich, Bette Davis and Greta Garbo. One other Nordic beauty boasted far more natural attributes, and contributed a lengthy variety of performances with many of the major directors of the day. Ingrid Bergman, known equally for her luminous loveliness and her 'immoral' (i.e. Swedish) love-life (for which a US senator denounced her as Hollywood's Apostle of Degradation), made her best

films early on. Here she relaxes at the Tower of London with director Alfred Hitchcock in 1948 before making *Under Capricorn*, a film that commenced the downward spiral of her career (2).

Dietrich was Paramount's answer to MGM's Greta Garbo – both embodied the alluring and ambiguous spirit of the Thirties, and both had relatively little success beyond it. While dancing in a revue Dietrich was spotted by the director Josef von Sternberg (overleaf, 1). He immediately cast her to play the part of the cabaret singer and *femme fatale* Lola opposite Emil Jannings as the ultimately destroyed professor in perhaps his – and her – most famous film, *The Blue Angel* (1930). For this Von Sternberg transformed Dietrich into his creature: suddenly blonde; exotically dressed in what was to become her masculine hallmark, including top hat and cigar; decadent rather than innocent. This whole new look was pursued by thousands of women who sought to start wearing the trousers. Paramount signed her for the astronomical fee of $125,000 a film, six of them to be made by 'Svengali' von Sternberg.

Brigitte Bardot came a generation later, a blonde sex kitten to Dietrich's sophisticate. Known in her native France as Bébé after both her initials and her babydoll looks, she made a string of little-remembered films in which her essential role was as the eternal feminine, personified in husband Roger Vadim's *And God Created Woman*. Here she causes head-scratching as she parades through the 1956 Cannes Film Festival, swinging her beads and her hips (overleaf, 2).

1

DAS Kino ist im Grunde ein Phänomen des 20. Jahrhunderts, und auch wenn Stummfilme ihre nostalgischen Verehrer haben, begann doch die eigentliche Blütezeit des Films erst mit dem ersten »talkie«, Al Jolsons *Der Jazzsänger* von 1927. Ein erster Höhepunkt waren die 30er Jahre mit der Entwicklung des Farbfilms und der Etablierung des Hollywood-Starsystems. Zu den größten Stars dieser Ära zählte Charlie Chaplin (1889-1977), knapp 25 Jahre lang weltweit der beliebteste Filmschauspieler überhaupt. Auch als Drehbuchautor, Regisseur, Produzent und Komponist von Filmmusiken leistete er Großes, doch vor allem war er natürlich ein begnadeter Schauspieler. Er schuf eine Gestalt, die Inbegriff ihrer Zeit und auch Inbegriff von Chaplin selbst war: den Tramp. Dazu borgte er sich von Fatty Arbuckle die zu weiten Hosen, von Mack Swain den struppigen Schnurrbart (drastisch getrimmt), von Ford Sterling die unförmigen Schuhe (und vertauschte rechten und linken), nahm eine enge Jacke und einen winzigen Bowler, und schon war der kleine Tramp geboren, stets abgerissen, der ewige Verlierer, immer auf Kollisionskurs mit der allzu schwierigen Welt. Dieses Standphoto von 1928 (vorige Seite, 1) zeigt uns Chaplin, wie er zum Inbegriff des Stummfilms wurde, zu einem Mann, der wie kein anderer dem Publikum Humor und Melancholie nahebrachte — und das Publikum liebte ihn dafür.

Die 30er und 40er Jahre glänzten mit hochstilisierten Filmgöttinnen wie Marlene Dietrich, Bette Davis und Greta Garbo. Eine andere nordische Schönheit gab sich im Vergleich dazu wesentlich natürlicher und spielte die verschiedensten Rollen unter einigen der bedeutendsten Regisseuren ihrer Zeit: Ingrid Bergman, für ihre strahlende Schönheit wie für ihren »unmoralischen« (sprich schwedischen) Lebenswandel bekannt (für den ein amerikanischer Senator sie »Hollywoods Apostel der Schamlosigkeit« nannte), drehte ihre besten Filme zu Anfang ihrer Karriere. Hier macht sie mit dem Regisseur Alfred Hitchcock einen Ausflug in den Londoner Tower, vor Beginn der Dreharbeiten zu *Sklavin des Herzens* (1948); das war der Film, mit dem der Niedergang ihrer Karriere begann (vorige Seite, 2).

Die Dietrich war Paramounts Antwort auf MGMs Greta Garbo — beide verkörperten den Typus der geheimnisvollen und verführerischen Frau der 30er Jahre, und beide kamen über diese Rolle nie hinaus. Dietrich wurde von Regisseur Josef von Sternberg (1) in einer Revuetruppe entdeckt. Er gab ihr auf Anhieb die Rolle der Nachtclubsängerin und *Femme fatale* Lola,

1

die in seinem — und vielleicht auch ihrem — berühmtesten Film, *Der blaue Engel* von 1930, Emil Jannings ins Verderben stürzt. Für diesen Film schuf Sternberg die Dietrich vollkommen neu: als Blondine, in exotisch-maskuliner Kleidung, die zu ihrem Markenzeichen werden sollte, mit Zylinder und Zigarre — ein Todes- und kein Unschuldsengel. Tausende von Frauen wollten nun selbst die Hosen anhaben und ahmten diesen Look nach. Paramount engagierte die Dietrich für astronomische 125.000 Dollar pro Film, und sechs davon sollte »Svengali« von Sternberg drehen.

Brigitte Bardot war der Star der nächsten Generation, eine sexy Blondine, ungleich unkomplizierter als die Dietrich. Zu Hause in Frankreich nannte man sie »Bébé«, ein Spiel mit ihren Initialen und ihrem Auftreten als naive Kindfrau, und in einer Unzahl von Filmen, die heute fast vergessen sind, verkörpert sie das Weibliche schlechthin, am überzeugendsten in dem Film ihres Ehemannes Roger Vadim, *Und immer lockt das Weib*. Hier kann sich ein Betrachter nur noch an den Kopf fassen, als sie 1956 ketten- und hüftschwingend zum Filmfestival in Cannes stolziert (2).

LE cinéma est essentiellement un phénomène du XXe siècle, et bien que les experts contemplent les films muets avec un brin de nostalgie, le véritable âge d'or du Septième Art n'a commencé qu'avec *Le Chanteur de jazz,* de Alan Crosland, premier film parlant, sorti en 1927 avec la voix de Al Johnson. Les années 30 ont vu un sommet d'activité avec les premiers films en couleurs et le développement du *star-system* à Hollywood. L'un des monstres sacrés fut Charlie Chaplin (1889-1977), considéré pendant près d'un quart de siècle comme la plus grande vedette populaire au niveau planétaire. Bien qu'il réalisât de grandes choses en tant qu'écrivain, réalisateur, producteur et musicien, il excellait surtout dans son activité de comédien. Il a créé une figure qui correspondait à la fois parfaitement à cette époque et à lui-même : le clochard. Pour cela, il emprunta les vastes pantalons de Fatty Arbuckle, la moustache touffue de Mack Swain (radicalement taillée), les chaussures démesurées de Fors Sterling (portées sur le « mauvais » pied), une veste étroite et un chapeau melon minuscule. Le petit clochard était né, toujours déguenillé, malchanceux et en perpétuel affrontement avec le monde alentour. Cette photo de 1928 (page précédente, 1) montre Charlie Chaplin au temps du muet, quand il présentait le tragique et le comique à un public qui le vénérait.

Les années 30 et 40 peuvent s'enorgueillir de divinités du grand écran aussi sophistiquées que Marlene Dietrich, Bette Davis et Greta Garbo. Une autre beauté nordique, qui possédait des atouts beaucoup plus naturels et interpréta des rôles très divers avec nombre des plus grands réalisateurs de l'époque, Ingrid Bergmann, était aussi connue pour son charme lumineux que pour sa vie amoureuse « immorale » (un sénateur américain la dénoncera d'ailleurs comme un agent de la dégradation hollywoodienne). Elle fit ses meilleurs films en début de carrière. Ici, elle se détend devant la Tour de Londres en compagnie d'Alfred Hitchcock, en 1948, avant de tourner *Les Amants du Capricorne,* un film qui amorce le début de son déclin (page précédente, 2).

Marlene Dietrich était la réponse de la Paramount à la Greta Garbo de la MGM. Elles incarnaient toutes les deux l'esprit séduisant et ambigu des années 30, et toutes deux connurent relativement peu de succès plus tard. Le réalisateur Josef von Sternberg découvrit Marlene Dietrich alors qu'elle se produisait comme danseuse dans une revue (1). Il l'engagea immédiatement pour lui faire jouer le rôle de Lola,

2

chanteuse de cabaret et femme fatale qui donne la réplique à Emil Jannings, le professeur qu'elle finira par détruire, dans ce qui fut peut-être, à l'un comme à l'autre, leur plus grand film, *L'Ange bleu* (1930). Pour ce faire, von Sternberg créa une nouvelle Marlene : blonde, vêtue de ce qui deviendra sa marque « masculine », haut-de-forme et cigare, incarnant plus la décadence que l'innocence. Cette mode entièrement nouvelle fut suivie par des milliers de femmes qui demandaient à porter le pantalon. Paramount l'engagea pour la somme astronomique de 125 000 dollars par film ; six d'entre eux furent réalisés par « Svengali » von Sternberg.

La génération suivante fut celle de Brigitte Bardot, blonde coquette et sexy. Connue sous le nom de B.B., elle réalisa une série de films où elle incarnait l'éternel féminin, comme dans *Et Dieu créa la femme,* réalisé par son mari Roger Vadim. Ici les hommes restèrent sans voix quand elle parada en 1956 à l'occasion du Festival de Cannes, faisant sauter ses perles et roulant des hanches (2).

3

(*Previous pages*)

PERHAPS the most famous film made by Fritz Lang was *Metropolis* (1926), which played on the fundamental fears of a post-industrial age. In it time becomes all-controlling and the clock cannot be turned back (3); the demands of the market-place lead to child slavery (2); and a flood threatens an apocalyptic finale (1).

(*vorige Seiten*)

DER berühmteste Film Fritz Langs ist wohl *Metropolis* (1926), in dem er die tiefsitzenden Ängste eines postindustriellen Zeitalters zum Thema macht. Zeit wird zum alles beherrschenden Faktor, und keiner kann die Uhr zurückdrehen (3); die Anforderungen des Marktes versklaven die Kinder (2); und eine große Flutwelle droht mit einem apokalyptischen Finale (1).

(*Pages précédentes*)

LE film le plus célèbre de Fritz Lang est certainement *Métropolis* (1926), qui joue sur les craintes fondamentales de l'ère post-industrielle. C'est le temps qui contrôle tout et il est impossible de reculer les aiguilles de l'horloge (3) ; sur la place du marché les enfants sont vendus comme esclaves (2), et une inondation menace de l'apocalypse finale (1).

FIFTEEN years of Charlie Chaplin's film career: from *The Kid* (1) with Jackie Coogan in the eponymous part (1920) to *Modern Times* with Paulette Goddard (2). The playing-card posters came captioned: 'A gentleman from Paris sent us these French posters used over there to advertise Charlie. I had them posted up and photographed. Charlie liked the centre top and lower right ones' (3).

FÜNFZEHN Jahre in Charlie Chaplins Filmkarriere: *Das Kind* mit Jackie Coogan als Titelheld »the kid« (1920, 1) bis hin zu *Moderne Zeiten* mit Paulette Goddard (2). Die Unterschrift zu dem Bild mit den Spielkarten-Plakaten lautete: »Ein Herr aus Paris schickte uns diese Plakate, mit denen dort für Charlie Werbung gemacht wird. Ich ließ sie ankleben und aufnehmen. Charlie mochte besonders die Bilder oben in der Mitte und unten rechts (3).«

QUINZE années de la carrière cinématographique de Charlie Chaplin : depuis *Le Kid* (1) avec Jackie Coogan dans le rôle éponyme (1920) aux *Temps modernes* avec Paulette Goddard (2). Les affiches en forme de cartes à jouer

2

3

devinrent légendaires : « Un monsieur de Paris nous a envoyé ces affiches françaises utilisées là-bas pour faire de la publicité à Charlie. Je les ai installées et photographiées. Charlie aimait celle d'en haut au centre et celle d'en bas à droite. (3). »

A deck of the most accomplished silent screen comedians who made it into the 'talkies'. Harold Lloyd was reckoned to be even more popular than Chaplin. Like the latter's 'tramp' character, Lloyd's 'Glasses' became swiftly identified with what would later be called a yuppie – college-educated, on the make and bent on success. Here, 'Glasses' dolefully pursues that sought-after acclaim among a large party of children at a picture theatre (1). Buster Keaton was equally popular, demonstrating stoical fortitude in the face of every eventuality. His experiments with cinema's technical potential – image manipulation and other special effects – are mimicked by this conversation he's having with a miniaturized version of himself (2). Stan Laurel and Oliver Hardy were a lovable duo who relied on heavy stereotyping and comforting familiarity, never varying from the weedy pathos of the one and the plump bluster of the other. They take a break from performing at the London Palladium in 1947 to drive the inaugural train on the reopened Hythe and Dymchurch line (3).

EIN Kleeblatt der beliebtesten Stummfilmkomiker, die den Sprung in die »talkies« schafften. Harold Lloyd war seinerzeit womöglich noch bekannter als Chaplin. Lloyds Brille wurde genauso zum Markenzeichen wie Chaplins Trampkostüm, und sie symbolisierte Eigenschaften, die man später dem Yuppie zuordnen sollte — gebildet, aufstrebend und erfolgreich. Hier tut Lloyd etwas für diesen Erfolg und läßt sich, wenn auch etwas halbherzig, mit einer ganzen Schar Schulkinder in einem Kino aufnehmen (1). Nicht weniger populär war Buster Keaton, der selbst die größten Katastrophen mit stoischer Miene meisterte. Er experimentierte auch mit den technischen Möglichkeiten des Films — mit nachträglichen Veränderungen des Bildes und anderen »special effects« —, und hier scheint er im Zwiegespräch mit seinem miniaturisierten Alter ego darüber nachzudenken (2). Stan Laurel und Oliver Hardy waren ein liebenswertes Duo, dessen Erfolgsrezept immer wiederkehrende Stereotypen waren; und zeit ihres Lebens mimten sie den sentimentalen Umstandskrämer und den tolpatschigen Tatmenschen. Hier nehmen sie sich von ihren Auftritten im Londoner Palladium (1947) einen Tag frei und sind Lokomotivführer im ersten Zug der wiedereröffneten Miniatureisenbahn von Hythe nach Dymchurch (3).

SUR le pont, les comédiens les plus accomplis du cinéma muet qui continuèrent dans le « parlant ». Harold Lloyd était même plus populaire que Charlie Chaplin. Comme plus tard le rôle de « clochard » de Charlot, les lunettes d'Harold Lloyd le firent rapidement identifier à ce qu'on appellera plus tard un « yuppie », de formation supérieure, programmé pour la réussite. Ici, l'homme aux célèbres lunettes rondes pose d'un air morne dans un cinéma au milieu d'une grande fête donnée pour des enfants (1). Buster Keaton, tout aussi populaire, faisait preuve d'un courage imperturbable dans l'adversité. Ces expériences avec les possibilités techniques du cinéma — manipulation des images et autres effets spéciaux — sont rendues ici par la conversation qu'il tient en ce moment avec sa propre version miniature de lui-même (2).

Stan Laurel et Oliver Hardy formaient un duo adorable qui associait le stéréotype lourd et la familiarité réconfortante ; l'un invariablement mauviette tragique et souffreteuse, l'autre colérique et bien en chair. Ici, un moment de détente pendant la représentation au Palladium de Londres en 1947 : ils conduisent le train inaugurant la ligne Hythe et Dymchurch de nouveau en circulation (3).

THE Marx Brothers were not only the most variously talented comedy team in Hollywood but the precursors of the zany 'Jewish humour' of later US comedians such as Mel Brooks and Woody Allen (2, photographed here in 1971). Groucho's droopy slouch, eyebrows and moustache; Chico's Italianate gobbledy-gook and magical piano-playing; Harpo's silly wig, dumb insolence and – of course – harp, with fourth brother Zeppo as a foil in the earlier movies, were fought over by the major film companies. While they made *Monkey Business*, *Horsefeathers* and *Duck Soup* (1) with Paramount, they added *A Night at the Opera*, *A Day at the Races*, *At the Circus* and *Go West* to MGM's list, being criticized by supremo Irving Thalberg for being 'too funny'. Love interest was his solution, often in the somewhat surprising person of Margaret Dumont at her most stately.

DIE Marx Brothers waren seinerzeit die wohl begabteste Truppe in Hollywood, die Urahnen des kuriosen »jüdischen Humors« späterer amerikanischer Komiker wie Mel Brooks oder Woody Allen (2, hier in einer Aufnahme von 1971). Die großen Studios rissen sich um Groucho mit seinem schleichenden Gang, den buschigen Augenbrauen und dem aufgemalten Schnurrbart, Chico mit seinem italienischen Akzent und magischen Klavierspiel; sowie um Harpo mit der albernen Perücke, dem stummen Starrsinn und — wie der Name schon sagt — seiner Harfe, wobei anfangs der vierte Bruder,

Zeppo, noch für ein wenig ausgleichende Normalität sorgte. *Die Marx Brothers auf See*, *Horse Feathers* und *Die Marx Brothers im Krieg* (1) drehten sie für Paramount, während *Die Marx Brothers in der Oper, Ein Tag beim Rennen, At the Circus* und *Go West* das Repertoire von MGM zierten. Der dortige Boß, Irving Thalberg, fand sie »zu lustig«, und so kamen Liebeshandlungen hinzu, oft mit der pompösen Margaret Dumont.

LES Marx Brothers n'étaient pas seulement les comédiens aux talents les plus variés de Hollywood, ils furent aussi les précurseurs de « l'humour juif », type d'humour loufoque dont Mel Brooks et Woody Allen (2, photographié ici en 1971) seront les futurs représentants. L'allure avachie de Groucho, ses sourcils et sa moustache ; le charabia à l'italienne de Chico et son inimitable talent de pianiste ; la perruque impossible de Harpo, son insolence idiote et – évidemment – sa harpe, et Zeppo, faire-valoir dans les premiers films. Les plus grandes compagnies se battirent pour les engager. Pendant qu'ils tournaient *Monnaie de singe, Plumes de cheval* et *la Soupe au canard* (1) pour Paramount, ils ajoutaient *Une nuit à l'opéra, Un jour aux courses, Un jour au cirque* et *Chercheurs d'or* à la liste de MGM, critiqués par le grand chef Irving Thalberg parce que « *too funny* ». Pour remédier à cela, il eut l'idée de les rendre souvent amoureux, ce qui peut surprendre, de Margaret Dumont dans sa plus grande majesté.

UNITED Artists was founded by arguably the four greatest silent film giants in 1919: Douglas Fairbanks, Mary Pickford, D. W. Griffith and Charlie Chaplin (2), with the invisible assistance of US Treasury Secretary William McAdoo. Mack Sennett, nicknamed 'The King of Slapstick', produced – among others – W. C. Fields, but his company hit the rocks for a second and final time in 1937. This photo was taken on the Sennett film lot just before it was torn down, at a visibly dismal last lunch shared by Marion Davies, Will Haines, King Vidor, Ulric Bush and Eileen Percy (3). Mickey Mouse takes Walt Disney for a walk (1). Disney (1901-66) was not necessarily the most innovative but he was certainly the most businesslike of film animators. Mickey Mouse was born in 1928 and greatly helped Disney's company to win its 19 Oscars.

IM Jahre 1919 taten sich vier der einflußreichsten Persönlichkeiten der Stummfilmzeit zusammen — Douglas Fairbanks, Mary Pickford, D. W. Griffith und Charlie Chaplin — und gründeten die Filmgesellschaft United Artists (2), wobei William McAdoo vom US-Schatzamt hinter den Kulissen entscheidend mitwirkte. Mack Sennett, der »König des Slapstick«, produzierte unter anderem W. C. Fields, doch 1937 mußte seine schon zuvor in Schwierigkeiten geratene Firma endgültig Konkurs anmelden. Unser Bild zeigt die gedrückte Stimmung bei einem Abschiedsessen auf dem Gelände der Sennett-Studios, unmittelbar bevor sie abgerissen wurden (3). Mit von der Partie sind Marion Davies, Will Haines, King Vidor, Ulric Bush und Eileen Percy. Micky Maus bei einem Spaziergang mit Walt Disney (1). Disney (1901-1966) war vielleicht nicht der innovativste unter den Trickfilmzeichnern, aber er hatte zweifellos den besten Geschäftssinn von allen. Micky Maus kam 1928 zur Welt und trug seinen Teil zu den 19 Oscars bei, die die Disney-Studios errangen.

UNITED Artists a été fondée par les plus formidables géants du muet en 1919 : Douglas Fairbanks, Mary Pickford, D. W. Griffith et Charlie Chaplin (2) avec l'assistance invisible du secrétaire du ministère des Finances, William McAdoo. Mack Sennett, « le roi du slapstick », produisit – entre autres – W.C. Fields, mais sa compagnie fit naufrage une seconde et dernière fois en 1937. Cette photo a été prise sur le terrain des studios

Sennet, juste avant qu'ils ne fussent rasés. On y assiste à un dernier repas visiblement lugubre avec Marion Davies, Will Haines, King Vidor, Ulric Bush et Eileen Percy (3). Mickey Mouse emmène Walt Disney en promenade (1). Disney (1901-1966) ne fut pas nécessairement le plus inventif, mais certainement le plus efficace des animateurs du cinéma. Mickey Mouse, né en 1928, a beaucoup aidé la compagnie de Walt Disney à gagner ses 19 Oscars.

1   2

KNOWN for her sensuality and volatile temperament (the two fused when, having failed to seduce Marlon Brando during filming of *The Eagle has Two Heads*, she had him fired), Tallulah Bankhead changed leading men as rapidly as her exotic costumes. Here she is dressed to slay as the Spanish siren *Conchita* (1). Louise Brooks' press photos invite us to consider her as both demurely pensive (2) and as dressed in feather boa and high heels to undertake a little light exercise on her Hollywood home trapeze (3). Famous for her role in the German expressionist Pabst's *Pandora's Box* (1928), she captured the mood and set the hairstyle of the time.

TALLULAH Bankhead, bekannt für ihre Sinnlichkeit und ihr stürmisches Temperament, wechselte die Hauptdarsteller an ihrer Seite ebenso häufig wie ihre exotischen Kostüme. Sinnlichkeit und Temperament kamen bei den Dreharbeiten zu *The Eagle has Two Heads* zusammen: Als Marlon Brando ihren Verführungskünsten widerstand, sorgte sie dafür, daß er gefeuert wurde. Hier ist sie umwerfend als die spanische Sirene *Conchita* kostümiert (1). Louise Brooks wirkt auf den Pressephotos still und nachdenklich (2), aber auch in hochhackigen Schuhen und Federboa, bei ein paar Übungen auf dem Trapez ihres Hauses in Hollywood (3). Berühmt für ihre Rolle in *Die Büchse der Pandora* (1928) des deutschen Expressionisten G. W. Pabst, verkörperte sie wie keine andere die Stimmung jener Zeit, und alle Welt ahmte ihre Frisur nach.

CÉLEBRE pour son tempérament sensuel et volage (un mélange explosif, on le verra, quand n'ayant pu séduire Marlon Brandon durant le tournage de *L'Aigle à deux têtes*, elle le renvoya), Tallulah Bankhead changeait d'hommes aussi rapidement que de costumes. Ici, elle est vêtue en espagnole dans *Conchita* (1). Les photos de presse de Louise Brooks nous la montrent à la fois songeuse et réservée (2), ou en boa à plumes et hauts talons pour exécuter un petit exercice facile sur son trapèze dans sa maison de Hollywood (3). Fameuse pour son rôle dans le film de l'expressionniste allemand Pabst *Loulou* (1928), elle sut saisir l'esprit du temps et imposa un style de coiffure.

3

LILLIAN Gish (1) and Rudolph Valentino (2) were legends of the silent screen. Gish started as a child actress and often played alongside her sister, Dorothy, until the latter's death in 1968. However, her later films never had the impact of such epic masterpieces as *Birth of a Nation* (1914) and *Orphans of the Storm* (1922). Her most prolific year was 1926 when she played tragic lead roles in both *La Bohème* and *The Scarlet Letter* for MGM. Valentino also started young, alternating professional dancing with sidelines as (among other things) a gardener and a thief. The film that turned him into the hottest property of the 1920s was *The Four Horsemen of the Apocalypse* (1921), grossing over $4.5m. For five years, Valentino made films with titles like *The Sheikh* (1921) and *Blood and Sand* (1922) that established his reputation as a sultry and exotic screen lover. His sudden death in 1926, from a perforated ulcer brought on by overwork, brought street riots at his funeral and even female suicides.

LILLIAN Gish (1) und Rudolph Valentino (2) waren Legenden des Stummfilms. Gish stand schon als kleines Mädchen auf der Bühne, oft zusammen mit ihrer Schwester Dorothy, die 1968 starb. Doch ihre späteren Filme erreichten nie wieder die Kraft von *Die Geburt einer Nation* (1914) und *Orphans of the Storm* (1922). Ihr produktivstes Jahr war 1926, als sie bei MGM die tragischen Hauptrollen in *La Bohème* und in *Der scharlachrote Buchstabe* spielte. Auch Valentino begann jung und verband Auftritte als Tanzprofi mit Nebenverdiensten als (unter anderem) Gärtner und Dieb. Der Film, der ihn zum größten Star der Zwanziger machte und über viereinhalb Millionen Dollar einspielte, war *Die vier apokalyptischen Reiter* von 1921. Fünf Jahre lang drehte Valentino einen Film nach dem anderen, mit Titeln wie *Der Scheich* (1921) oder *Blood and Sand* (1922); mit seinem Schmollmund wurde er zum Inbegriff des exotischen Liebhabers auf der Leinwand. Sein plötzlicher Tod 1926 — ein Magengeschwürdurchbruch, die Folge seiner rastlosen Arbeit — führte zu erschütternden Szenen bei der Beerdigung, und manche Frauen begingen sogar Selbstmord deswegen.

2

LILIAN Gish (1) et Rudolf Valentino (2) font partie de la légende du cinéma muet. Lilian Gish fut actrice dès l'enfance et joua souvent aux côtés de sa soeur Dorothy jusqu'à la mort de celle-ci, survenue en 1968. Cependant, ses derniers films n'ont jamais eu l'impact des chefs-d'oeuvre épiques comme *Naissance d'une nation* (1914) et *À travers l'orage* (1922). 1926 fut son année la plus féconde : elle y joue de grands rôles tragiques dans *Au temps de la Bohême* et *La Lettre rouge* pour la MGM. Valentino débuta aussi très jeune dans le métier, alternant la danse professionnelle avec des activités secondaires dans le jardinage et le cambriolage. Le film *Les Quatre Cavaliers de l'Apocalypse* (1921) en a fait la star des années 20 et il généra à lui seul une recette de plus de 4,5 millions de dollars. Pendant cinq ans, Valentino tourna des films aux titres prometteurs comme *le Cheik* (1921) et *Arènes sanglantes* (1922) qui lui firent à l'écran une réputation d'amant, sensuel et exotique. Il mourut brusquement en 1926 d'un ulcère dû au surmenage. Au cours de ses funérailles, on assista à des émeutes dans les rues et des femmes se suicidèrent.

P1396-207

1

MIT ihrer sauberen, allem Anschein nach braven Art gehörten Cary Grant (1) und Gary Cooper (2) zu den größten Kassenschlagern jenseits des Atlantiks. Grant (1) kam aus armen Verhältnissen im englischen Bristol und ging nach Hollywood, um dort sein Glück zu machen: Die erste Gage bei Paramount waren immerhin schon 450 Dollar die Woche. Mit seinem guten Aussehen, dem vornehmen Akzent und seiner lässigen Nonchalance spielte er die männlichen Hauptrollen in Filmen mit Göttinnen wie Mae West, Marlene Dietrich und Katharine Hepburn. Cooper — hier zusammen mit William Anderson, dem »Mann, der ganz Hollywood füttert« (die fünfhundert Mann, die immer mit Außenaufnahmen beschäftigt waren, verköstigte er dreimal am Tag) — war 35 Jahre lang ein Star in Hollywood. Obwohl er in Western, Thrillern, Komödien und Literaturverfilmungen spielte (einmal sogar einen Baseballstar), verstand er sich immer als »der Amerikaner von nebenan«. Jemand hat einmal gesagt, die Bandbreite seiner Ausdrucksmittel reiche von »na klar« bis »von wegen«.

CARY Grant (1) et Gary Cooper (2), qui étaient deux des plus grandes attractions du box-office américain dans le genre « rasé de près », menaient apparemment une vie bien réglée. Abandonnant son milieu misérable de Bristol en Angleterre (1), Grant chercha fortune à Hollywood : son premier salaire à la Paramount s'élevait à 450 dollars par semaine. Son accent raffiné, son doux regard et sa nonchalance décontractée lui firent endosser des rôles qui l'opposaient à des déesses de l'écran comme Mae West, Marlene Dietrich et Katharine Hepburn. Gary Cooper, ici à côté de William Anderson, « l'homme qui nourrissait le cinéma » en procurant trois repas par jour aux 500 figurants, fut une star de Hollywood pendant trente-cinq ans. Bien qu'il ait travaillé dans tous les genres : westerns, thrillers, comédies, adaptations littéraires (il joua même une vedette du base-ball), il se décrit lui-même comme « Mr. Average Joe American ». On a dit de son envergure dramatique qu'elle allait du « ouais » au « non ».

CARY Grant (1) and Gary Cooper (2) were two of the biggest Stateside box office draws of the clean-shaven, apparently clean-living variety. Abandoning his poverty-stricken background in Bristol, England, Grant (1) was right to seek his fortune in Hollywood: his first Paramount salary was $450 a week. His refined accent, smooth looks and casual nonchalance brought him starring roles opposite such goddesses as Mae West, Marlene Dietrich and Katharine Hepburn. Cooper, here standing next to William Anderson, 'the man who feeds the movies' and provided three meals a day for the 500 people on location, was a Hollywood star for 35 years. Despite working across a range that covered westerns, thrillers, comedies, literary adaptations (he even played a baseball star), he described himself as 'Mr Average Joe American'. His dramatic span has been described as running from 'Yep' to 'Nope'.

2

1   2

BETTE Davis, Jean Harlow and Greta Garbo were all known as the vamps of the 1930s. The first became Hollywood's most enduring female star (1). Her tempestuous personality gave her a dark reputation, enhanced by a career renewed in the 1960s by the psychological thrillers *Whatever Happened to Baby Jane?* and *The Nanny*. Harlow was the 'blonde bombshell' whose locks were more platinum and cleavage more exposed than any other actress's (2). Paired with Clark Gable in five films, she played tough, funny and sexy through the 1930s. Her sudden death, aged only 26, made her last film *Saratoga* (1937) a huge box office success. Garbo's seductive but intelligent dreaminess made her 'the standard against which all other screen actresses are measured' (3). *Queen Christina*, *Ninotchka*, *Grand Hotel* and *Camille* afforded her most famous parts.

BETTE Davis, Jean Harlow und Greta Garbo galten als die drei Vamps der 30er Jahre. Bette Davis war wegen ihrer Temperamentsausbrüche gefürchtet (1). In den 60er Jahren erlebte sie mit Thrillern wie *Whatever Happened to Baby Jane?* und *The Nanny* noch einmal eine Blütezeit. Harlow war die »Sexbombe«, die platinblondere Locken und tiefere Ausschnitte hatte als jede andere Schauspielerin (2). In fünf Filmen mit Clark Gable spielte sie in den 30er Jahren ihren zähen, gewitzten und aufreizenden Frauentyp. Ihr plötzlicher Tod mit nur 26 Jahren machte aus ihrem letzten Film *Saratoga* (1937) einen Kassenschlager. Die verführerische, doch kluge Verträumtheit der Garbo macht sie zum »Standard, an dem alle anderen Schauspielerinnen sich messen müssen« (3). *Königin Christina*, *Ninotschka*, *Grand Hotel* und *Die Kameliendame* waren ihre größten Rollen.

BETTE Davis, Jean Harlow et Greta Garbo : les vamps des années 30. La première battit le record de longévité à Hollywood (1). Son caractère ombrageux lui fit une mauvaise réputation qu'un nouveau départ dans les années 60 avec les thrillers psychologiques *Qu'est-il arrivé à Baby Jane ?* et *La Nanny* ne fit qu'accentuer. Harlow était la « bombe blonde », aux boucles les plus platinées et au décolleté le plus large du cinéma d'alors (2). Avec Clark Gable, durant les années 30, elle joua dans cinq films qui la montrèrent solide, amusante et sexy. Sa mort soudaine, à l'âge de 26 ans, fit de son dernier film, *Saratoga* (1937), un énorme succès au box-office. Le caractère rêveur, séduisant, mais intelligent de Garbo firent d'elle « la norme à laquelle sont mesurées toutes les autres actrices » (3). *La Reine Christine*, *Ninotchka*, *Grand Hôtel* et *Camille* lui offrirent ses plus grands rôles.

CLARK Gable's reputation as King of Hollywood came with *Gone With the Wind* in 1939 (4). Later Hollywood heroes were James Dean (1) and the longer-lived Marlon Brando (5). Burt Lancaster's pin-up was taken while shooting *A Child is Waiting* with Judy Garland in 1966, at the height of his beef-cake popularity (3). His films became subtler and more inventive as he aged, ranging from Louis Malle's *Atlantic City* in 1980 to Bill Forsythe's *Local Hero* in 1983. Gregory Peck was caught during the filming of *The Million Pound Note* in 1953 (2).

2

3

4

5

CLARK Gable erwarb sich seinen Ruf als König von Hollywood im Jahre 1939 mit *Vom Winde verweht* (4). Spätere Hollywood-Stars waren James Dean (1) und Marlon Brando (5). Das Starphoto von Burt Lancaster entstand 1966, als er mit Judy Garland *Ein Kind wartet* drehte, auf dem Höhepunkt seiner Karriere als Muskelprotz (3). Im Alter wurde sein Spiel subtiler und charaktervoller, von Louis Malles *Atlantic City, USA* von 1980 bis zu *Local Hero* von Bill Forsythe, 1983. Das Bild von Gregory Peck entstand bei der Verfilmung von Mark Twains *Die Million-Pfund-Note* im Jahre 1953 (2).

EN 1939, Clark Gable devint le roi de Hollywood avec *Autant en emporte le vent* (4). Parmi les héros de Hollywood plus jeunes étaient James Dean (1) et l'éternel Marlon Brando (5). La photo de Burt Lancaster a été prise pendant le tournage de *Un enfant attend* avec Judy Garland en 1966. À l'époque, il était l'un des rois du « beefcake » (3). À mesure qu'il vieillissait, ses films devinrent plus subtils et plus inventifs, allant d'*Atlantic City* de Louis Malle, en 1980, à *Local Hero* de Bill Forsythe en 1983. Gregory Peck a été saisi sur le vif en 1953 pendant le tournage de l'adaptation du livre de Mark Twain, *Un pari de milliardaires* (2).

1

2

MAE West (2, in 1954) was accused of looking more female impersonator than sex symbol. She became as known for her witty ripostes as for her overblown allure (George Raft commented: 'In this picture, Mae West stole everything but the cameras'). Brigitte Bardot was the St-Tropez version, who never quite recognized the funnier aspects of some of her movies. In 1971, clearly too much *Private Life* led to her fainting while on set, and to being mobbed as she was carried off (1). Sophia Loren in the 1960s co-starred with 'cowboy actor' John Wayne in *Legend of the Lost*, coming off set in Libya to do a little extra dance for the press cameras (3).

ÜBER Mae West (2, 1954) hörte man gelegentlich, sie sehe eigentlich eher wie ein Transvestit als wie ein Sexsymbol aus. Sie war ebenso bekannt für ihre schlagfertigen Antworten wie für ihre grenzenlosen Allüren (George Raft meinte dazu: »In diesem Film hat Mae West alles gestohlen außer den Kameras«). Das Gegenstück in St.-Tropez war Brigitte Bardot, die nie so ganz durchschaute, wie unfreiwillig komisch manche ihrer Filme sind. 1971 wurde sie, wahrscheinlich wegen zuviel *Privatleben*, bei Dreharbeiten ohnmächtig, und die Schaulustigen drängten sich, als sie abtransportiert wurde (1). Sophia Loren spielte in den 60er Jahren an der Seite des Cowboydarstellers John Wayne in *Legend of the Lost*; hier gibt sie am Drehort in Libyen eine extra Tanzvorführung für die Presse (3).

ON a dit de Mae West (2, en 1954) qu'elle était plus une parodie de la femme qu'un sex-symbol. Ses ripostes spirituelles la rendirent aussi populaire que son allure extravagante (commentaire de George Ralf : « Sur cette photo, Mae West vole tout sauf les caméras. »). Brigitte Bardot, la version Saint-Tropez, ne reconnut jamais vraiment les aspects plus drôles de certains de ses films. En 1971, *Vie privée* l'a manifestement affaiblie : elle s'évanouit durant un tournage avant d'être assaillie par la foule alors qu'on la transporte (1). Sophia Loren, dans les années 60, jouant aux côtés du cow-boy de l'écran, John Wayne, dans *La Cité disparue*. Venue tourner en Lybie, elle fait quelques pas de danse devant les caméras de presse (3).

2

MARILYN Monroe (1) conserved her little-girl-lost vulnerability, dying, aged 36, of a drugs overdose before age would have caused her to outlive it. Her fragile sexiness and breathy singing are best seen and heard in *Gentlemen prefer Blondes* and *How to Marry a Millionaire* (both 1953); *The Seven Year Itch* (1955); *Bus Stop* (1957) and *Some Like it Hot* (1959). Seeking to go beyond her dumb blonde/gold-digger roles, in 1961 she starred in *The Misfits*, written for her by the leading playwright (and her last husband) Arthur Miller. British playwright Terence Rattigan was also the author of *The Prince and the Showgirl*, in which she starred with Laurence Olivier. Here, in 1957, Monroe and Miller are on their way to attend a party given by Rattigan (2).

MARILYN Monroe erweckte bis zuletzt das Bild des verirrten kleinen Mädchens und starb mit 36 an einer Überdosis Tabletten, bevor sie zu alt für diese Rolle wurde. Ihre fragile Erotik und die schüchterne Singstimme sind am besten in *Blondinen bevorzugt*, *Wie angelt man sich einen Millionär?* (beide 1953), *Das verflixte siebente Jahr* (1955), *Bus Stop* (1957) und *Manche mögen's heiß* (1959) zu sehen und zu hören. Sie wollte mehr spielen als nur das blonde Dummchen, und so übernahm sie die weibliche Hauptrolle in *Nicht gesellschaftsfähig* (1961) nach einem Stück des führenden amerikanischen Dramatikers Arthur Miller, der auch ihr letzter Ehemann war. Millers britischer Kollege Terence Rattigan lieferte die Vorlage zu *Der Prinz und die Tänzerin*, in dem sie zusammen mit Laurence Olivier spielte. Hier sieht man die Monroe und Miller 1957, unterwegs zu einer Party bei Rattigan (2).

MARYLIN Monroe (1) resta la petite fille désemparée, disparue à 36 ans d'une overdose avant que l'âge lui fît perdre sa vulnérabilité. On la voit et on peut écouter sa voix fragile, sensuelle et un rien haletante dans des films comme *Les Hommes préfèrent les blondes*, et *Comment épouser un millionnaire* (tournés en 1953) ; *Sept Ans de réflexion* (1955) ; *Bus Stop* (1957) et *Certains l'aiment chaud* (1959). Cherchant à aller au-delà de ses rôles de petite blonde niaise/chercheuse d'or, elle jouera en 1961 dans *Les Désaxés*, écrit pour elle par le grand dramaturge Arthur Miller, son dernier mari. Le dramaturge britannique, Terence Rattigan, était également l'auteur du *Prince et la Danseuse,* où elle donne la réplique à Laurence Olivier. Ici, en 1957, Marylin Monroe et Arthur Miller au cours d'une fête donnée par Rattigan (2).

1

IM Laufe ihrer außerordentlich langen Karriere errang Katharine Hepburn vier Oscars als beste Hauptdarstellerin, mehr als jede andere (1). Zwei ihrer liebsten Filme, *Leoparden küßt man nicht* und *Holiday* (beide 1938), fielen beim zeitgenössischen Publikum durch, so daß sie als »Kassengift« galt. Doch sowohl die neun Filme, die sie mit Spencer Tracy drehte, von der frühen *Philadelphia Story* an (1939, ein Film, an dem sie mit ihrem bemerkenswerten Geschäftssinn auch die Rechte erwarb) wie auch die späte *African Queen* (1951), wo sie zusammen mit Humphrey Bogart spielte, waren sehr erfolgreich. Lauren Bacall war natürlich nicht nur auf der Leinwand, sondern auch im Leben Bogarts Partnerin (2). Ihre größten Erfolge waren *Tote schlafen fest* (1946), *Dark Passage* (1947) und *Gangster in Key Largo* (1948); später kehrte sie zu den Broadway-Shows zurück, in denen sie angefangen hatte, und eroberte sich ein neues Publikum.

FAIT sans précédent, Katharine Hepburn obtint quatre fois l'Oscar de la meilleure interprète au cours de sa carrière exceptionnellement longue (1). Deux de ses films favoris, *L'impossible Mr. Bébé* et *Vacances* (tous deux tournés en 1938), n'ont pas connu le succès à l'époque, lui valant la réputation de « poison » du box-office. Mais les neuf films qu'elle réalisa avec Spencer Tracy, ainsi que *Philadelphia Story* en 1939 (dont Katharine Hepburn acquit les droits, faisant aussi preuve d'un grand sens des affaires) et le film ultérieur *African Queen* (1951), qui la met face à Humphrey Bogart, furent de grands succès. Lauren Bacall était évidemment la partenaire de Bogart à l'écran comme en privé (2). Ses plus grands succès restent *Le Grand Sommeil* (1946), *Les Passagers de la nuit* (1947) et *Key Largo* (1948), bien qu'elle recommençât plus tard une carrière et conquis un nouveau public avec des spectacles à la mode à Broadway.

KATHARINE Hepburn won an unprecedented four Oscars for Best Actress throughout her exceptionally long career (1). Two of her own favourites (*Bringing Up Baby* and *Holiday*, both 1938) were contemporary flops, giving her the label of 'box office poison'. But the nine films she made with Spencer Tracy, as well as the earlier *Philadelphia Story* (1939, to which, with considerable business acumen, Hepburn bought film rights) and the later *African Queen* (1951), playing opposite Humphrey Bogart, were hugely successful. Lauren Bacall was, of course, Bogart's partner on and off screen (2). Their greatest hits were *The Big Sleep* (1946), *Dark Passage* (1947) and *Key Largo* (1948), though latterly she returned to and won new audiences in mainstream Broadway shows.

FOLLOWING the stunning impact of *The Blue Angel* (1), Marlene Dietrich became the first of a generation of smoky-voiced, androgynous stars of both screen and cabaret (2). Despite the lampshade millinery she excelled in elegance in such films as *Blonde Venus* (1932), *The Scarlet Empress* (1934) and *The Devil is a Woman* (3). It was after the latter film that in 1935 she applied to become a US citizen, in order to elude Hitler's reiterated invitations to her to 'return home' and – paradoxically – her career dived. It began to revive with *Destry Rides Again* (1939), in which she was teamed with James Stewart in an inspired bit of casting.

MIT dem gewaltigen Eindruck, den sie im *Blauen Engel* (1) machte, wurde Marlene Dietrich zum Prototyp einer ganzen Generation von Leinwand- und Kabarettstars, allesamt androgyn und mit rauchiger Stimme (2). Selbst mit einem Lampenschirm auf dem Kopf war sie noch ein Muster an Eleganz in Filmen wie *Die blonde Venus* (1932), *Die scharlachrote Kaiserin* (1934) und *Die spanische Tänzerin* (3). Nach diesem Film, 1935, beantragte sie die amerikanische Staatsbürgerschaft, um sich Hitlers wiederholten Einladungen zur »Rückkehr nach Hause« zu entziehen. Paradoxerweise ging es danach mit ihrer Karriere abwärts, und ihr nächster Erfolg kam erst 1939 mit *Der große Bluff* an der Seite von James Stewart.

1 2

3 SUITE à l'impact stupéfiant que connut *L'Ange bleu* (1), Marlene Dietrich devint la première d'une génération de stars de l'écran et du cabaret à la silhouette androgyne et au timbre voilé par le tabac (2). En dépit de la coiffure en abat-jour qu'elle porte ici, elle brillait par son élégance dans des films comme *Blonde Vénus* (1932), *L'Impératrice rouge* (1934) et *La Belle Ensorceleuse* (3). C'est après ce dernier film qu'elle demanda, en 1935, la citoyenneté américaine afin de mettre fin aux invitations répétées de Hitler, qui lui demandait de « rentrer à la maison » et – paradoxalement – sa carrière en pâtit. Le succès lui sourit à nouveau avec des films comme *Les Deux Cavaliers* (1939), où elle a pour partenaire James Stewart.

1

HUMPHREY Bogart and Katharine
Hepburn, not up the Zambesi but at
Britain's Isleworth studios during the
filming of a storm-lashed scene from *The
African Queen* (1). As soon as this last scene
was shot, Bogart bailed out and scrambled
on board the Île de France to sail for home
with wife Lauren Bacall and son Stevie.

Some years before, in 1938, Hepburn
proved she was no slouch, practising an
acrobatic feat for *Holiday* with Cary Grant
(2). Audrey Hepburn on set, discussing
what must be her most unlikely role as the
Cockney flower-seller Eliza in *My Fair
Lady* with director George Cukor in 1964
(3).

HUMPHREY Bogart und Katharine
Hepburn fahren den stürmischen
Sambesi hinauf, und zwar in den
englischen Isleworth-Studios während
der Aufnahmen zu *African Queen* (1). Als
diese letzte Szene im Kasten war, hielt
Bogart nichts mehr: Er ging an Bord der
Île de France und fuhr mit Ehefrau
Lauren Bacall und Sohn Stevie nach
Hause. Ein paar Jahre zuvor, 1938,

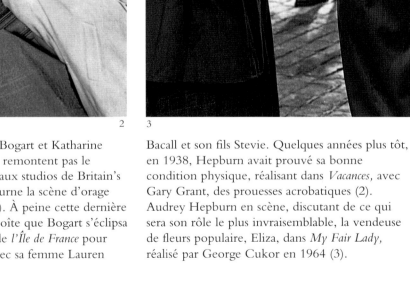

2

3

bewies Hepburn ihre akrobatischen Talente in *Holiday* mit Cary Grant, hier bei der Probe (2). Audrey Hepburn bei Aufnahmen im Jahre 1964 (3). Sie diskutiert mit Regisseur George Cukor ihre Rolle als Cockney-Blumen-mädchen Eliza in *My Fair Lady*, unter allen Figuren, die sie verkörperte, diejenige, die man sich am wenigsten bei ihr vorstellen konnte.

H UMPHREY Bogart et Katharine Hepburn ne remontent pas le Zambèze, ils sont aux studios de Britain's Isleworth où se tourne la scène d'orage d'*African Queen* (1). À peine cette dernière scène fut-elle en boîte que Bogart s'éclipsa et grimpa à bord de l'*Île de France* pour rentrer chez lui avec sa femme Lauren

Bacall et son fils Stevie. Quelques années plus tôt, en 1938, Hepburn avait prouvé sa bonne condition physique, réalisant dans *Vacances,* avec Gary Grant, des prouesses acrobatiques (2). Audrey Hepburn en scène, discutant de ce qui sera son rôle le plus invraisemblable, la vendeuse de fleurs populaire, Eliza, dans *My Fair Lady,* réalisé par George Cukor en 1964 (3).

Screen lovers: Ingrid Bergman and Paul Henreid in a scene from *Casablanca*, the 1942 masterpiece that was slated to have Ronald Reagan and Ann Sheridan in the leads (1). *Gone with the Wind* swept Clark Gable and Vivien Leigh (who was cast only *after* the burning of Atlanta scene) into a desperate love story that also caught the mood of the times (1939). Rhett Butler's infamous 'Frankly, my dear, I don't give a damn' became the statutory rat's farewell, against the epic backdrop of the Civil War (2). Claude Rains, known for bouffant hair-styles and boxes to add height to his love scenes, here plays to Bette Davis in *Deception* (3). James Mason and Margaret Lockwood donned stagecoach costume for *The Wicked Lady* (4) and Richard Burton breeches and doublet for his *Hamlet* to Claire Bloom's balletic Ophelia (5). Gloria Swanson and William Holden (6) have a lovers' tiff in Billy Wilder's *Sunset Boulevard* (1950).

PAARE auf der Leinwand: Ingrid Bergman und Paul Henreid in einer Szene aus *Casablanca*, dem Meisterwerk von 1942, für dessen Hauptrollen ursprünglich Ronald Reagan und Ann Sheridan vorgesehen waren (1). *Vom Winde verweht* warf Clark Gable und Vivien Leigh (die erst für die Rolle ausgesucht wurde, als der Brand Atlantas schon gedreht war) in eine verzweifelte Liebesgeschichte, die ganz der Stimmung der Zeit entsprach (1939). Rhett Butlers berüchtigtes »Offen gesagt ist mir das gleichgültig« vor dem epischen Hintergrund des Bürgerkriegs wurde zum Standard-Abschiedsgruß des Leinwandschurken (2). Claude Rains, der mit fülligem Haar und manchmal auch mit einer Kiste seinen Liebesszenen Größe verlieh, hier zusammen mit Bette Davis in *Deception* (3). James Mason und Margaret Lockwood warfen sich für *The Wicked Lady* in Kostüme der Postkutschenzeit (4), Richard Burton für *Hamlet* in Wams und Kniehose zu Claire Blooms Ophelia, die eher wie eine Balletteuse wirkt (5). Bei Gloria Swanson und William Holden geht es in Billy Wilders *Sunset Boulevard* (1950) hoch her (6).

LES amants du cinéma : Ingrid Bergmann et Paul Henreid dans une scène de *Casablanca*, le chef-d'oeuvre de 1942 qui faillit compter Ronald Reagan et Ann Sheridan dans les rôles principaux (1). *Autant en emporte le vent* entraîne Clark Gable et Vivian Leigh (qui ne joua le rôle qu'après la scène de l'incendie d'Atlanta) dans une histoire d'amour désespérée qui reflétait aussi l'esprit du temps (1939). Le mot infâme de Rhett Butler : « Franchement, mon petit, je m'en fiche comme d'une guigne » devint l'adieu notoire du traître, sur la toile de fond épique de la guerre civile (2). Claude Rains, connu pour ses coiffures bouffantes et ses gifles censées donner de l'épaisseur à ses scènes amoureuses, joue ici à côté de Bette Davis dans *Déception* (3). James Mason et Margaret Lockwood, en costumes de diligence pour tourner *The Wicked Lady* (4) ; Richard Burton en chausses et pourpoint dans *Hamlet,* avec Claire Bloom en Ophélie dansante (5). Gloria Swanson et William Holden (6) ont une petite querelle amoureuse dans *Boulevard du crépuscule* (1950).

6

THUNDER and lightning on set to accompany Maurice Chevalier's 20th Century Fox hit *Folies Bergère* in 1935 (1). Since Chevalier was made to take second billing to actress Grace Moore, he did not return to Hollywood until 1956. Similar musical style is adopted by a dancing James Cagney in Warner Bros' *Yankee Doodle Dandy* (3). Paul Whiteman as *The King of Jazz* and his orchestra making music on a grand scale (2), seated at a piano built for ten hands (1930).

EIN Bühnengewitter für Maurice Chevaliers *Folies Bergères*, 1935 ein großer Erfolg der 20th Century Fox (1). Chevalier verließ Hollywood aus Empörung darüber, daß sein Name erst an zweiter Stelle nach Partnerin Grace Moore genannt wurde, und kehrte erst 1956 zurück. Ähnliche Musical-Elemente verwendete *Yankee Doodle Dandy* der Warner Bros., das einen tanzenden James Cagney zu bieten hatte (3). Paul Whiteman macht mit seinem Orchester in *The King of Jazz* Musik im großen Stil (2), an einem Klavier für zehn Hände (1930).

TONNERRE et lumières accompagnent le succès de la 20th Century Fox : *Folies Bergère* (1935) avec Maurice Chevalier (1).

Comme Chevalier devait passer au programme à la suite de l'actrice Grace Moore, il ne remit plus les pieds à Hollywood avant 1956. James Cagney a adopté un style similaire pour danser dans *Yankee Doodle Dandy* (3) de Warner Bros. Paul Whiteman, *Le Roi du jazz* et son orchestre font de la musique à grande échelle (2), assis devant un piano construit pour dix mains (1930).

ORSON Welles as Harry Lime in Carol Reed's adaptation of Graham Greene's story *The Third Man*. Made in 1949, it was one of the few films to tackle directly the sensitive theme of war racketeering by Allied Forces and the growing rift between east and west Europeans in the divided city of Vienna. Its most famous scenes were set at the top of the Ferris wheel in the Prater Gardens and inside the city's underground sewers.

ORSON Welles als Harry Lime in *Der dritte Mann*. Carol Reeds 1949 entstandener Film nach einer Vorlage von Graham Greene war einer der wenigen, die sich wirklich mit dem heiklen Thema des Schwarzhandels der Alliierten in der geteilten Stadt Wien und mit der immer größer werdenden Kluft zwischen Ost- und Westeuropa auseinandersetzten. Die berühmtesten Szenen spielten auf dem Riesenrad im Prater und in den Abwasserkanälen der Stadt.

ORSON Welles interprétant Harry Lime dans l'adaptation cinématographique par Carol Leed du livre de Graham Greene, *Le Troisième Homme*. Réalisé en 1949, ce fut un des rares films à attaquer de front le sujet délicat des activités criminelles des forces alliées durant la guerre, et la fissure croissante entre les Européens de l'Est et de l'Ouest à Vienne, cité en pleine division. Les scènes les plus célèbres ont été prises au sommet de la Grande Roue dans les jardins du Prater et dans les égouts souterrains de la ville.

FRED and his sister Adele Astaire dance on the roof of London's Savoy Hotel in 1923 (1); a diminutive Mickey Rooney and Judy Garland attend the Ice Follies (2); and Bogie, Bacall and son Stevie stroll on Southampton docks in 1951 before going home (3).

FRED Astaire tanzt mit seiner Schwester Adele auf dem Dach des Londoner Savoy-Hotels, 1923 (1); der kleine Mickey Rooney besucht mit Judy Garland eine Eisrevue (2); und Bogie, Bacall und Sohn Stevie machen 1951 einen Spaziergang in den Docks von Southampton, bevor sie das Schiff zur Heimfahrt besteigen (3).

FRED Astaire et sa soeur, Adele, dansent sur le toit de l'hôtel Savoy à Londres en 1923 (1) ; Mickey Rooney, minuscule, et Judy Garland assistent aux Ice Follies (2) ; Bogie, Bacall et leur fils Stevie flânent sur les quais de Southampton en 1951 avant de rentrer chez eux (3).

PAUL Newman gets behind the camera to check a shot (1). The 20-month-old Natasha Richardson shoves her camera in for a close-up of newborn sister Joely (2), held by their famous actress mother, 27-year-old Vanessa Redgrave (1965). Peter Sellers takes the director's chair from his Swedish wife Britt Ekland during filming of Vittorio de Sica's *Caccia alla Volpe* at Sant'Angelo d'Ischia (3).

PAUL Newman begibt sich hinter die Kamera, um eine Einstellung zu prüfen (1). Die zwanzigmonatige Natasha Richardson macht eine Nahaufnahme von ihrer erst ein paar Tage alten Schwester Joely im Arm ihrer Mutter, der damals 27jährigen Vanessa Redgrave (1965, 2). Peter Sellers läßt sich im Stuhl seiner Ehefrau Britt Ekland nieder, in Sant'Angelo d'Ischia während der Dreharbeiten zu Vittorio de Sicas *Jagt den Fuchs* (3).

PAUL Newman surveille la prise de vue derrière la caméra (1). Natacha Richardson, âgée de vingt mois, pousse son appareil-photo pour faire un gros plan de sa soeur Joely, laquelle vient de naître (2). Leur mère, la célèbre actrice Vanessa Redgrave, 27 ans, lui vient en aide (1965). Peter Sellers emprunte le fauteuil de régie de son épouse suédoise Britt Ekland sur le tournage du film de Vittorio de Sica *La Chasse au renard* à Sant'Angelo d'Ischia (3).

SCHOOLCHILDREN in 1937, queuing to see a matinée performance of *Flash Gordon* in East London. Saturday cinema rapidly gained popularity as a whole new experience, a definite improvement on merely reading about comic strip heroes, and the ultimate in safe and relatively cheap babysitting for harassed working parents. Here the cinema manager polices an orderly queue of unaccompanied children, many wearing their school caps and all clutching their penny-ha'penny (less than 1p) admission money (1). For this they would get two full-length feature films and a newsreel that would only change every few months, and often functioned more as a piece of geographical reportage and political propaganda than as up-to-the-minute news. Still, to judge from both the extent of the preparation (the usher going down the checklist in front of the mirror, for one – 2) and the results (the children shrinking from the action in delighted horror – 3), everyone emerged well satisfied.

SCHULKINDER stehen im Londoner East End an, um eine Matinee-vorstellung von *Flash Gordon* zu sehen. Der samstägliche Besuch im Kino erfreute sich großer Beliebtheit und war ein ganz neuartiges Erlebnis, viel besser, als wenn man über die Comic-Helden nur lesen konnte — und für überbeanspruchte Eltern das Ideal eines sicheren und vergleichsweise billigen Kinderhorts. Hier sorgt der Leiter des Kinos dafür, daß sie ordentlich antreten, viele in Schulkappen und alle mit den anderthalb Pence (weniger als ein heutiger Penny) Eintrittsgeld in der Hand (1). Dafür bekamen sie zwei ganze Filme und eine Wochenschau zu sehen, die oft nur alle paar Monate wechselte und daher wenig Neues, dafür aber geographisches Lehrmaterial und politische Propaganda brachte. Doch wohlvorbereitet, wie alles war (zum Beispiel hatte der Platzanweiser einen Spiegel mit Checkliste, damit er immer adrett aussah, 2), und auch nach dem Blick in den Saal zu urteilen (Kinder, die freudiges Entsetzen angesichts der Geschehnisse auf der Leinwand mimen, 3), waren alle zufrieden.

DES écoliers font la queue en 1937 dans l'Est de Londres pour voir la projection de *Flash Gordon* en matinée. Le cinéma du samedi gagne rapidement en popularité : c'est une expérience nouvelle, une amélioration par rapport à la simple lecture des bandes dessinées, et fin du fin pour des parents harassés par le travail et voulant faire garder leurs enfants sans danger et à bon marché. Ici, le directeur du cinéma fait se ranger les enfants non accompagnés en une belle file. Beaucoup portent leurs casquettes d'écolier et tous tiennent bien serré leur *penny-ha'penny* (moins qu'un penny), prix d'entrée de la séance (1). Pour ce prix, ils assisteront à deux films long métrage et à des actualités qui restent plusieurs mois à l'affiche. Ce sont plus souvent des reportages géographiques et de la propagande politique que des nouveautés. En tout cas, à en juger par l'étendue des préparatifs (le placeur étudie les différents points de la liste de contrôle dans le miroir, 2) et les résultats (les enfants blottis dans leurs fauteuils sont en proie à une terreur délicieuse, 3), chacun sort fort satisfait.

3

HOLLYWOOD became synonymous with cinema in the 1930s and 40s. Many exiles from Nazi Europe joined the westward drift to contribute to the rapid expansion of the silver screen. The Californian climate also gave rise to a fresh dimension of the American Dream. If everyone was to own a smart car, then cinemas themselves would have to accommodate this. In the 1950s, a time of gas-guzzling Chevrolets, Oldsmobiles and Thunderbirds, roadsters with white tyres, wide wings and chromium teeth – the 'drive-in' was born (1). Your car was an additional fashion accessory, an extra-flashy outfit; bus-boys came and served the regulation hot dog and soda on a tray hooked into the window; the giant screen afforded but part of the entertainment, which also involved going as far as you could with your girl, or stopping the next driver from necking with his. That said, in this instance one driver is a woman, a far more common sight than in Europe at the time (2).

IN den 30er und 40er Jahren wurde Hollywood zum Synonym für Kino. Viele Flüchtlinge aus Nazideutschland ließen sich weiter nach Westen treiben und trugen ihren Teil zum kometenhaften Aufstieg der Filmstadt bei. Das kalifornische Klima gab auch dem Amerikanischen Traum eine ganz neue Dimension. Wenn nun jeder mit einem schicken Wagen kam, dann mußte auch das Kino entsprechend dafür eingerichtet sein. In den 50er Jahren, in der Zeit der Chevrolets, Oldsmobiles und Thunderbirds — der Straßenkreuzer mit ihren Weißwandreifen, Heckflossen und gewaltigen Chromkühlern —, entstand das »Drive-in« (1). Der eigene Wagen wurde zu einem Teil der Mode, er war ein eleganter Anzug; Servierer hängten ein Tablett am Fenster ein und brachten den unvermeidlichen Hot Dog mit Sodawasser; die gewaltige Leinwand war dabei nur ein Teil der Attraktion, denn es ging ja auch darum, bei seinem Mädchen so weit zu kommen wie nur möglich oder wenigstens den Nachbarn daran zu hindern, mit seinem zu knutschen. Immerhin haben wir hier einmal eine Frau am Steuer (2), in Amerika damals schon weit häufiger zu sehen als in Europa.

C'EST au cours des années 30 et 40 que le mot Hollywood devint synonyme de cinéma. De nombreux exilés, fuyant le nazisme en Europe, arrivèrent et contribuèrent à la rapide expansion du septième art. En outre, le climat californien fit beaucoup pour conférer une dimension nouvelle au rêve américain. Tandis que tout un chacun désirait posséder une voiture chic, les cinémas eux-mêmes devaient s'en accommoder. Ce sont les années 50, à l'époque des Chevrolet, Oldsmobile, Thunderbird et autres gouffres à essence — les routières à pneus blancs, larges ailes et dents de chrome —, qui ont vu naître le drive-in. La voiture, devenue un accessoire à la mode, était d'un tape-à-l'oeil extrême ; les garçons de bus venaient et servaient les hot dogs et cocas de rigueur sur un plateau accroché à la fenêtre ; l'écran géant, qui ne représentait qu'une partie du divertissement, invitait à aller aussi loin que possible avec sa petite amie ou empêchait le conducteur d'à côté d'embrasser la sienne. Cela dit, scène bien plus répandue qu'en Europe, ici c'est une femme qui tient le volant (2).

The Changing Role of Women

SINCE at least Roman times there has been debate over whether women who 'sell themselves' into arranged matches with wealthy men are in essence doing anything very different from the women who offer a more short-term sexual union in return for money. The 'season' of débutante parties (such as this 1950s Red Cross ball, 1) and social events which still takes place in Britain and to a lesser extent elsewhere is a vestige of the arranged marriage system.

Throughout history women were bartered much as other forms of investment or currency. The brokers were usually men, a father if the 'marriage market' were being played; a pimp if the girl were being sold on the streets. It was only when women themselves could become the agents of change that their situation altered.

The long campaign to obtain the vote for women aimed to help them to step from the domestic to the political arena. Women had been grudgingly accorded token recognition within various education systems, so long as their betterment should not lead them beyond the home to outside spheres of influence. It was further determined that women's voting be tied to property rights – a way of reducing both the gender and the class component of the franchise, since women were considerably less likely to be house-owners. Switzerland was the last 'developed' country to grant women the vote – only in 1971.

Worldwide, even in the 1990s, women compose half of the world's population; perform two-thirds of its work; earn 10 per cent of its income and own 1 per cent of its wealth. Even recent campaigns such as that for 'equal work for equal pay', which resulted in the 1976 Equal Pay and Sex Discrimination Acts in Britain, still leave a majority of women worse off than their male counterparts. And if it is hard to achieve even the implementation of existing legislation based on broad consensus, it is far harder to guarantee equal rights in more controversial areas to do with female sexuality and fertility; childcare and education; sexual harassment and exploitation.

1

MINDESTENS seit den Zeiten der alten Römer wird darüber debattiert, ob Frauen, die sich für eine ausgehandelte Ehe mit einem reichen Mann »verkaufen«, nicht im Grunde das Gleiche tun wie Frauen, die in zeitlich begrenzterem Rahmen ihren Körper für Geld feilbieten. Die »Saison« der Debütantinnenbälle und anderer sozialer Ereignisse (hier ein Rotkreuzball in den 50er Jahren, 1), die es auch heute noch in Großbritannien und in geringerem Maße in anderen Ländern gibt, ist ein Überbleibsel der Zeit, als Ehen ausgehandelt wurden.

In vergangenen Zeiten wurden Frauen wie Investitionsgüter oder Geld gehandelt. Die Händler waren meist Männer — der Vater, wenn es um den »Ehemarkt« ging, ein Zuhälter, wenn es ein Straßenmädchen war. Erst als Frauen die Macht bekamen, selbst etwas dagegen zu unternehmen, änderten sich die Verhältnisse.

Das Wahlrecht, um das die Frauen so lange kämpften, sollte das Mittel sein, von der häuslichen in die politische Arena zu gelangen. Nur widerwillig war den Frauen Zugang zu gewissen Bildungseinrichtungen gewährt worden, und auch das nur pro forma und nicht mit dem Ziel, daß sie mit ihrer Universitätsbildung hinaus in die Öffentlichkeit gingen und Einfluß nahmen. Außerdem war das Frauenwahlrecht noch lange an Grundbesitz geknüpft, wodurch Frauen sexuell wie sozial diskriminiert wurden, denn sie waren weitaus seltener Hausbesitzer. Die Schweiz war die letzte unter den Industrienationen, die Frauen das Wahlrecht gewährte — erst 1971.

Selbst heute stellen Frauen zwar die Hälfte der Weltbevölkerung und leisten zwei Drittel aller Arbeit, doch verdienen sie nur zehn Prozent des Gesamteinkommens und besitzen nur ein Prozent aller Vermögen. Auch nach den Kampagnen unserer Tage wie etwa den Aktionen unter dem Motto »gleicher Lohn für gleiche Arbeit«, die 1976 in Großbritannien zu Antidiskriminierungsgesetzen führten, steht ein Großteil der Frauen schlechter da als vergleichbare Männer. Und wenn es schon schwer ist, bestehende Gesetze durchzusetzen, die von einer breiten Mehrheit befürwortet werden, dann ist es noch weitaus schwieriger, Gleichberechtigung in strittigeren Bereichen zu erlangen, in Fragen der weiblichen Sexualität, der Kindererziehung und der sexuellen Belästigung und Ausbeutung.

LE débat date au moins de la Rome antique : les femmes des unions arrangées avec des hommes riches font-elles vraiment autre chose que monnayer leurs corps ? Le « bal des débutantes » (ici, par exemple en 1950, le bal de la Croix-Rouge, 1) et d'autres événements de la vie sociale qui ont toujours existé en Grande-Bretagne et à un degré moindre ailleurs, sont un vestige du système des mariages arrangés.

Tout au long de l'Histoire, les femmes ont été échangées plus que toute autre forme d'investissement ou de monnaie. Les courtiers étaient habituellement des hommes, un père si on jouait au « marché du mariage » ; un souteneur, si la fille devait être vendue dans les rues. La situation des femmes ne changea que lorsqu'elles purent devenir elles-mêmes agents de change.

La longue campagne en vue d'obtenir le droit de vote pour les femmes visait à les aider à sortir de l'arène domestique pour entrer dans l'arène politique. On avait accordé aux femmes, de mauvaise grâce, une reconnaissance symbolique par des systèmes variés d'éducation, aussi longtemps que leurs progrès ne les amenaient pas à sortir de leur foyer pour entrer dans les sphères extérieures d'influence. De plus, on avait décidé que le vote des femmes serait lié aux droits à la propriété – une façon de réduire à la fois le nombre de participants féminins aux élections et de manipuler la composition sociale, puisque les femmes étaient probablement assez rarement propriétaires de leur maison. La Suisse a été le dernier pays « développé » à reconnaître le droit de vote aux femmes – ce fut seulement en 1971.

À l'échelle planétaire, même dans les années 90, les femmes composent près de la moitié de la population mondiale ; elles exécutent les deux tiers du travail ; gagnent 10 % des revenus et possèdent 1 % des richesses. Même si des campagnes récentes, dans le genre « à travail égal, salaire égal », qui résultent des lois de 1976 sur l'égalité du salaire et la discrimination sexuelle, la plupart des femmes restent, aujourd'hui encore, moins bien payées que leurs homologues masculins. Et s'il est déjà difficile de seulement imposer l'application de la législation existante basée sur un consensus général, il s'avère plus compliqué encore de garantir l'égalité des droits dans des domaines plus controversés traitant de la sexualité de la femme et de sa fertilité ; des crèches et de l'instruction ; du harcèlement sexuel et de l'exploitation.

2

THESE Barcelona 'ladies of the night' bargain with a prospective client under posters advertising a comedy called *If Eve were a Flirt* (1). Although firmly prohibited from street-soliciting by Franco's draconian laws, in 1951 these women were so hungry that their fee was a loaf of bread. In 1940s Hamburg there was already a street licensed for prostitution. Each girl has her own room and washroom – and her own windowsill from which to dangle her legs (2).

SCHÖNHEITEN der Nacht« in Barcelona verhandeln mit einem interessierten Kunden unter Plakaten für eine Filmkomödie namens *Wenn Eva flirtet* (1). Zwar war die Straßenprostitution unter den drakonischen Gesetzen Francos streng verboten, doch diese Frauen im Jahre 1951 waren so hungrig, daß sie es für einen Laib Brot taten. In Hamburg gab es schon in den 40er Jahren eine Straße mit legaler Prostitution. Jedes Mädchen hatte sein eigenes Zimmer mit Waschgelegenheit — und ein eigenes Fensterbrett, von dem sie die Beine baumeln lassen konnte (2).

CES « reines de la nuit » barcelonaises négocient avec un client potentiel sous des affiches présentant une comédie intitulée *Si Ève était coquette* (1). Malgré la ferme interdiction du racolage, promulguée en 1951 par Franco, ces femmes avaient si faim qu'elles se vendaient pour une miche de pain.

En 1940, à Hambourg, il existait déjà une rue où l'on permettait la prostitution. Chaque fille disposait de sa chambre, de sa salle de bains et de son rebord de fenêtre, comme celui sur lequel cette femme est assise, les jambes pendantes (2).

1   2

3

BROTHEL keeper Cyn Payne, Madam
Cyn (1), clearly showed initiative on
more than the choice of her name. In the
1980s she claimed to have been visited by
many eminent Tory Party members. In
wartime Berlin, club hostesses also offered
to discipline Nazi officers (2), while

humbler punters took to the streets where
the women posed at their windows (3).
Baghdad has a 'shopping street' for the
trade in women's bodies (5), while in
1930s Calcutta (4) and Cairo (6) women
are transported and caged like animals in
order to force them into prostitution.

DIE Bordellbesitzerin Cyn Payne,
genannt Madam Cyn (1), behauptete
in den 80er Jahren, ihr Etablissement sei
von zahlreichen Mitgliedern der
Konservativen Partei frequentiert worden.
In den Berliner Clubs schwangen zu
Kriegszeiten Animiermädchen für
Nazioffiziere auch die Peitsche (2),

4

5

6

während der einfache Mann durch die Straßen zog, wo Frauen sich an den Fenstern feilboten (3). Bagdad hat eine »Ladenstraße« für Frauenhaut (5); in den 30er Jahren hingegen wurden Frauen in Kalkutta (4) und Kairo (6) in Käfigen gehalten wie Tiere und zur Prostitution gezwungen.

LA tenancière de maison close Cyn Payne, Madame Cyn (1), a fait preuve d'une initiative manifeste. En 1980, elle a affirmé avoir reçu la visite de membres éminents du parti conservateur. À Berlin, pendant la guerre, des hôtesses de club offraient aussi de « punir » les officiers nazis

(2), pendant que les clients plus humbles allaient dans les rues où les femmes posaient (3). Bagdad a une rue marchande réservée au commerce du corps féminin (5), pendant qu'à Calcutta (4) et au Caire (6) les femmes étaient parfois transportées dans des cages et obligées à se prostituer.

2

STRIPPERS are professional (1) as well as amateur (2). The task to fathom during training is how to handle a mink stole, a silk stocking, or a gilt chair while keeping the audience's attention and the sticking-plasters in place.

STRIPTEASE, professionell (1) oder als Amateur (2). Es kam alles darauf an zu wissen, wie man mit einer Nerzstola, einem Seidenstrumpf und einem vergoldeten Stuhl umging, ohne die Aufmerksamkeit des Publikums oder die Pflästerchen zu verlieren.

LE strip-tease est l'affaire des professionnelles (1) et des amatrices (2). Pendant l'entraînement on apprend à manipuler une étole en vison, un bas de soie ou une chaise dorée, tout en s'efforçant de garder l'attention du public et les sparadraps à leur place.

1

THE difference is in the address... and therefore the price. The Monte Carlo Follies of 1935 at Grosvenor House offer a fine if fluffy display in apparent emulation of the frill on a lamb cutlet (1). In 1973 Soho, bookshops, strip joints and parts of Berwick Street market were given over entirely to the sex industry (2): quite a displacement for an area that once boasted illustrious (and sometimes scurrilous) residents like the Duke of Monmouth, Mozart, the author Hazlitt, and the King of Corsica.

DIE Adresse macht den Unterschied... und bestimmt den Preis. Die Monte Carlo Follies, 1935 im Grosvenor House aufgenommen, scheinen mit diesem gefiederten Auftritt die Form der Banderolen nachzuahmen, die man an Lammkoteletts findet (1). Eine Aufnahme aus Soho zeigt, daß

Buchläden, Lokale und Teile des Markts in der Berwick Street 1973 ganz zum Geschäft mit dem Sex übergegangen waren (2): ein tiefer Fall für ein Viertel, in dem einst so illustre (oder auch dubiose) Gestalten wie der Herzog von Monmouth, Mozart, der Schriftsteller Hazlitt und der König von Korsika wohnten.

LA différence est dans l'adresse, et surtout dans le prix. Les Monte Carlo Follies de 1935, à Grosvenor House, offraient un spectacle duveteux (1). En 1973 à Soho, les librairies, les tripots et des tronçons de la Berwick Street se

consacrèrent entièrement à l'industrie du sexe (2) : une drôle d'évolution pour un endroit qui avait vu défiler des habitants illustres (et quelquefois bizarres) comme le Duc de Monmouth, Mozart, l'écrivain Hazlitt et le roi de Corse.

APPARENTLY the first British Women's Institute opened in a summerhouse on Anglesey Island. By the 1950s it had a membership of over half a million, and a considerable lobbying voice in all sectors of government, standing particularly firm on matters relating to the family and Christianity. Their domestic concerns were often summarized as 'jam and Jerusalem', which refers to their fund-raising through home-produced goods and the hymn (with words by the eighteenth-century poet William Blake) they always sing at the end of their national rally. Here members from Eastgate participate in some lively outdoor country dancing at Weardale, County Durham.

DER erste britische Frauenverein wurde offenbar in einem Sommerhaus auf der Insel Anglesey gegründet. In den 50er Jahren hatte der Verein bereits über eine halbe Million Mitglieder und konnte beträchtlichen Druck auf alle Bereiche der Regierung ausüben; besonders vehement setzten die Frauen sich für alles ein, was mit Familie und mit Christentum zu tun hatte. Sie bekamen den Spitznamen »Marmelade und Jerusalem«, weil sie sich das Geld für ihre Unternehmungen meist mit selbstge-machten Lebensmitteln verschafften und am Ende ihrer Landestreffen immer das Kirchenlied »Jerusalem« (nach einem Text des Dichters William Blake) sangen. Hier sieht man Mitglieder aus Eastgate bei einem fröhlichen Tanz auf dem Lande, in Weardale, Grafschaft Durham.

LE premier Institut pour les femmes de Grande-Bretagne s'ouvrit apparemment dans une résidence d'été des îles d'Anglesey. Durant les années 50, il comptait plus de 500 000 membres, et son influence en tant que groupe de pression était importante dans tous les domaines du gouvernement, particulièrement quant aux sujets relevant de la famille et du christianisme. Les affaires domestiques des femmes étaient souvent résumées sous la devise « Confiture et Jérusalem », parce qu'elles collectaient des fonds par la vente d'aliments fabriqués à la maison et entonnaient immanquablement un hymne (avec un texte du poète du XVIIIe siècle William Blake) à la clôture de leur rassemblement national. Ici, à Weardale, comté de Durham, quelques membres d'Eastgate participent à un charmant bal de campagne en plein air.

A parallel British organization stemming from Edwardian times was the Mothers' Union, meeting here in a church hall in their hats and wire-rimmed spectacles (1). In the 1940s, too, Russian women decorated for service in the Second World War march through Red Square on a Victory Day Parade (3). And in Bradford, Yorkshire, Spinsters' Club members go public in their campaign for a national pension (2).

EINE ähnliche britische Organisation, die vom Anfang des Jahrhunderts stammte, war die Mothers' Union (Mütterverein), die sich hier in einem Kirchensaal trifft, alle mit Hüten und den typischen Nickelbrillen der Zeit (1). Diese russischen Frauen (3), ebenfalls in den 40er Jahren, sind als Kriegsheldinnen ausgezeichnet worden und nehmen an einer Parade auf dem Roten Platz zum Jahrestag des Kriegsendes teil. In Bradford, Yorkshire, demonstrieren Frauen des Spinsters' Club (Verein unverheirateter Frauen) für eine staatliche Rente (2).

L'UNION des mères était une organisation britannique remontant à Édouard VII. On les voit ici dans une église, coiffées de leurs chapeaux et arborant des lunettes cerclées de fer (1). Au cours des années 40, également, des femmes russes décorées pour leurs bons et loyaux services durant la Seconde Guerre mondiale traversent la Place rouge pour célébrer le jour de la Victoire (3). À Bradford, dans le Yorkshire, les membres du Spinsters'Club manifestent pour la retraite nationale (2).

2

3

WOMEN have had a long and dynamic connection with pacifism. In 1923 a Women's Rally of the Workers' Union deplored the millions of sons and husbands lost in the Great War and opposed rearmament (1). In 1936 thousands of women donned hideous paper gas-masks for the Assembly for Peace in Trafalgar Square (2).

FRAUEN spielen schon lange eine wichtige Rolle für den Pazifismus. 1923 gedachten die Frauen der Arbeitergewerkschaft der Millionen von Söhnen und Männern, die im Ersten Weltkrieg umgekommen waren, und protestierten gegen die Wiederaufrüstung (1). 1936 setzten Tausende von Frauen bei einer Friedensdemonstration am Trafalgar Square häßliche Papier-Gasmasken auf (2).

LES femmes ont eu une relation longue et dynamique avec le pacifisme. En 1923 un rassemblement féminin de l'Union des travailleurs déplorait les millions de fils et de maris disparus pendant la Grande Guerre et s'opposait au réarmement (1). En 1936, des milliers de femmes portent d'horribles masques à gaz en papier pendant l'Assemblée pour la paix à Trafalguar Square (2).

SUPPORTERS of the anti-nuclear Com-
mittee of a Hundred are carted away
from Parliament Square (2). These marchers
declare their intention of withholding
income tax designated for nuclear arms (1).
Jean Shrimpton spends a hungry Christmas
protesting at British complicity in the 1967–
70 Biafra conflict (3).

ATOMKRAFTGEGNERINNEN werden
vom Londoner Parliament Square
getragen (2). Die Demonstrantinnen wollen
ihre Einkommensteuer zurückbehalten, weil
sie für nukleare Aufrüstung verwendet
werden soll (1). Jean Shrimpton in
weihnachtlichem Hungerstreik aus Protest
gegen die britische Haltung im Biafrakrieg
(1967–70) (3).

DES manifestants du Comité
antinucléaire des Cent sont emportés
hors du Parliament Square (2). Ceux-ci
refusent l'impôt sur le revenu devant financer
les armes nucléaires (1). Jean Shrimpton passe
un Noël en faisant la grève de la faim pour
protester contre la complicité britannique
dans la guerre du Biafra en 1967-1970 (3).

A woman, in the 1950s, wears a mask under the watchful and sceptical eyes of a copper and a city gent, flagging a meeting for equal pay to be addressed at London's largest rallying hall by MP Edith Summerskill and Labour premier Clement Attlee (1). By 1971, women are still making the same demand. Tired of waiting, they hand in a petition to Prime Minister Edward Heath at No. 10 Downing Street, calling for equal educational and job opportunities; equal pay now; free contraception and abortion on request; and free 24-hour child care centres (2).

EINE Frau, in den 50er Jahren, hat sich eine Maske umgebunden und ruft zu einer Versammlung für Lohngerechtigkeit auf. In London werden die Parlaments-abgeordnete Edith Summerskill und der Labour-Premierminister Clement Attlee sprechen (1). 1971 sind die Forderungen noch dieselben. Diese Frauen haben das Warten satt und sind zur Downing Street No. 10 gezogen, wo sie dem Premier-minister Edward Heath eine Petition überreichen, in der sie Gleichstellung bei Ausbildungs- und Arbeitschancen fordern, sofortige Angleichung der Löhne, das Recht auf Abtreibung sowie Verhütungsmittel und Ganztags-Kinderhorte auf Staatskosten (2).

AU cours des années 50, une femme masquée porte une pancarte sous les yeux attentifs et sceptiques d'un policier et d'un citadin. Elle indique le rassemblement organisé par MP Edith Summershill et le Premier ministre travailliste Clement Attlee, qui demande l'égalité des salaires et qui se déroule dans la plus grande salle de Londres (1). En 1971, les femmes demanderont toujours la même chose. Fatiguées d'attendre, elles présentent une pétition au Premier ministre Edward Heath au n° 10, Downing Street, demandant l'égalité en termes d'éducation et de droit au travail ; le salaire égal maintenant ; la contraception libre et l'avortement sur demande ; et des crèches ouvertes 24 heures sur 24 (2).

2

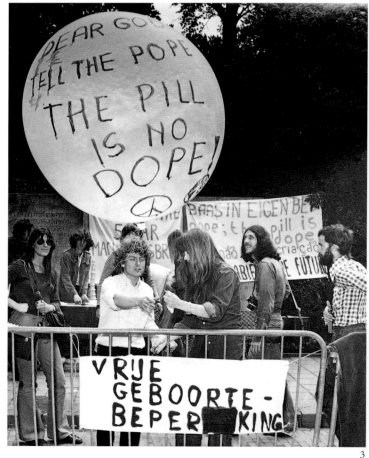

THROUGH the 1970s, women appeared to be on the march across the world. In the United States there emerged a clash between those, led here by Bella Abzug, who regarded a pregnancy as purely a transient condition of the female body (1), and the 'right-to-lifers' who considered abortion as tantamount to infanticide (2). In 1973 Dutch members of 'Dolle Mina' marked the fifth anniversary of the papal encyclical *Humanae Vitae* by releasing a balloon with the message: 'Dear God – tell the Pope the Pill is no Dope!' (3). In Italy, seat of the Vatican and country with the lowest birth rate in the world, women protest at the detention of a gynaecologist who performed abortions on demand (4).

IN den 70er Jahren erhoben Frauen überall auf der Welt ihre Stimmen. In den Vereinigten Staaten kam es zu Auseinandersetzungen zwischen denen, die Schwangerschaft lediglich als einen vorübergehenden Zustand des weiblichen Körpers betrachteten (1), und der »Recht-auf-Leben«-Fraktion, für die eine Abtreibung einem Kindesmord gleichkam. 1973 begingen Mitglieder der holländischen Gruppe »Dolle Mina« den fünften Jahrestag der päpstlichen Enzyklika *Humanae vitae* damit, daß sie einen Ballon mit der Aufschrift in den Himmel steigen ließen: »Lieber Gott — sag dem Papst, daß die Pille kein Haschisch ist!« (3). In Italien, dem Sitz des Vatikans und dem Land mit der weltweit geringsten Geburtenrate, protestieren Frauen gegen die Verhaftung eines Gynäkologen, der auf Bitten von Patientinnen Abtreibungen vorgenommen hatte (4).

AU cours des années 70, la cause des femmes semble faire bouger le monde entier. Aux États-Unis, on voit apparaître des divergences entre Bella Abzug et ses disciples. Les unes estiment que la grossesse n'est qu'un état passager du corps féminin (1) tandis que les autres, « Droit à la vie », assimilent l'avortement à l'infanticide (2). En 1973, les membres néerlandais de la « Dolle Mina » marquent le cinquième anniversaire de l'encyclique papale *Humanae Vitae*, lâchant à cette occasion un ballon porteur d'un message à Dieu. Il postule ceci : « Dis au pape que la pilule n'est pas de la drogue ! » (3). En Italie, siège du Vatican, pays où le taux de natalité est le plus faible, les femmes protestent contre la détention d'un gynécologue qui a procédé à des interruptions de grossesse (4).

4

1

A New York woman police officer in the 1970s demonstrates to a quizzical audience how to disarm an assailant armed with a knife (1). According to the caption: 'Ravishing good looks may lure an assailant, but [she] tackles the problem with cool counterstrategy. There's daggers in her eyes!' Following a succession of rapes and sexual assaults near Stockport, Cheshire, youth leader (and ex-commando) George Ashton started training girls in 'how to say no to a rapist' (2). The classes were particularly popular with girls on local factory night shifts, or indeed anyone who wanted to learn 'how to blind your attacker' or 'how to cripple him by stamping on his feet'.

EINE New Yorker Polizistin der 70er Jahre zeigt einem nachdenklichen Publikum, wie man jemanden entwaffnet, der einen mit dem Messer bedroht (1). Die Bildunterschrift lautete: »Wenn eine Frau so gut aussieht, kann das einen Angreifer schon provozieren, aber sie weiß, wie sie damit fertig wird. Und ihre Augen schießen Pfeile!« Nachdem es in der Gegend von Stockport, Cheshire, mehrfach zu Vergewaltigungen und Fällen von sexueller Belästigung gekommen war,

begann der Jugendführer George Ashton (ehemals Mitglied einer Kommandotruppe) mit Kursen, in denen er den Mädchen beibrachte, »wie man Nein zu einem Vergewaltiger sagt« (2). Die Kurse fanden besonderen Zuspruch bei Mädchen, die auf Nachtschicht in den Fabriken arbeiteten, zogen aber auch andere an, die wissen wollten, »wie man dem Angreifer die Augen aussticht« oder »wie man ihm die Füße zertritt«.

À New York, dans les années 70, une femme agent de police enseigne à un public narquois comment désarmer un attaquant muni d'un couteau (1). La légende précise : « Une belle apparence peut tromper un assaillant, mais [elle] s'attaque au problème avec une contre-stratégie froide. Il y a des poignards dans ses yeux ! » Suite à une série de viols et d'agressions sexuelles près de Stockport, dans le Cheshire, George Ashton, chef

d'un centre de jeunes (et ancien membre de commando) a initié un programme d'entraînement destiné aux filles qui s'appelle « Comment dire non à un violeur » (2). Les cours étaient particulièrement populaires auprès des filles des équipes de nuit des usines locales, de toutes celles qui voulaient apprendre « comment aveugler un attaquant » ou « comment l'estropier en lui marchant sur les pieds ».

Music and Dance

THE musical scene in the twentieth century brought wildly varying styles and extraordinary new techniques. While composers such as Richard Strauss (1864-1949) and Edward Elgar (1857-1934) were happy to develop in the mainstream as the natural successors of Wagner and Brahms, others went out on a limb. Arnold Schoenberg (1874-1951) devised the twelve-tone compositional method, in which 'old-fashioned' concepts of key and chromaticism were thrown out and instead a 'row' of twelve notes arranged in unrelated order was used as a thematic basis. His disciples, Berg and Webern, also used this method, although less rigidly. But it cannot be said that the average music-lover finds it easy to whistle a snatch or two of many of their works, despite the unquestioned merits of such operas as *Wozzeck* and *Lulu*. A later generation headed by the Frenchman Pierre Boulez and the German Karlheinz Stockhausen turned to electronic music, mixing tapes with live performance and using newly invented instruments such as the *ondes martenot*, a type of synthesizer. Their works, too, have met with critical attention rather than widespread popularity.

Stockhausen (1, overleaf) was born in 1928. In 1971 he created a programme of 'Anthems' of concrete sound to last all evening. Divided into four sections, each of which featured the national anthem of a different country, it provided a natural accompaniment of sounds ranging from the breathing of jungle animals to that of the instrumentalists. Asked if the listener could tell the difference and whether it mattered, the composer replied: 'Music is a state of being. It is a means to a new awareness.' Boulez (b. 1925) founded the Paris-based IRCAM institute in 1976 for research into experimental composition techniques. He is an outstanding conductor, of Wagner in particular, somewhat surprisingly.

As ballet branched away from Russia and underwent a revitalization at the hands of Serge Diaghilev (1872-1929), the young Igor Stravinsky was coming to the fore. His three early works (*Firebird*, *Petruchka*, *Rite of Spring*) are among the best ballet scores of this or any century, and indeed are as thrilling in the concert hall as in the theatre. Diaghilev had a supremely catalytic quality, bringing together magnificent artists and composers as well as dancers like Nijinsky, now legends in the history of ballet. The influence of his splendid company percolated to Britain and the USA, and the eventual result was the establishment of the Royal Ballet in London and Balanchine's New York City Ballet. Britain produced another legend in Margot Fonteyn, while the vigorous American style was epitomized by Martha Graham and many others.

A true English opera at last became a reality with the stunning première of Benjamin Britten's *Peter Grimes* in 1945. On the face of it a gloom-laden tragedy, the opera is so gripping, with such marvellous music, that audiences emerge exhilarated and moved rather than downcast. American opera too has become firmly established over the last fifty years, through the setting up of world-class companies and performing centres throughout the United States.

Leonard Bernstein (1) was immensely successful at combining a classical training with a common touch. Born in the United States to immigrant parents in August 1918, he became internationally known as an electrifying conductor, becoming music director of the New York Philharmonic, and for the realism of his own compositions, in tune with popular rhythms and phraseology. Nowhere was this plainer than in his watershed musical *West Side Story*, a 'Romeo and Juliet' in which Montagues and Capulets are replaced by Sharks and Jets, the warring factions of New Yorkers and *newyorquinos*. His symphonies and sacred compositions are in a completely different vein.

DIE Musikszene des 20. Jahrhunderts zeichnet sich durch eine große Vielfalt der Stile und durch außerordentliche neue Techniken aus. Während Komponisten wie Richard Strauss (1864-1949) und Edward Elgar (1857-1934) mit großem Erfolg die Traditionen von Wagner und Brahms fortentwickelten, begannen andere ganz von vorn. Arnold Schönberg (1874-1951) erfand die Zwölftontechnik, in der »veraltete« Vorstellungen von Tonart und Chromatik über Bord geworfen wurden und statt dessen eine »Reihe« von zwölf unverbundenen Tönen die thematische Basis lieferte. Seine Schüler Berg und Webern komponierten ebenfalls nach dieser Methode, handhaben sie jedoch flexibler. Die meisten Musikfreunde fanden es nicht gerade leicht, die Melodien aus diesen Werken nachzupfeifen, auch wenn der Rang von Opern wie *Wozzeck* oder *Lulu* außer Frage steht. Die nächste Generation wandte sich unter Führung des Franzosen Pierre Boulez und des

Deutschen Karlheinz Stockhausen der elektronischen Musik zu, sie brachten Tonbandmusik in ihre Konzertauftritte und arbeiteten mit neuerfundenen Instrumenten wie etwa den *ondes martenot*, einer Art Synthesizer. Auch ihre Arbeiten haben eher bei den Kritikern als beim großen Publikum Anerkennung gefunden.

1971 führte Stockhausen (1), Jahrgang 1928, ein abendfüllendes Programm konkreter Musik mit dem Titel »Hymnen« auf. Im Mittelpunkt jedes der vier Teile stand die Nationalhymne eines Landes, und dazu wurden Geräusche eingespielt, vom Atem eines wilden Tieres bis hin zum Atem der Instrumentalisten. Auf die Frage, ob der Zuschauer denn zwischen beiden unterscheiden könne und ob das von Bedeutung sei, entgegnete der Komponist: »Musik ist ein Seinszustand. Sie ist ein Mittel zur Erweiterung des Bewußtseins.« Der 1925 geborene Boulez gründete 1976 in Paris das IRCAM-Institut zur Erforschung experimenteller Kompositionstechniken. Er ist ein bedeutender Dirigent und hat sich — was man bei seinen sonstigen Vorlieben wohl kaum vermutet hätte — besonders als Wagner-Interpret hervorgetan.

Als das Ballett seine russische Heimat verließ und unter Sergej Diaghilew (1872-1929) eine Verjüngungskur machte, trat der junge Igor Strawinsky auf den Plan. Seine frühen Werke *Der Feuervogel*, *Petruschka* und *Le sacre du printemps* zählen zu den bedeutendsten Ballettwerken dieses Jahrhunderts, wenn nicht aller Zeiten, und sind im Konzertsaal nicht weniger faszinierend als im Theater. Diaghilew war ein genialer Katalysator und brachte die bedeutendsten bildenden Künstler und Komponisten zusammen, dazu natürlich Tänzer wie Nijinsky, die heute Ballettlegende sind. Der Einfluß seiner Truppe reichte bis nach England und in die Vereinigten Staaten und war mitverantwortlich dafür, daß das Royal Ballet in London und Balanchines New York City Ballet gegründet wurden. Eine weitere Tanzlegende, Margot Fonteyn, kam aus Großbritannien, und Inbegriff des energischen amerikanischen Stils war, unter anderen, Martha Graham.

Mit der atemberaubenden Premiere von Benjamin Brittens *Peter Grimes* im Jahre 1945 wurde der Traum von einer echt englischen Oper endlich Wirklichkeit. Auf den ersten Blick ist es eine finstere Tragödie, doch die Oper ist so packend und die Musik so mitreißend, daß das Publikum nicht etwa niedergeschlagen aus dem Saal kommt, sondern gerührt und geläutert. Auch im amerikanischen Kulturleben hat sich die Oper in den letzten fünfzig Jahren einen festen Platz erobert, mit erstklassigen Truppen und Opernhäusern im ganzen Land.

Leonard Bernstein (1, vorige Seite) verstand es, klassische Ausbildung mit einer volkstümlichen Art zu verbinden. Als Einwanderersohn im August 1918 in Amerika geboren, wurde er für seine faszinierende Dirigentenkunst (er wurde Chef der New Yorker Philharmoniker) weltbekannt, ebenso für die Realistik seiner eigenen Kompositionen, in denen er volkstümliche Rhythmen und Gesangsstile verarbeitete. Nirgendwo war das offensichtlicher als in seinem Durchbruchswerk, dem Musical *West Side Story*, einem »Romeo und Julia«, bei dem an die Stelle der Montagues und der Capulets die Sharks und die Jets getreten sind, die verfeindeten Banden der einheimischen New Yorker und der lateinamerikanischen Einwanderer. Bernsteins Symphonien und Sakralwerke sind dagegen vollkommen anders im Ton.

Au cours des années 20, des styles très variés et des techniques nouvelles apparurent dans le monde de la musique. Alors que des compositeurs comme Richard Strauss (1864-1949) et Edward Elgar (1857-1934) étaient heureux d'évoluer dans la tendance générale comme les successeurs naturels de Wagner et Brahms, d'autres sortaient des rangs. Arnold Schoenberg (1874-1951) conçut le système dodécaphonique, qui rejetait les concepts « démodés » de clés et de chromatisme et les remplaçait par une succession de douze sons n'ayant de rapport qu'entre eux. Ses disciples Berg et Webern utilisèrent aussi cette méthode, bien que de manière moins rigide. Mais il est difficile pour le mélomane de siffler facilement un extrait ou deux de nombre de leurs oeuvres, et cela malgré l'incontestable interêt des opéras comme *Wozzeck* et *Lulu*. La génération suivante, menée par le Français Pierre Boulez et l'Allemand Karlheinz Stockhausen, se tourna vers la musique électronique, mélangeant des enregistrements avec des prises en direct et utilisant des instruments nouveaux.

Stockhausen (1) est né en 1928. En 1971, il a créé un programme d' « anthems », de son concret persistant toute une soirée. Divisé en quatre sections, chacun d'eux caractérisant l'anthem national des différents pays, il propose un accompagnement naturel de sons allant de la respiration des animaux de la jungle à celle des musiciens. Quand on lui demanda si l'auditeur pourrait établir la différence, et si cela avait de l'importance, le compositeur répondit : « La musique est un état de l'existence. C'est un moyen d'arriver à un nouvel " éveil " ». Boulez (né en 1925) a fondé l'IRCAM (Institut de recherche et de coordination acoustique musique) à Paris en 1976. Il est en outre un chef d'orchestre remarquable, de Wagner en particulier, ce qui ne laisse de surprendre.

L'heure sonna pour le jeune Igor Stravinsky à l'époque où les ballets évoluèrent loin de la Russie et furent revitalisés par Serge Diaghilev (1872-1929). Les trois premières oeuvres de Stravinski (*L'Oiseau de feu*, *Petrouchka*, *Le Sacre du printemps*) font partie des ballets les plus prestigieux et Diaghilev possédait un talent suprêmement catalytique, réunissant autant d'artistes et de compositeurs magnifiques que de danseurs comme Nijinsky, entré dans la légende de l'histoire des ballets. L'influence de sa troupe superbe se fit sentir en Grande-Bretagne et aux États-Unis, et aboutit finalement à la création du Royal Ballet à Londres et du City Ballet de Ballantine à New York. La Grande-Bretagne donna naissance à une autre légende en la personne de Margot Fonteyn, pendant que le vigoureux style américain était porté aux nues par Martha Graham et d'autres encore.

Enfin, un véritable opéra anglais vit le jour avec la première étonnante de *Peter Grimes,* de Benjamin Britten en 1945. Cet opéra, tragédie lugubre à première vue, est si passionnant, la musique est si belle que le public en sort plus vivifié et ému que mortifié. L'opéra américain, lui aussi, s'est solidement établi au cours des cinquante dernières années.

Leonard Bernstein (1918-1990) connut un succès immense en combinant une formation classique et une touche talentueuse (1, page précédente). Né aux États-Unis, il se fit connaître du monde entier comme un chef d'orchestre galvanisant, qui devint le directeur musical du Philharmonic de New York, et pour le réalisme de ses propres compositions en accord avec les rythmes et la phraséologie populaires. La simplicité est à son comble dans sa comédie musicale progressiste *West Side Story*, un « Roméo et Juliette » dans lequel les Montagu et les Capulet sont remplacés par les Shark et les Jet, les groupes de New-Yorkais en guerre et les *Newyorquinos*.

1

IGOR Stravinsky created a sensation when, aged 28 in 1910, he scored Diaghilev's ballet *The Firebird*. Fellow Russian Leon Bakst designed the costumes and the lead role was danced by Tamara Karsavina. In 1911 there followed the first performance of his ballet *Petruschka* in Paris, the beseechingly romantic puppet danced by Nijinsky, with costumes designed by Alexandre Benois. In 1913 uproar greeted the Théâtre des Champs-Elysées première of *The Rite of Spring*, described by one critic as composed of 'pounding, reiterated rhythms, and savage discords'. The pictures show Stravinsky in later life, conducting at a recording of Bach's *Von Himmel Hoch* and his own *The Rake's Progress* in London in 1964. The cellist Mstislav Rostropovich congratulates him at the end (5).

4

MIT der Musik, die er 1910 im Alter von 28 Jahren für Diaghilews Ballett *Der Feuervogel* schrieb, sorgte Igor Strawinsky für eine Sensation. Sein russischer Landsmann Leon Bakst entwarf die Kostüme, und Primaballerina war Tamara Karsawina. 1911 folgte die Erstaufführung seines Balletts *Petruschka* in Paris, die flehende romantische Puppe von Nijinsky getanzt, mit Kostümen von Alexandre Benois. Als *Le sacre du printemps* 1913 im Théâtre des Champs-Élysées uraufgeführt wurde, gab es Tumulte; ein Kritiker schrieb, das Werk bestehe aus »stampfenden, immergleichen Rhythmen und wilden Mißklängen«. Die Bilder zeigen Strawinsky in späteren Jahren bei Schallplattenaufnahmen von Bachs *Vom Himmel hoch* und seinem eigenen *The Rake's Progress* in London 1964. Am Ende beglückwünscht ihn der Cellist Mstislaw Rostropowitsch (5).

IGOR Stravinsky fit sensation lorsqu'il écrivit en 1910, à l'âge de 28 ans, la musique du ballet de Diaghilev, *L'Oiseau de feu*. Son compatriote Leon Bakst dessina les costumes et le rôle principal était dansé par Tamara Karsavina. En 1911 suivit la première de son ballet *Petrouchka* à Paris : le pantin pathétique est incarné par Nijinsky, et les costumes sont d'Alexandre Benois. En 1913 eut lieu au Théâtre des Champs-Élysées la première tumultueusement saluée du *Sacre du Printemps*. Un critique la décrit comme un ensemble de « rythmes martelés, répétés et de dissonances sauvages ». Les photographies montrent Stravinsky à la fin de sa vie, dirigeant un enregistrement du *Von Himmel Hoch* de Bach et sa composition personnelle *The Rake's Progress* à Londres en 1964. Il est ici félicité par le violoncelliste Mstislav Rostropovitch (5).

2

3

(Overleaf)
IN 1980 the eighty-two-year-old Japanese violinist and tutor Shinichi Suzuki visited Britain to demonstrate his teaching methods. The lack of Suzuki teachers led to this demonstration at the British Suzuki Institute in Hertfordshire by the inventor of the technique himself (1). Back home in Tokyo, 2000 little fiddlers (aged 3-10) from across Japan gathered in 1970 for a mass violin concert attended by their admiring parents (2, 3).

(Page suivante)
EN 1980, le violoniste et professeur particulier japonais Shinichi Suzuki, âgé de 82 ans, se rendit en Grande-Bretagne pour exposer ses méthodes d'enseignement. Les enseignants qui utilisaient cette méthode étant rares, l'inventeur de la technique en

personne fait une démonstration au British Suzuki Institute de Hertfordshire (1). 2 000 petits violonistes âgés de trois à dix ans, venus de toutes les régions du Japon se rassemblèrent en 1970 à Tokyo pour un gigantesque concert de violons auquel assistaient leurs parents admiratifs (2,3).

(folgende Seite)
IM Jahre 1980 kam der zweiund-achtzigjährige japanische Geiger und Geigenlehrer Shinichi Suzuki nach Großbritannien und führte seine Lehrmethoden vor. Es fehlte an Lehrern, und deshalb führt der Erfinder der Suzuki-Methode sie hier im British Suzuki Institute in Hertfordshire selbst vor (1). Zu Hause in Tokio versammelten sich 1970 zweitausend kleine Geigenvirtuosen aus ganz Japan (zwischen drei und zehn Jahren alt) und gaben für die stolzen Eltern ein Großkonzert (2, 3).

5

1

WHILE *Tosca* was the lush apotheosis of nineteenth-century Italian opera, Alban Berg's *Lulu* was among the most daring operatic works of the present century (although it remained incomplete at Berg's death). Both are thematically realistic works, dominated by the tragedy of a powerful but doomed woman. And both are here played by outstanding singers who gave a unique interpretation to their roles: Maria Callas (2, with Tito Gobbi) in the former, Karan Armstrong (1, with Erik Saeden) in the latter. Puccini's Tosca goes beyond other contemporary heroines (such as Violetta in *La Traviata*) in having a political as well as a romantic dimension. *Lulu* deals with the theme of the *femme fatale*, bringing musical inventiveness to the heroine's parabolic rise and fall and the sleazy fate which even she was unable to manipulate.

DER Überschwang von *Tosca* ist der Höhepunkt der italienischen Oper, Alban Bergs *Lulu* (die der Komponist nicht mehr vollenden konnte) zählt zu den gewagtesten Opernwerken unseres Jahrhunderts. Beide sind vom Thema her realistische Werke, und im Mittelpunkt steht jeweils die Tragödie einer machtvollen, doch dem Untergang geweihten Frau. Beide werden sie hier von Sängerinnen verkörpert, deren Interpretation Geschichte machte: Maria Callas (2, mit Tito Gobbi) als Tosca, Karan Armstrong (1, mit Erik Saeden) als Lulu. Was Puccinis Tosca vor anderen Opernheldinnen ihrer Zeit (wie etwa Violetta in *La Traviata*) auszeichnet, ist die politische Dimension, die zur Liebeshandlung hinzukommt. Das Thema von *Lulu* ist die Femme fatale, und mit bis dahin ungekannten musikalischen Mitteln werden der parabelhafte Aufstieg und Fall der Heldin und die Verwicklung des Schicksals vorgeführt, das nicht einmal sie beeinflussen konnte.

SI *Tosca* est l'apothéose luxueuse de l'opéra italien du XIXe siècle, le *Lulu* d'Alban Berg fait partie des œuvres les plus audacieuses de l'opéra du XXe siècle (bien qu'elle soit restée inachevée à la mort de Berg). Les deux œuvres sont thématiquement réalistes, dominées par la tragédie d'une femme forte mais condamnée par le destin. Et les deux opéras sont joués par des cantatrices exceptionnelles qui donnent une interprétation unique de leurs rôles : Maria Callas (2, avec Tito Gobbi) dans *Tosca* et Karan Armstrong (1, avec Erik Saeden) dans *Lulu*. La Tosca de Puccini surpasse les héroïnes de son époque (par exemple la Violetta de *La Traviata*) par sa dimension aussi bien politique que romantique. *Lulu* traite du thème de la femme fatale, et met son inventivité musicale au service de l'ascension et la chute allégorique de l'héroïne, de son destin malheureux qu'elle est incapable de diriger.

2

LONDON'S Royal Opera House – originally founded in 1732 – returned to a central position on the musical map in the 1950s. Here Joan Sutherland (1) spreads her bloodstained skirts and her tumbling locks in the mad scene from Donizetti's *Lucia di Lammermoor*. In her audience was Maria Callas, the Greek 'Tigress', chatting to German fellow-soprano Elisabeth Schwarzkopf (2). Schwarzkopf also goes into a huddle with conductor Wolfgang Sawallisch for further musical exchanges following their recording of Richard Strauss's *Der Rosenkavalier* (3).

DAS Londoner Royal Opera House, schon 1732 gegründet, konnte Mitte der 50er Jahre an einstige Größe anknüpfen. Hier (1) zeigt Joan Sutherland ihr blutbeflecktes Gewand und die wallenden Locken in der Wahnsinnsszene aus Donizettis *Lucia di Lammermoor*. Im Publikum saß auch die griechische »Tigerin« Maria Callas, die hier mit ihrer deutschen Kollegin, der Sopranistin Elisabeth Schwarzkopf, plaudert (2). Nach der Aufnahme von Richard Strauss' *Der Rosenkavalier* fachsimpelt die Schwarzkopf mit dem Dirigenten Wolfgang Sawallisch (3).

LE Royal Opera House de Londres – fondé en 1732 – retrouva une position centrale sur la scène musicale dans les années 50. Joan Sutherland (1) étale ici ses jupes trempées de sang et ses boucles en cascade dans la scène de la folie de *Lucie de Lammermoor* de Donizetti. Maria Callas, la « tigresse » hellénique bavarde avec le soprano allemand Elisabeth Schwarzkopf (2). Elisabeth Schwarzkopf avec le chef d'orchestre Wolfgang Sawallisch pour des échanges musicaux plus poussés après leur enregistrement du *Chevalier à la rose* de Richard Strauss (3).

2

3

1 2

FRANCIS Egerton sings the Captain to Welsh baritone Sir Geraint Evans in the title role of Alban Berg's *Wozzeck* in this 1978 production at the Royal Opera House, London (1). A very different treatment of a military theme was revived, also at Covent Garden, in 1966 with Donizetti's *Fille du Régiment* with (left to right) a relatively slender Luciano Pavarotti, Joan Sutherland and Spiro Malas (3). The 1973 Wagner Festival at Bayreuth opened with *Die Meistersinger von Nürnberg*: the master's grandson Wolfgang Wagner directs René Kollo as Walther von Stolzing (2).

FRANCIS Egerton singt den Hauptmann, der walisische Bariton, Sir Geraint Evans, die Titelrolle in dieser Produktion von Alban Bergs *Wozzeck* im Londoner Royal Opera House, 1978 (1). Eine ganz andere Sicht des Militärs kommt 1966, ebenfalls in Covent Garden, in dieser Inszenierung von Donizettis *Die Regimentstochter* zum Ausdruck, mit (von links nach rechts) einem damals noch vergleichsweise schlanken Luciano Pavarotti, Joan Sutherland und Spiro Malas (3). Die Festspiele in Bayreuth eröffneten 1973 mit den *Meistersingern von Nürnberg*. Hier gibt Wolfgang Wagner, der Enkel des Meisters, René Kollo, der den Walther von Stolzing singt, seine Anweisungen (2).

FRANCIS Egerton chante le Capitaine au baryton gallois Sir Geraint Evans dans le rôle principal de *Wozzek* d'Alban Berg produit en 1978 par la Royal Opera House de Londres (1). Le thème militaire est traité tout à fait différemment et revivifié à Covent Garden en 1966 dans *La Fille du régiment* de Donizetti qui réunit (de gauche à droite) un Luciano Pavarotti relativement svelte, Joan Sutherland et Spiro Malas (3). Le Festival de Bayreuth de 1973 ouvrit ses portes avec *Les Maîtres chanteurs de Nuremberg* : le petit-fils du maître, Wolfgang Wagner, dirige ici René Kollo qui interprète Walther von Stolzing (2).

(Overleaf)

THE opening of the 1934 Glyndebourne opera season brought forth Lady Diana Cooper, aristocratic leader of the social scene and author of a racy literary autobiography (2). Five years later the German photographer Felix Man (formerly Baumann) took this image of an interval in the grounds of the stately home where operas are staged (1). Despite the summer season, several of the women find it necessary to attend in their furs. Similar fashions, including buttonholes, accompany first-nighters attending the opening of the 1937 season at the Royal Opera House, picking their way through the crates of vegetables at Covent Garden (3).

(folgende Seite)

LADY Diana Cooper, damals erste Dame der englischen Gesellschaft (und Verfasserin einer skandalträchtigen Autobiographie), erscheint zur Eröffnung der Festivalsaison in Glyndebourne, 1934 (2). Fünf Jahre später nahm der deutsche Photograph Felix Man (vormals Baumann) dieses Bild von einer Aufführungspause im Park des aristokratischen Opernhauses auf (1). Obwohl es Sommer ist, finden einige der Damen Pelz angebracht. Ähnlich gekleidet, komplett mit Knopflochnelke, kommen diese Besucher zur Eröffnung der 1937er Saison im Royal Opera House (3). Ihr Weg führt sie zwischen den Gemüsekisten am Markt von Covent Garden hindurch.

avec les muses (1) dans *Apollon Musagète* et Serge Diaghilev (à droite), avec Jean Cocteau (2). En 1909, Diaghilev fonda la troupe des Ballets Russes à Monte-Carlo et les fit connaître en Occident, réunissant les plus grands talents de la danse et de la musique de l'époque : Pavlova, Nijinsky, Fokine, Massine, Balanchine, Stravinsky et Prokofiev.

(Overleaf)

THE famous portraitist Kleboe's picture of the young Scottish ballerina Moira Shearer (b. 1926) as she appeared in the 1948 film *The Red Shoes*, one of the most successful ballet films, directed by Powell and Pressburger.

(folgende Seite)

DIESES Bild des berühmten Porträtphotographen Kleboe zeigt die junge schottische Ballerina Moira Shearer (geboren 1926) bei ihrem Auftritt 1948 in *Die roten Schuhe* von Powell und Pressburger, einem der erfolgreichsten Ballettfilme aller Zeiten.

(Page suivante)

LA jeune ballerine écossaise Moira Shearer (née en 1926) photographiée par le célèbre portraitiste Kleboe lors de son apparition en 1948 dans le film *Les Chaussons rouges,* réalisé par Powell et Pressburger, un des films-ballets qui connut le plus de succès.

ANNA Pavlova (1881-1931) became the world's most famous exponent of classical ballet, basing herself in this house (Ivy Lodge) in London's Golders Green (3). The carefully posed swan is a heavy allusion to her signature solo, Mikhail Fokine's *Dying Swan* of 1905. Other important Russians in the world of dance at this time included Serge Lifar, posed with the muses (1) in *Apollon Musagète*, and Serge Diaghilev (on the right), with Jean Cocteau (2). In 1909 Diaghilev founded the *Ballets Russes* in Monte Carlo. From here, he brought Russian ballet to the west, introducing all the star composers, choreographers and dancers of the period: Pavlova, Nijinsky, Fokine, Massine, Balanchine, Stravinsky and Prokofiev.

ANNA Pawlowa (1881-1931) war die weltweit berühmteste Tänzerin des klassischen Balletts, und dieses Haus, Ivy Lodge im Londoner Golders Green, war ihr Hauptquartier (3). Der Schwan im Vordergrund steht für die Rolle, die sie zu ihrem Markenzeichen machte, Michel Fokines *Sterbenden Schwan* von 1905. Andere bedeutende Russen in der Welt des Tanzes waren damals Serge Lifar, hier (1) mit den Musen in *Apollon Mussagète* zu sehen, und Sergej Diaghilew (rechts), mit Jean Cocteau (2). 1909 hatte Diaghilew seine *Ballets Russes* in Monte Carlo gegründet. Von dort aus exportierte er russisches Ballett in den Westen und machte alle bedeutenden Komponisten, Choreographen und Tänzer der Zeit damit vertraut: Pawlowa, Nijinsky, Fokine, Massine, Balanchine, Strawinsky und Prokofieff.

ANNA Pavlova (1881-1931) devint la plus célèbre représentante du ballet académique, se fixant dans cette maison (Ivy Lodge) de Golders Green à Londres (3). Le cygne posant à ses côtés est une lourde allusion au *Cygne* de Mikhaïl Fokine, qu'elle créa en 1905. Parmi les autres Russes qui ont compté à cette époque dans le monde du ballet, on note ici la présence de Serge Lifar posant

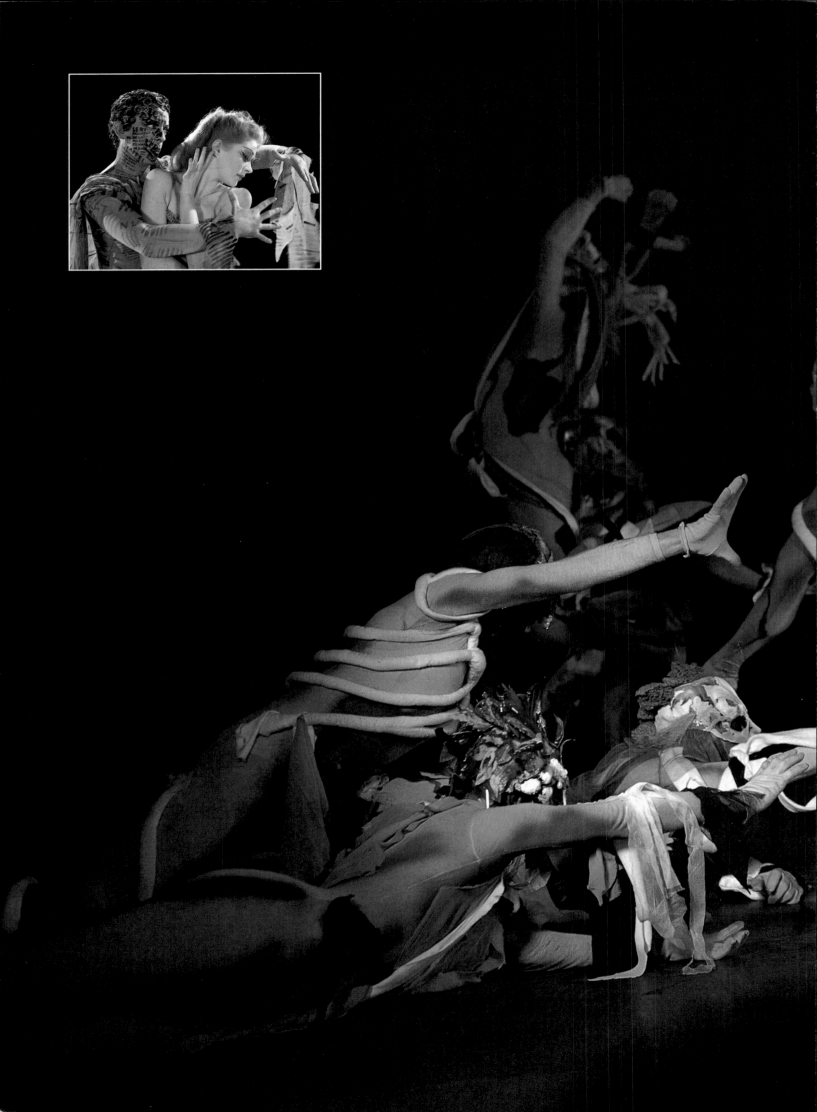

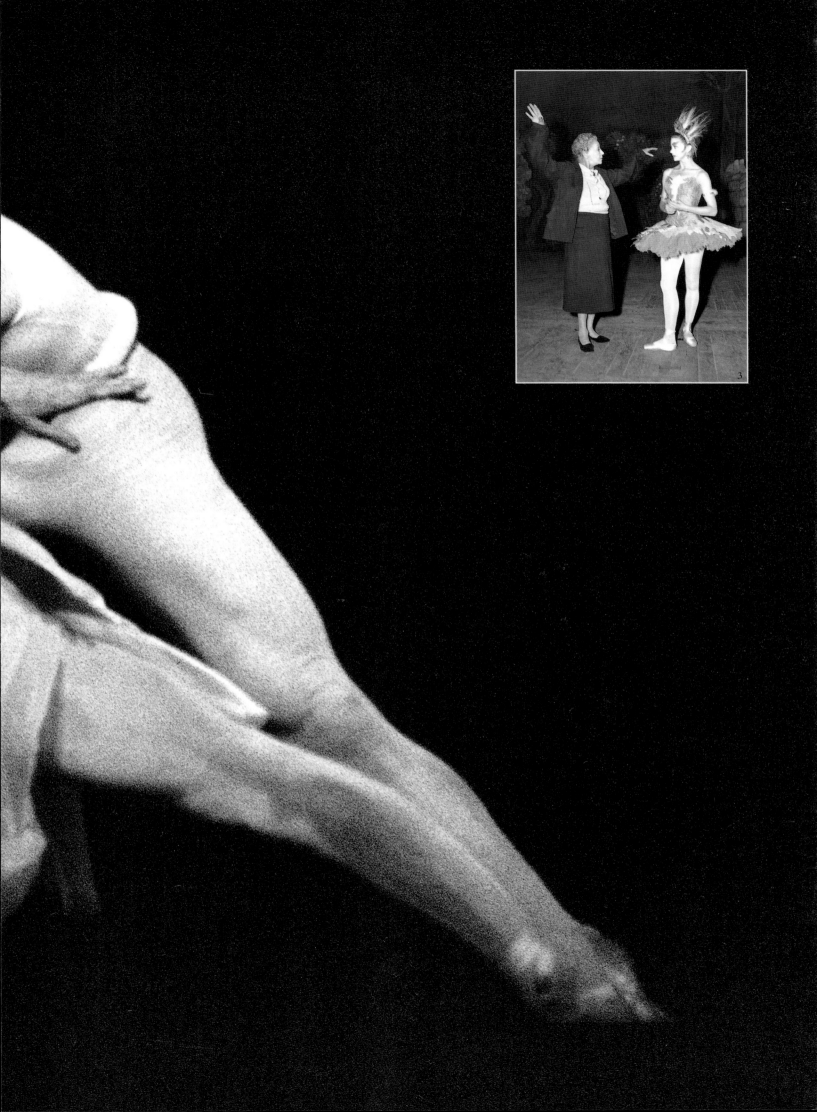

3

1

THE American Martha Graham (1894-1991) in her 1927 dance *Strike* (1). The Russian-born choreographer George Balanchine (1904-83) founded the New York City Ballet. Here, with British choreographer Frederick Ashton (second from left), he rehearses them in 1950 (2).

DIE Amerikanerin Martha Graham (1894-1991) in ihrem Tanz *Strike* 1927 (1). Der aus Rußland stammende Choreograph Georges Balanchine (1904-83) begründete das New York City Ballet. Hier bei einer Probe im Jahre 1950 mit seinem britischen Kollegen Frederick Ashton (zweiter von links, 2).

L'AMÉRICAINE Martha Graham (1894-1991) dans un ballet de 1927, *Strike* (1). Le chorégraphe d'origine russe George Balanchine (1904-1983) fonda le New York City Ballet. Ici, en 1950, répétant avec le chorégraphe britannique Frederick Ashton (second à partir de la gauche, 2).

(Previous pages)

MARGOT Fonteyn (1919-1991) made her debut with the Vic-Wells Ballet in 1934. After her first *Giselle* in 1937 (1, in practice dress), she rapidly became a world star. Here she is in one of the roles she made her own: Stravinsky's *Firebird*, for which she was coached by Tamara Karsavina, the original Firebird (3). Her later career was revitalized by her partnership with the young Russian émigré Rudolf Nureyev. The pair are shown in the final rehearsal for the gala of *Pelléas et Mélisande* in 1969 (2).

(vorige Seiten)

MARGOT Fonteyn (1919-1991) gab ihr Debüt beim Vic-Wells-Ballett, 1934. Ihre erste *Giselle* 1937 (1, bei der Probe) machte sie zum Weltstar. Hier ist sie in einer ihrer Leib- und Magenrollen zu sehen, Strawinskys *Feuervogel*, für den sie Unterricht von Tamara Karsawina bekam (3). Später gab die Partnerschaft mit dem jungen russischen Emigranten Rudolf Nurejew ihrer Karriere neuen Schwung. Das Bild zeigt die beiden bei der letzten Probe zu einer Galavorstellung von *Pelléas et Mélisande* 1969 (2).

(Pages précédentes)

MARGOT Fonteyn (1919-1991) fit ses débuts en 1934 avec le Vic-Wells Ballet. Après son premier *Giselle*, en 1937 (1, pendant l'entraînement), elle devint vite une star internationale. On la voit ici dans, *L'Oiseau de feu* de Stravinsky, tandis qu'elle écoute les conseils de Tamara Karsavina, l'Oiseau de feu original (3). Sa carrière connut un nouvel essor grâce Rudolf Noureev (1938-1993). On peut voir le couple lors de la dernière répétition pour le gala de *Pelléas et Mélisande* en 1969 (2).

NINETTE de Valois (1, extreme left) rehearses the Sadlers Wells (later the Royal Ballet) *corps de ballet* in 1943. Marie Rambert founded the Ballet Rambert in 1926 (2). The British choreographer Frederick Ashton studied with Léonide Massine and Marie Rambert before joining the Vic-Wells ballet in 1935, creating numerous roles for Margot Fonteyn. Director of the Royal Ballet 1963-70, he is seen here rehearsing *Monotones* to music by Erik Satie (3), and dancing with Robert Helpmann as the Ugly Sisters in Prokofiev's *Cinderella* (5, right). John Cranko rehearses Gillian Lynne in *New Cranks* at London's Lyric Theatre in 1960 (4).

NINETTE de Valois (1, ganz links) trainiert die Truppe von Sadlers Wells (das spätere Royal Ballet), 1943. Marie Rambert begründete das Ballet Rambert 1926 (2). Der britische Choreograph Frederick Ashton studierte bei Léonide Massine und Marie Rambert, bevor er sich 1935 dem Vic-Wells-Ballett anschloß, wo er zahlreiche Rollen für Margot Fonteyn schuf. 1963-70 war er Direktor des Royal Ballet; und hier sieht man ihn bei der Probe zu *Monotones* mit Musik von Erik Satie (3) und zusammen mit Robert Helpmann als häßliche Schwestern in Prokofieffs *Aschenbrödel* (5, rechts). John Cranko probt mit Gillian Lynne für *New Cranks* im Londoner Lyric Theatre, 1960 (4).

NINETTE de Valois (1, à gauche) fait répéter le corps de ballet du Sadlers Wells (plus tard Royal Ballet) en 1943. Marie Rambert fonda le Ballet Rambert en 1926 (2). Le chorégraphe britannique Frederick Ashton fit ses études avec Léonide Massine et Marie Rambert avant de rejoindre le ballet de Vic-Wells en 1935, créant de nombreux rôles pour Margot Fonteyn. Directeur du Royal Ballet de 1963 à 1970, on le voit ici faisant répéter *Monotones* sur une musique d'Érik Satie (3), et interprétant avec Robert Helpmann le rôle des Ugly Sisters du *Cendrillon* de Prokofiev (5, à droite). John Cranko fait répéter Gillian Lynne dans *New Cranks* au Lyric Theatre de Londres en 1960 (4).

MANY social changes occurred through Fifties popular culture. Even the skifflers here look faintly suspicious of the women choosing to jive on the pavement with one another, watched by a crowd of men (1). Girls out shopping together in the heyday of the gramophone go into a listening booth to check out a record before buying (2). Other teenagers with interchangeable hats and sandals sip identical milk-shakes in an identical pose (3).

VIELE gesellschaftliche Veränderungen kamen durch die Popkultur der 50er Jahre in Gang. Diese Skiffle-Musiker scheinen den beiden Frauen selbst nicht ganz zu trauen, die da vor einer großen Zahl männlicher Zuschauer einen Jive aufs Parkett des Bürgersteiges legen (1). Es war

die große Zeit der Schallplatte: Mädchen hören sich beim Einkaufsbummel eine Platte in der Hörkabine des Ladens an, bevor sie entscheiden, ob sie sie kaufen (2). Diese Teenager haben alle die gleichen Sandalen, die gleichen Hüte, die gleichen Posen und die gleichen Milkshakes (3).

DE nombreux bouleversements sociaux se produisent à travers la culture populaire des années 50. Même les musiciens, d'un air légèrement soupçonneux, observent les femmes qui dansent le rock sous les yeux d'une foule masculine (1). C'est l'âge d'or du tourne-disques ; des filles écoutent ensemble un microsillon avant de l'acheter (2). D'autres adolescentes à chapeaux et sandalettes interchangeables sirotent les mêmes milk-shakes dans une pose identique (3).

1

2

3

4

DIE Tanzstile wurden im Laufe des Jahrhunderts immer lockerer. Im Jahre 1927 nimmt Mrs. Harradine aus Wood Green, Nord-London, Unterricht im Black Bottom (1). Auch mit 87 Jahren möchte sie, wie sie sagt, auf dem laufenden bleiben, damit sie mit den jüngeren Familienmitgliedern Schritt halten kann. Eine andere Variante war der »Affentanz«, so genannt, weil Miss Jola Cohen aus Chicago und Arthur Murray sich die Schritte von der Äffin La Bella Pola beibringen ließen (5). Fred Astaire unterrichtet in seinem Atelier an der New Yorker Park Avenue gleich hundert Tanzlehrer in seinen Techniken. Zwei von ihnen demonstrieren den typischen Astaire-Tanz, eine Mischung aus Jitterbug, Foxtrott und einem geheimnisvollen »Jersey Bounce« (2). Das ist natürlich »der Astaire«. Latin Lovers wie Ramon Navarro führten einen »neuen Tango« ein, und im Londoner Piccadilly-Hotel eifern Josephine Head und Albert Zapp ihm nach (3). In den 60er Jahren kam es, wie es kommen mußte: Als es nicht mehr weiter voranging, konnte es nur noch rückwärts gehen (4) — und zwar bis ganz nach unten. Wer im Glenlyn Ballroom Dancing Club keinen Twist tanzt, der ist rettungslos verloren.

LA danse s'échauffe et s'agite au cours du siècle. Pour rester à la page à 87 ans et danser le Black Bottom en 1927, Mme Harradine, de Wood Green, au nord de Londres, écoute les instructions (1) pour demeurer, comme elle dit, « en paix avec les plus jeunes membres de la famille ». Une autre variation était la « danse du singe » — appelée ainsi depuis que le singe, La Bella Pola, avait appris un pas ou deux à Miss Jola Cohen de Chicago et Arthur Murray lui-même (5). Fred Astaire a transmis sa technique à cent instructeurs dans son propre studio de Park Avenue à New York. Deux d'entre eux font une démonstration de sa danse qui allie le jitterburg, le fox-trot et un énigmatique « bond de Jersey » (2). C'est, bien sûr, la « Astaire ». Des « latin lovers », à la façon de Ramon Novarro, ont remis le tango au goût du jour. Au Picadilly Hotel de Londres, Josephine Head et Albert Zapp s'y exercent intensément (3). Durant les années 60, arriva ce qui devait arriver : quand tout mouvement vers l'avant a été fait, on ne peut plus qu'aller vers l'arrière (4) — à plat sur le dos. Au club de danse de Glenlyn, vous êtes vieux jeu si vous ne dansez pas le twist.

DANCE styles loosened up and shook down through the course of the century. Anxious to get with it and do the Black Bottom in 1927, 87-year-old Mrs Harradine of Wood Green, North London, takes instruction (1) in order, she says, 'to keep pace with the younger members of the family'. Another variation was the 'Monkey Dance', so-called since the monkey La Bella Pola taught Miss Jola Cohen of Chicago and Arthur Murray himself a step or two (5). Fred Astaire's technique is passed on to 100 instructors at his own studio on Park Avenue, New York. Two of them demonstrate his signature dance, which combines jitterbug, fox-trot and a mysterious 'Jersey bounce' (2). It is, of course, 'the Astaire'. Latin lovers like Ramon Novarro created a taste for a 'new-fangled tango'. At the Piccadilly Hotel, London, Josephine Head and Albert Zapp are in hot pursuit of it (3). The 1960s brought the predictable outcome: when every forward move has been made, there's nowhere to go but back (4) – flat on your back. At the Glenlyn Ballroom Dancing Club, if you're not in a Twist you're a Square.

FRENCH night-life always had a certain *je ne sais quoi*. The Folies Bergère in 1929 was so grand and glamorous that it (and Maurice Chevalier) transferred direct to Hollywood's silver screen (4). Inside, the girls all acquired the same bobbed hairstyle – and the same high-kicking technique for pulling up their stockings (3). Josephine Baker was a legend in her two lifetimes: firstly as a dancer who brought her colour to the European stage and sexily sent up every racist prejudice with her oiled body, bouncing bananas and jungle seductions (1); secondly as the 'mother of a hundred' deprived and abandoned children she adopted and cherished. Edith Piaf's impoverished background; her past as a prostitute; her addiction to morphine and alcohol to help overcome the physical and emotional scars, all would have rendered her the quintessential victim, had it not been for her voice (2). Its tremendous power, combined with her fragile frame dressed always in black, made period songs like *La Vie en Rose* and *Non, je ne regrette rien* into her personal anthems.

4

DAS Nachtleben in Frankreich hatte schon immer ein gewisses *je ne sais quoi*. Die Folies Bergère waren 1929 so grandios, daß man sie (und Maurice Chevalier) schnurstracks nach Hollywood verfrachtete (4). Drinnen hatten die Mädchen alle die gleiche Kurzhaarfrisur — und die gleiche Technik, um die Strümpfe anzuziehen (3). Josephine Baker wurde gleich zweimal zur Legende, in den zwei Leben, die sie führte: zuerst als Tänzerin, die Farbe auf die Bühnen Europas brachte und allen rassistischen Vorurteilen mit ihrem geölten Körper, den hüpfenden Bananen und ihrer Dschungelerotik die Spitze nahm (1), zum zweiten als Mutter von hundert verlassenen Kindern, die sie adoptierte und aufzog. Edith Piaf schien zum Opfer geboren, bei den ärmlichen Verhältnissen, aus denen sie kam, ihrer Vergangenheit als Prostituierte, ihrer Morphium- und Alkoholsucht; doch ihre Stimme rettete sie (2). Die enorme Kraft dieser Stimme, die in einem solchen Kontrast zu der zerbrechlichen, stets in Schwarz gekleideten Gestalt stand, machte Lieder wie *La vie en rose* oder *Non, je ne regrette rien* zu ihren ganz persönlichen Hymnen.

EN France, la vie nocturne possède un certain « je-ne-sais-quoi ». En 1929, le prestige et l'attrait des Folies-Bergère était tels qu'on les transposa directement (avec Maurice Chevalier) sur le grand écran hollywoodien (4). À l'intérieur, les filles avaient toutes la même coupe au carré et une technique identique pour enfiler leur bas (3). Joséphine Baker fut deux fois légendaire : une première fois, en tant que danseuse de couleur en tournée européenne, elle ridiculisa tous les préjugés racistes avec son corps luisant, ses bananes bondissantes et ses attraits exotiques (1) ; une seconde fois en adoptant une centaine d'enfants abandonnés. Le milieu misérable d'où était issue Édith Piaf, son passé dans la prostitution, sa dépendance à l'alcool et à la morphine qui l'aidait à faire face aux problèmes physiques et émotionnels, tout cela aurait fait d'elle la quintessence de la victime s'il n'y avait pas eu sa voix (2). Celle-ci émanait de sa fragile silhouette toujours vêtue de noir. Grâce à elle, son nom est indissolublement lié à des chansons comme « La vie en rose » et « Non, je ne regrette rien ».

Billie Holiday (1); Ella Fitzgerald in 1962 (3); Thelonius Monk (2); Louis Armstrong in the 1960s (4).

Billie Holiday (1); Ella Fitzgerald, 1962 (3); Thelonious Monk (2); Louis Armstrong in den 60er Jahren (4).

Billie Holiday (1) ; Ella Fitzgerald en 1962 (3) ; Thelonius Monk (2) ; Louis Armstrong dans les années 60 (4).

The Sixties

THE decade opened with a bang, with Africa dominant. In 1960 Harold Macmillan's 'wind of change' speech unintentionally inaugurated a period of unprecedented bloodshed, which started when unarmed civilians attending a public meeting at Sharpeville were mown down as armed police opened fire without warning. That, of course, did most to radicalize both African and world opinion against apartheid. In the United States too the Civil Rights Movement was taking off, partly inspired by a time of rising expectations with Kennedy's presidential nomination in 1960. He won against Nixon, by only 120,000 votes, and promised in his inaugural speech that: 'The old era is ending. The old ways will not do.'

Kennedy's assassination in 1963 did not stem the tide of America's rise to the heights. In 1961 the US had put a chimpanzee named Ham into space; the Russians followed with their dog Laika – and, ahead of the US, their man, Yuri Gagarin. The Space War gradually turned into Star Wars: a hundred million viewers tuned in their television sets in 1969 to watch Neil Armstrong land on the moon, taking 'one small step for man, one giant leap for mankind'.

From August 1964, the US became heavily embroiled in the Vietnam war. By 1965 international protest was growing. In Washington candle-lit vigils were held outside the White House; in London 250,000 demonstrated before the US Embassy. 'Agent Orange', used in the war to defoliate trees and starve the local population, was perhaps one of the instigators of the backlash against environmental warfare.

Outstripping everything in popularity was 'Beatlemania', however fierce the defendants of the altogether rawer and raunchier Rolling Stones. The Beatles starred at the Royal Command Perform-ance and walked away with their CBEs: by 1964 they were the country's most popular tourist attraction. Beatlemania was said to be primarily female, primarily below the belt. Even stay-up stockings sported pictures of the Fab Four.

London was swinging: more specifically, King's Road, Chelsea, was swinging to the sounds of British and West Coast bands and the fashions of Mary Quant, Ossie Clark and Barbara Hulanicki ('Biba'). Despite a radical student movement – causing the closure of numerous European universities, particularly in Britain, Germany and France – and the Black Power movement in the United States, there was a mood of positive optimism abroad. The world was youth's oyster: international travel was suddenly cheap (especially if you hitched the hippie trail); love was suddenly 'free' (at a time when the Pill was new and AIDS unheard-of); music was both poignant and danceable (and folk was pop while blues made the classics); and politics could still be about 'liberation movements' rather than 'the stuff of corruption and negativism'.

DAS Jahrzehnt begann mit einem Paukenschlag, ganz besonders in Afrika. Harold Macmillans Rede von 1960, in der er von einem »frischen Wind« sprach, löste unbeabsichtigt eine Welle beispielloser Bluttaten aus, die damit begann, daß unbewaffnete Zivilisten, Teilnehmer einer öffentlichen Versammlung in Sharpeville, von der Polizei niedergemäht wurden, die ohne Vorwarnung das Feuer eröffnete. Mehr brauchte es nicht, um Afrika und die ganze Welt auf die Barrikaden gegen die Apartheid zu bringen. In den Vereinigten Staaten kam die Bürgerrechtsbewegung in Gang, nicht zuletzt beflügelt von den großen Erwartungen der Nominierung Kennedys als Präsidentschaftskandidat im Jahre 1960. Mit nur 120.000 Stimmen Vorsprung setzte er sich gegen Nixon durch. In seiner Antrittsrede erklärte er: »Die alten Zeiten sind vorbei. Aber die guten Traditionen nicht.«

Die Ermordung Kennedys im Jahre 1963 konnte den Aufstieg der USA zu neuen Höhen nicht aufhalten. 1961 hatten die Amerikaner einen Schimpansen namens Ham in den Weltraum geschickt; die Russen folgten mit ihrer Hündin Laika — und vor den Amerikanern mit dem ersten Menschen im Weltraum, Juri Gagarin. Aus dem Wettlauf im Weltall wurde allmählich ein Sternenkrieg: 100 Millionen Menschen saßen 1969 an ihren Fernsehgeräten, um Neil Armstrong auf dem Mond zu sehen, wie er »einen kleinen Schritt für einen Menschen, doch einen großen Sprung für die Menschheit« machte.

Vom August 1964 an engagierten die Vereinigten Staaten sich verstärkt im Vietnamkrieg. 1965 kam es weltweit zu Protesten. Vor dem Weißen Haus in Washington wurden Mahnwachen gehalten; in London demonstrierten 250.000 vor der amerikanischen

Botschaft. Das Entlaubungsmittel »Agent Orange«, das die Einheimischen dem Hungertod preisgab, war mitverantwortlich dafür, daß eine Kampagne gegen ökologische Kriegführung in Gang kam.

Populärer als alles andere war die »Beatlemania«, so sehr sich die Verehrer der handfesteren Rolling Stones auch ins Zeug legten. Die Beatles waren es, die vor der Queen auftraten und mit Orden dekoriert wurden — schon 1964 waren sie Großbritanniens größte Touristenattraktion. Von der Beatlemania, heißt es, waren hauptsächlich die weiblichen Fans betroffen, und sie wirkte eher unter der Gürtellinie. Selbst halterlose Strümpfe zierten das Bild der Pilzköpfe.

Es war die Zeit des »Swinging London«; genauer gesagt, war es die King's Road in Chelsea, die zu den Klängen britischer und kalifornischer Bands swingte, mit Mode von Mary Quant, Ossie Clark und Barbara Hulanicki (»Biba«). Trotz Studentenunruhen — die zur zeitweiligen Schließung zahlreicher Universitäten führten, vor allem in England, Deutschland und Frankreich — und der Black-Power-Bewegung in den Vereinigten Staaten war es ein durch und durch optimistisches Jahrzehnt. Die ganze Welt stand der jungen Generation offen: Auslandsreisen waren plötzlich billig (besonders wenn man als Hippie per Anhalter reiste); Liebe war plötzlich »frei« (zu einer Zeit, als die Pille eben erst erfunden war und noch niemand von AIDS gehört hatte); die Musik hatte Tiefe, und man konnte trotzdem dazu tanzen (und Folk war Pop, und Blues war Klassik); und in der Politik konnte es noch um Befreiungsbewegungen gehen statt um Korruption und allgemeinen Niedergang.

L ES années 60. La décennie s'est ouverte sur un véritable coup de tonnerre en Afrique du Sud. En 1960, le discours du Britannique Harold MacMillan à propos d'un certain « vent de changement » inaugura une époque d'épanouissement sans précédent, qui, paradoxalement, débuta à Sharpeville par un massacre. En effet, la police sud-africaine ouvrit le feu sans sommations sur des civils désarmés qui assistaient à un meeting public. Tout cela contribua évidemment beaucoup à durcir l'opinion africaine et mondiale contre l'apartheid.

Au États-Unis, c'est porté par une époque riche d'espoirs, dont l'élection de Kennedy à la présidence, que démarra le Mouvement pour les droits civils. Le nouveau président n'obtint que 120 000 voix de plus que Nixon et déclara dans son discours d'ouverture : « L'ère ancienne est révolue. Les vieilles méthodes ne fonctionnent plus. »

En 1963, son assassinat ne freina en rien l'ascension américaine. Dès 1961, les États-Unis avaient envoyé dans l'espace un chimpanzé du nom de Ham ; les Russes leur emboîtèrent le pas en lançant leur chienne Laïka sur orbite et, précédant les États-Unis dans ce domaine, il lancèrent Youri Gagarine. La guerre de l'espace se mua progressivement en guerre des étoiles : en 1969, pas moins de cent millions de téléspectateurs assistèrent à la sortie de Neil Armstrong sur la Lune et l'entendirent prononcer le fameux « petit pas pour l'homme, pas de géant pour l'humanité » qui restera dans la postérité.

À partir du mois d'août 1964, les États-Unis furent étroitement mêlés à la guerre du Viêt-nam. Dès 1965, on assista à une vive recrudescence des protestations internationales. À Washington, on organisait des veillées aux chandelles devant la Maison Blanche ; à Londres, ce furent 250 000 personnes qui manifestèrent devant l'ambassade des États-Unis. L'agent orange, un défoliant utilisé pendant la guerre, destiné à affamer la population locale, inspira peut-être le « retour de manivelle » contre la guerre écologique.

Aussi populaires qu'ils fussent, les Rolling Stones, dans l'ensemble plus crus et plus sensuels que les Beatles, ne parvinrent jamais à égaler l'enthousiasme provoqué par la « beatlemania ». Les Beatles furent les vedettes de la Royal Command Performance avant de devenir « Compagnons de l'Ordre de l'Empire britannique » ; en 1964, ils incarnaient la principale attraction touristique de la nation britannique. On a prétendu que la « beatlemania », à connotation sexuelle, était surtout le fait des filles. Même les bas-jarretelles arboraient les portraits des quatre célèbres garçons.

Londres, ou plus spécialement King's Road, Chelsea, dansait au rythme des groupes britanniques et occidentaux, et s'habillait à la mode de Mary Quant, Ossie Clark et Barbara Hulanicki, « Biba ». En dépit d'un mouvement lancé par des étudiants radicaux — qui causa la fermeture de nombreuses universités européennes, en particulier en Grande-Bretagne, en Allemagne et en France — et du mouvement du Black Power aux États-Unis, on sentait à l'étranger un sentiment d'optimisme positif. En effet, la jeunesse avait le monde à ses pieds : les voyages internationaux étaient soudain devenus bon marché (en particulier sur le mode hippy) ; tout à coup l'amour devenait « libre » (en ces temps où la pilule était une nouveauté et le sida inconnu) ; la musique était à la fois émouvante et se prêtait à la danse tandis que les politiques s'occupaient davantage des « mouvements de libération » que des retombées liées aux affaires de corruption et au négativisme ambiant.

4

1

MARY Quant was fashion's contribution to 'Swinging London' (1). Even the staid *Time* magazine noted that: 'In a decade dominated by youth, London has burst into bloom. It swings: it is the scene'. Noted for swinging skirts and flares at near-High Street prices, and for her angular, heavily fringed haircut, Quant also attracted publicity when her husband trimmed her pubic hair into a heart-shape. Sandie Shaw (2), better known as a Eurovision Song Contest winner (with *Puppet on a String* in 1964), also launched a fashion boutique in 1967. Her perennially bare feet contrast with Quant's clumpy platform soles.

MARY Quant war der Beitrag der Modewelt zum »Swinging London« (1). Selbst die hausbackene Zeitschrift *Time* vermerkte: »In einem Jahrzehnt, das von der Jugend beherrscht wird, ist London erblüht. Es swingt: hier ist was los.« Quant war für ihre schwingenden Röcke und Schlaghosen bekannt, die sie zu Preisen verkaufte, die kaum über denen der Kaufhäuser lagen, und für den kantigen Haarschnitt mit dem tief in die Stirn gezogenen Pony. Sie erregte auch Aufsehen damit, daß ihr Mann ihr das Schamhaar herzförmig frisierte. Sandie Shaw (2), eher als Siegerin des Eurovisions-Schlagerwettbewerbes bekannt (1964, mit *Puppet on a String*), eröffnete 1967 ihre eigene Modeboutique. Der Kontrast zwischen den nackten Füßen — ihrem Markenzeichen — und Mary Quants klobigen Plateausohlen könnte nicht größer sein.

MARY Quant était une haute figure de la mode au « Swinging London » (1). Même le *Time*, plutôt collet monté, notait : « Dans une décennie dominée par la jeunesse, Londres s'est épanoui. Il se balance : il est la scène. » Rendue célèbre par ses jupes courtes et ses pantalons à pattes d'éléphant, à des prix presque High-Street, mais également pour sa coiffure en casque à lourde frange, Mary Quant bénéficia des retombées publicitaires, lorsque son mari arrangea les poils de son pubis en forme de cœur. Sandie Shaw (2), que sa première place au concours de l'Eurovision de la chanson en 1964, avec « *Puppet on a String* » a rendu célèbre, ouvrit aussi une boutique de mode en 1967. Ses pieds, perpétuellement nus, contrastent avec les massives semelles à plateau de Mary Quant.

(Previous pages)

YVES St Laurent with models (1). Space is big news even in 1969 fashion swimsuits (2). If a face summarized the mood of the times, it was Twiggy's – doe-eyed, freckle-nosed, topped with cropped hair (4). Her gestures and bare feet seemed designed to underline her nickname (3).

(vorige Seiten)

YVES Saint-Laurent mit Mannequins (1). 1969 dreht sich alles um die Raumfahrt, selbst in der Bademode (2). Wenn es ein typisches Gesicht gab, dann war es das von Twiggy, mit ihren Kulleraugen, der sommersprossigen Nase und dem kurzen Haar (4). Mit ihrer Haltung und den nackten Füßen schien sie ihren Spitznamen (»Zweiglein«) noch zu unterstreichen (3).

(Pages précédentes)

YVES Saint-Laurent avec des mannequins (1). L'espace est à la une en 1969, et même les maillots de bain n'y échappent pas (2). Avec ses yeux de biche, ses taches de son sur le nez et ses cheveux courts, Twiggy est, à de multiples égards, représentative de cette époque (4). Ses gestes et ses pieds nus semblaient souligner son apparence de « petite branche » (3).

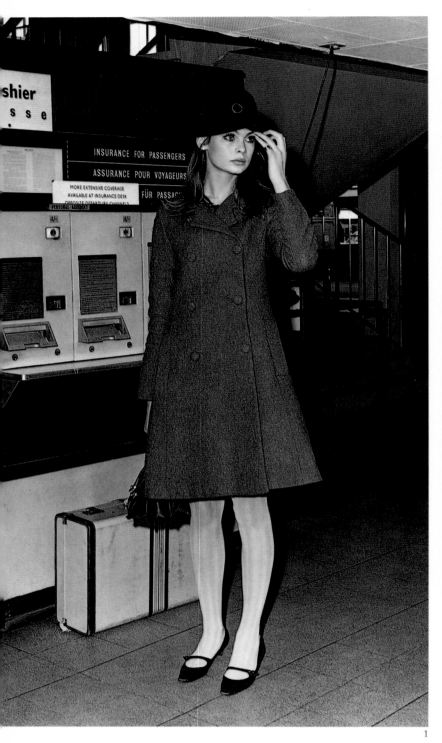

1

2

JEAN 'the Shrimp' Shrimpton was the sleek end of the fashion market. Known for her elegant taste, in antiques and pictures as much as her outfits, the model was heavily promoted by the photographer, and her lover, David Bailey as 'the face – and the figure'. She was constantly in transit at airports (1, 2, 3), although the Chanel suit (4) was worn at Melbourne races.

JEAN »the Shrimp« Shrimpton war für die kostspieligere Seite der Mode zuständig. Als Model, das nicht nur in der Mode, sondern auch bei Antiquitäten und Kunstwerken immer nur das Feinste nahm, wurde sie von dem Photographen David Bailey, mit dem sie zusammenlebte, als »das Gesicht — und die Figur« vermarktet. Sie war ständig unterwegs, hauptsächlich sah man sie auf Flughäfen (1, 2, 3); die Aufnahme im Chanel-Kostüm (4) entstand hingegen beim Rennen in Melbourne.

3

4

JEAN Shrimpton, surnommée la « *Shrimp* » (crevette), représentait le côté bien lisse du marché national. Connue pour son goût raffiné aussi bien en matière d'antiquités et de tableaux que de vêtements, le mannequin fut efficacement lancé par le photographe David Bailey, son amant, comme « *the face and the figur* ». On la voyait toujours entre deux avions (1,2,3), et c'est en tailleur Chanel qu'elle assistait aux courses de Melbourne.

IN 1965 Bob Dylan and his girlfriend Joan Baez were still folk-singers, rooted in the 'white blues' of Woody Guthrie and Pete Seeger (1). Composers, songwriters, singers and performers, they fulfilled new ideals of new troubadours. John Lennon and his second wife, the Japanese film-maker Yoko Ono, mock another established tradition in appearing on the Eamonn Andrews Show.

While Eamonn gets to lie in the bed they made famous by taking to it for world peace, they occupy a sheet sleeping-bag at its feet (2). Having denuded themselves before the camera, they were to remove another layer by shaving their heads. And they still maintained their opposition to the Vietnam War, along with their fellow long-haired 'peaceniks'.

IM Jahre 1965 waren Bob Dylan und seine damalige Freundin Joan Baez noch Folksänger, verwurzelt im »weißen Blues« von Woody Guthrie und Pete Seeger (1). Als Komponisten, Liedermacher, Sänger waren sie die idealen Troubadoure einer neuen Zeit. John Lennon und seine zweite Frau, die japanische Fluxus-Künstlerin Yoko Ono, verspotten in der Eamonn

1

2

Andrews Show wieder einmal eine ehrwürdige Tradition. Eamonn liegt in dem Bett, das sie mit ihren Friedensdemonstrationen weltberühmt machte, und die beiden sitzen in einem Schlafsack ihm zu Füßen (2). Sie blieben weiterhin Vietnamkriegsgegner, wie ihre langhaarigen Freunde, die anderen »Peaceniks«.

E N 1965, Bob Dylan et sa petite amie Joan Baez étaient encore des interprètes de musique folk, laquelle prenait ses racines dans les blues blancs de Woody Guthrie et Pete Seeger (1). Compositeurs, paroliers, chanteurs et interprètes, ils correspondaient au nouvel idéal du troubadour moderne. John Lennon et sa seconde épouse, la réalisatrice japonaise Yoko Ono, apparaissent dans le Eamonn Andrews Show. Tandis qu'Eamonn se couche dans le lit support de la campagne du couple en faveur de la paix dans le monde, ils se sont enroulés à ses pieds dans un drap blanc (2). Soutenus et accompagnés de nombreux pacifistes, jamais ils ne cesseront de s'opposer à la guerre du Viêt-nam.

THE 1960s were little if not exuberantly heterogeneous. While Stateside 'women's libbers' burnt their bras (even if only once and for a press-orchestrated publicity stunt), Hugh Hefner, head of the Playboy empire, stuffed his 'bunny girls' into ever-tighter, upward-thrusting corsets (1). An historic moment was reached in Vienna when, 16 years after the city's partition in 1945, President Kennedy exchanged handshakes with Prime Minister Krushchev (2). The 1963 Profumo scandal brought down a minister and, subsequently, a government. Prostitute Christine Keeler was said to have bowed to the machinations of society doctor Stephen Ward, who used extensive connections to procure her high-class clients. Here she is

seen waiting outside the courtroom at his trial (4). She made a comeback of sorts at a 1969 photocall for photographer David Bailey's book *Goodbye baby and Amen*, alongside model Penelope Tree and singer Marianne Faithfull (3).

DAS Bemerkenswerteste an den 60er Jahren war ihre Widersprüchlichkeit. Während in Amerika Feministinnen ihre BHs verbrannten, steckte Hugh Hefner, Chef des Playboy-Imperiums, seine »Bunnies« in immer engere Korsetts (1). Ein historisches Ereignis fand in Wien statt, wo Präsident Kennedy sechzehn Jahre nach der Teilung der Stadt dem russischen Premierminister Chruschtschow die Hand reichte (2). Der Profumo-Skandal von

3

4

1963 brachte in England einen Minister und am Ende eine ganze Regierung zu Fall. Es heißt, die Prostituierte Christine Keeler sei dem Arzt der High Society, Stephen Ward, gefällig gewesen, und dieser habe seine vielfältigen Kontakte spielen lassen, um ihr Kunden aus der besten Gesellschaft zu vermitteln. Hier wartet sie beim Prozeß gegen Ward vor dem Gerichtssaal (4). 1969 hatte sie eine Art Comeback, als der Photograph David Bailey der Presse sein Buch *Goodbye Baby and Amen* präsentierte. Die beiden anderen sind Model Penelope Tree und Sängerin Marianne Faithfull (3).

LES années 60 n'ont pas connu la même évolution dans chaque pays. Alors qu'aux États-Unis, les adeptes du Women's Lib brûlaient leurs soutiens-gorge (en fait un seul devant les photographes et journalistes invités), Hugh Heffner, à la tête de l'empire Playboy, affublait ses Bunnys de corsets moulants qui mettaient en valeur leurs attributs (1). Vienne vécut un moment historique quand, seize ans après le partage de la ville, le président Kennedy échangea une poignée de main avec Khrouchtchev, alors Premier ministre de l'Union soviétique (2). En 1963, le scandale Profumo ne causa rien moins que la démission d'un ministre et la chute d'un gouvernement. La prostituée Christine Keeler était mêlée aux intrigues de Stephen Ward, médecin de la bonne société lui fournissant une clientèle haute gamme. On la voit ici pendant son procès, attendant devant le tribunal (4). Elle revint en 1969, en posant pour l'album du photographe David Bailey, *Goodbye Baby and Amen*, aux côtés du mannequin Penelope Tree et de la chanteuse Marianne Faithfull (3).

FILM faces of the 1960s. Michael Caine, at home with his mother and brother in 1964 (1), the epitome of a working-class lad made good who still loved his mum. His flat South London accent and square specs were as much a part of his act as the tough-guy parts he played. Polish film director Roman Polanski married Californian starlet Sharon Tate in January 1968 (2). Nothing in the sinister oddness of his fantasy world anticipated the horror that resulted. In August 1969, Tate and their unborn child along with four friends were murdered by maniac cult leader Charles Manson and three female accomplices. And in Venice for the 1963 Film Festival, British stars Julie Christie and Tom Courtenay captured the look and spirit of a decade in the hugely successful *Billy Liar* (3).

FILMSTARS der Sechziger. Michael Caine, zu Hause mit Mutter und Bruder im Jahre 1964 (1), ganz der brave Sohn aus einfachem Hause. Der Südlondoner Akzent und die breiten Brillengläser waren ebenso eine Rolle, die er spielte, wie der harte Typ, den er so oft verkörperte. Der polnische Regisseur Roman Polanski heiratete das kalifornische Starlet Sharon Tate im Januar 1968 (2). Doch auch die abseitigsten Phantasien seiner Filme

bereiteten niemanden auf das vor, was kommen sollte. Im August 1969 wurden Sharon Tate und ihr ungeborenes Kind zusammen mit vier Freunden von dem wahnsinnigen Sektenführer Charles Manson und drei Anhängerinnen ermordet. 1963, beim Filmfestival in Venedig, waren die britischen Stars Julie Christie und Tom Courtenay ganz auf der Höhe des Jahrzehnts, und ihr Film *Billy Liar* war ein großer Erfolg (3).

VISAGES de cinéma des années 60. Michael Caine, posant en modèle de garçon de la classe ouvrière et de fils aimant, chez lui avec sa mère et son frère en 1964 (1). Son parler, dépourvu des intonations du sud de Londres, et ses lunettes démodées revêtaient une grande importance dans les rôles d'homme confirmé qu'il devait interpréter. C'est en janvier 1968 que le réalisateur polonais, Roman Polanski, épousa la petite actrice californienne Sharon Tate (2). En août 1969, alors que Sharon Tate était enceinte, un nommé Charles Manson, gourou d'un culte satanique, et trois femmes complices, assassinèrent l'actrice et quatre de ses amis. En 1963, au Festival de Venise, les vedettes britanniques Julie Christie et Tom Courtenay surent capter l'allure et l'esprit d'une décennie dans *Billy Liar* (3), un énorme succès.

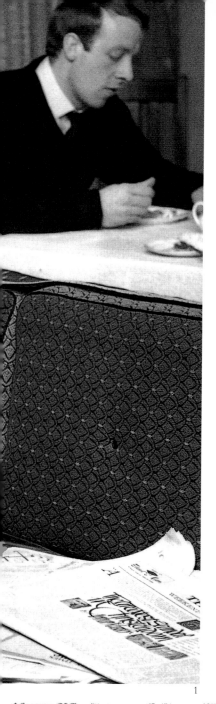

1 2

3

(Overleaf)

OUTDOOR pop festivals became big business through the 1960s and 1970s. Windsor (1), Woburn, Bath, the Isle of Wight and Hyde Park were all popular venues. And even if you couldn't hear the music, you could paint your own (or someone else's) body (2) and roll your own smoke, using an unlikely cigarette-holder (3).

(folgende Seiten)

FREILUFT-POPFESTIVALS waren in den 60er und 70er Jahren ein großes Geschäft. Windsor (1), Woburn, Bath, die Isle of Wight und der Hyde Park waren die populärsten Orte. Man konnte sich den Körper bemalen (oder den einer Freundin) (2), oder etwas Selbstgedrehtes rauchen, wie hier mit dieser originellen Zigarettenspitze (3).

(Page suivante)

LES festivals de musique pop en plein air prirent une grande ampleur durant les années 60 et 70. À Windsor (1), Woburn, Bath, l'Île de Wight ou à Hyde Park, s'il était parfois difficile d'écouter la musique, on pouvait peindre son corps (ou celui de quelqu'un d'autre) (2) ou encore utiliser ce style de fume-cigarette (3).

2 3

JIMI Hendrix shortly before dying of a heroin overdose in 1970 (1). Mary Wilson, Diana Ross and Cindy Birdsong in 1968 attained stardom as the Supremes (2). In 1967, the Rolling Stones enhanced their 'bad boys' image: Mick Jagger and Keith Richards sentenced for drug offences (3) .

JIMI Hendrix 1970, kurz bevor er an einer Überdosis Heroin starb (1). Mary Wilson, Diana Ross und Cindy Birdsong 1968, als sie schon als »Supremes« berühmt waren (2). Die Rolling Stones 1967: Mick Jagger und Keith Richards werden wegen Drogenbesitzes verurteilt (3).

JIMI Hendrix, en 1970, avant qu'il ne succombe à une overdose d'héroïne (1). Mary Wilson, Diana Ross et Cindy Birdsong en 1968, qui devinrent plus tard les Supremes (2). En 1967, Mick Jagger et Keith Richards, des Rolling Stones, furent condamnés pour usage de stupéfiants (3), accentuant leur image de mauvais garçons.

3

1 2

3 4

5

6

Elvis Presley's phenomenal career (1) went into almost equally dramatic decline as drugs took over his life. Michael Jackson with the family pop group at Heathrow in 1972 (2). Bob Marley (5) made it ahead of other reggae singers because of exceptional talent, as a composer, musician and singer. The Everly Brothers (3), made fame last by staying the same, while 'husband-and-wife pop singers Sonny & Cher' (6) are no more, but Sonny Bono is mayor in California and Cher keeps churning out the movies. Stevie Wonder (4) in 1965, 'little' boy Wonder with his harmonica.

Elvis Presleys Aufstieg war kometenhaft, doch beinahe ebenso steil war sein Fall, als Medikamentensucht sein Leben ruinierte (1). Michael Jackson mit der singenden Familie auf dem Londoner Flughafen Heathrow, 1972 (2). Bob Marley (5) hatte mehr Erfolg als jeder andere Reggaesänger. Den Everly Brothers (3) blieb der Erfolg treu; für Sonny & Cher (6) sind die Zeiten als singendes Ehepaar vorbei, doch Sonny Bono ist Bürgermeister in Kalifornien, und Cher dreht einen Film nach dem anderen. Stevie Wonder 1965, als er noch der nette Junge mit der Mundharmonika war (4).

La carrière phénomènale d'Elvis Presley (1), à l'image de sa déchéance physique, connut un déclin dramatique. Michael Jackson avec le groupe pop familial en 1972 à Heathrow (2). Le talent de Bob Marley (5) en tant que compositeur, musicien et chanteur en fit le pape du reggae. C'est en restant les mêmes que les Everly Brothers (3) devinrent célèbres. Le couple de chanteurs pop Sonny & Cher (6) a cessé d'exister depuis longtemps. Sonny Bono est maire en Californie et Cher se produit au cinéma. Stevie Wonder (4) en 1965 avec son harmonica.

THE punk movement of the 1970s (1) was largely launched by the likes of the Sex Pistols pop group. In October 1978 Sid Vicious was arrested by New York police and charged with murdering Nancy Spungeon while the two were high on drugs. In February 1979 he died of a heroin overdose. Just as in the 1960s, supporters of different political and musical factions had their uniforms, despite a measure of crossover. Skinheads and bovver boots were the primary prerogative of the neo-Nazi white supremacist British Movement (2), while 'crusties' in the 1990s (3), following hippie style, adopted the New Age garb of colourful dreadlocks, crazy hats and fabrics and a definitely unwashed look.

DIE Punk-Bewegung der 70er Jahre (1) wurde von Gruppen wie den Sex Pistols begründet. 1978 wurde Sid Vicious von der New Yorker Polizei festgenommen und des Mordes an Nancy Spurgeon angeklagt; beide standen zur Tatzeit unter Drogen. Im Februar 1979 starb er an einer Überdosis Heroin. Genau wie in den 60er Jahren hatten die Anhänger bestimmter politischer Fraktionen oder Musikrichtungen ihre Uniformen, auch wenn die Grenzen nicht mehr ganz so scharf gezogen waren. Kahlgeschorene Köpfe und Springerstiefel waren Erkennungszeichen der Neonazis (die es auch in England als rassistisches »British Movement« gab, 2), wohingegen die »crusties« der 90er Jahre (3) sich in New-Age-Gewänder hüllten, mit bunten Dreadlocks, verrückten Hüten und Stoffen, und einen ausgesprochen ungewaschenen Eindruck machten.

LE mouvement punk des années 70 (1) a en grande partie été popularisé par les faits et gestes des Sex Pistols. En octobre 1978, Sid Vicious était arrêté par la police de New York pour avoir tué Nancy Spungeon, alors qu'ils étaient tous deux sous influence de la drogue. C'est en février 1979 qu'il disparut à la suite d'une overdose d'héroïne. Dans les années 60, les supporters de différentes factions politiques et musicales arboraient l'uniforme. La tête rasée et les bottes cloutées furent la prérogative du mouvement britannique des blancs néonazis (2). Les « crusties » des années 90 (3) ont, pour leur part, adopté la panoplie New Age : des mèches rasta passées à la teinture, des chapeaux et tissus excentriques et un look irrévocablement négligé.

1

2

St-Tropez, made famous by its yachts and by Brigitte Bardot's residence there, continued to flaunt fashion's bottom line into the 1970s. Buttock-cutting jeans (3), studded mini-shorts (2) and a scarf (4) – at times only a string – were rare concessions to dress when leaving the nudist beaches for the boutiques and cafés lining the boardwalks. The striped outfit (1) has more lasting appeal than the outrageous platforms (5) or the babydoll smock and bell-bottoms (6).

St.-Tropez – bekannt für seine Jachten und dafür, daß Brigitte Bardot sich dort niedergelassen hatte – machte auch in den 70er Jahren noch Mode. Hautenge Hüfthosen (3), nietenbewehrte, ultrakurze Shorts (2) und ein Tuch (4) — manchmal sogar nur ein String — waren die einzigen

4   5   6

Zugeständnisse, die man machte, wenn man von den Nacktbadesträanden zu den Boutiquen und Straßencafés herüberkam. Der Streifenanzug (1) kann heute eher noch überzeugen als die verrückten Plateausohlen (5) oder die Babydoll-Bluse mit Schlaghosen (6).

Saint-Tropez, fameuse pour ses yachts et la maison de Brigitte Bardot, continua, au cours des années 70, à montrer le style à suivre: des pantalons serrés (3), des mini-shorts cloutés (2) et un foulard (4) — qui tenait plus de la ficelle à l'époque — étaient les rares concessions faites par ceux qui quittaient les plages nudistes pour les boutiques et les cafés qui s'alignaient le long des trottoirs. Les vêtements à rayures (1) présentent un attrait plus durable que les semelles à plateau incroyablement hautes (5) ou les blouses babydoll et autres pantalons à pattes d'éléphant (6).

DEMONSTRATIONS had their fashions too. While feminist marches in the United States and Britain could not fail to be reported as packed with 'dungarees-wearing, burly lesbians', the Italians had their own inimitable style, linking sunglasses and furs with demands for preschool provision and curriculum reform (1). Meanwhile rock'n'roll revivalists (2) and Notting Hill carnival celebrants (3) show a perhaps surprising convergence of glamorous and androgynous intentional vulgarity.

DEMONSTRATIONEN hatten ihre eigenen Moden. In den angelsächsischen Ländern konnte man sich darauf verlassen, daß in einem Bericht über einen feministischen Protestmarsch von »kräftigen Lesben in Latzhosen« die Rede sein würde, während Italienerinnen stilvoller in Sonnenbrille und Pelz auftraten, wenn sie für Kindergärten und Schulreformen demonstrierten (1). Es mag erstaunen, wie beim Rock 'n' Roll-Revival (2) und beim Karneval in Notting Hill (3) Glamour und ein androgyner, bewußt anstößiger Stil zusammenkommen.

LES manifestations suivent également la mode. Alors que les marches féministes aux États-Unis et en Grande-Bretagne ne manquaient pas d'être attribuées à des « lesbiennes bien charpentées vêtues de salopettes », les Italiennes, avec un style inimitable, défilaient en manteaux de fourrure, arborant des lunettes de soleil pour réclamer davantage d'écoles maternelles et une réforme des programmes d'études (1). Pendant ce temps, ceux qui faisaient revivre le rock'n'roll (2) et qui célébraient le carnaval de Notting Hill (3) montraient, curieusement peut-être, la même vulgarité provocatrice, séduisante et androgyne.

1

2   3

2   3

BLACK culture gave British male fashion a necessary fillip, lifting it out of its longstanding dullness. When the ex-troopship *Empire Windrush* docked at Tilbury in 1948 with 482 Jamaicans aboard, little did anyone imagine that it was Messrs Hazel, Wilmot and Richards's talents as natty dressers rather than as carpenters that would hit the headlines (1). Their chic tweeds contrast somewhat drastically with Mr Ruben Torres's 'ideal suit', which looks more appropriate to a moon landing than to Kew Gardens Railway Station (2). George Best, known for his antics off as well as on the football pitch, also fell foul of the dangling flares and the 'let it all hang out' school of fashion (3, right).

DIE Kultur der Schwarzen gab der britischen Herrenmode einen dringend benötigten Vitaminstoß und befreite sie aus ihrer althergebrachten Langeweile. Als der ehemalige Truppentransporter *Empire Windrush* 1948 mit 482 Jamaikanern an Bord in den Docks von Tilbury festmachte, hätte es niemand für möglich gehalten, daß die Herren Hazel, Wilmot und Richards eher wegen ihrer auffälligen Kleider in die Zeitung kamen, als daß sie Arbeit als Zimmerleute fanden (1). Ihre schicken Tweeds stehen in gewissem Kontrast zu Mr. Ruben Torres' »Idealanzug«, der eher zu einer Mondlandung als zum Bahnhof Kew Gardens zu passen scheint (2). George Best (3, rechts) hatte auch außerhalb des Spielfelds seinen eigenen Kopf und hielt nichts von Schlaghosen und der schreienden Mode dieser Zeit.

LA culture noire donna à la mode masculine britannique le coup de fouet dont elle avait besoin pour se libérer de la grisaille qu'elle cultivait depuis trop longtemps. Quand l'ancien navire de troupes, l'*Empire Windrush*, jeta l'ancre à Tilbury en 1948 avec 482 Jamaïcains à bord, personne n'aurait imaginé que MM. Hazel, Wilmot et Richards seraient bientôt plus connus (1) pour leur chic vestimentaire que pour leur maîtrise de la charpente. Leurs tweeds élégants contrastent quelque peu avec le costume « idéal » de Ruben Torres que l'on imaginerait mieux sur la Lune qu'à la gare de Kew Gardens (2). George Best, reconnu autant pour ses bouffonneries que pour ses qualités de footballeur, s'est mis à dos les pantalons à pattes d'éléphant et les tenues « pendantes » (3, à droite).

THE 1950s British youth revolt began with the 'teddy boys', so-called after the Edwardian style of draped suits and slicked hair they adopted (1). Two decades later the hippie movement stretched from California to Katmandu, supposedly spreading 'peace and love' – and long hair, paisley tablecloths and knitted skullcaps – across the globe (2).

DIE britische Jugendrevolte der 50er Jahre begann mit den »Teddyboys«, so benannt nach ihrem Outfit im Stil der Jahrhundertwende, als König Edward regierte (1). Zwei Jahrzehnte darauf gab es Hippies von Kalifornien bis Katmandu, und sie verbreiteten weltweit »Frieden und Liebe« — und lange Haare, Paisley-Tischtücher und Strickmützen (2).

DURANT les années 50, la jeunesse britannique se révolta avec les « Teddy boys ». Ils devaient leur nom à leurs costumes prince de Galles et à leur chevelure bien peignée (1). Vingt ans plus tard, le mouvement hippie, qui était né en Californie et s'étendait à Katmandou, faisait entendre son message – amour et paix – et popularisait son style : longs cheveux, nappes aux motifs cachemire et calottes tricotées (2).

(Overleaf)
In June 1967 the Beatles released *Sergeant Pepper's Lonely Hearts Club Band* to massive sales and acclaim. Fifteen years after he first heard the final track 'A Day in the Life', Leonard Bernstein wrote that it 'still sustained and rejuvenated me'.

(folgende Seiten)
IM Juni 1967 veröffentlichten die Beatles *Sergeant Pepper's Lonely Hearts Club Band*, und der Verkaufserfolg war enorm. Fünfzehn Jahre nachdem er »A Day in the Life« zum ersten Mal gehört hatte, schrieb Leonard Bernstein: »Es nährt und erquickt mich bis heute.«

(Page suivante)
EN juin 1967, les Beatles sortent l'album *Sergeant Pepper's Lonely Hearts Club Band*, qui se vendra à des millions d'exemplaires. Quinze ans après « *A Day in the Life* », Leonard Bernstein écrivait : « Cela me soutient et me rajeunit toujours. »

Aviation and Space

AVIATION has been one of the greatest forces for change in the modern world. Just a dozen years after the Wright Brothers achieved their historic first mission in 1903, air warfare was being introduced. Despite the new terror of being hit from the skies during the Great War, it was only in the Second World War that air power became a deciding factor.

The development of airships at the end of the 1920s was intended to provide a major new transport system. The R100 flew from Britain to Montreal in 78 hours. However, the disaster which overtook its sister ship, the R101, effectively put a stop to this innovation. The danger was always that poor weather could reduce command control and result in a collision and then an explosion. With 5.5 million cubic feet of hydrogen on board, the disaster was bound to be near-total.

English-language signpost 1,000 miles north of Oslo (1) gives an accurate estimate of air-travel time in 1955 (sponsorship crest from Scandinavian Airlines). These times are a far cry from Wilbur Wright's winning the Michelin Cup for flying 124 kms (77 miles) in 2 hours 44 years earlier; 44 years on, times would have been shortened by an even greater ratio. In 1990, the Oslo-New York run would have taken no more than five hours by the shortest route and the journey to Paris about 2 hours.

KAUM etwas hat die moderne Welt so sehr verändert wie die Luftfahrt. Nur zwölf Jahre nach dem historischen ersten Flug der Brüder Wright im Jahre 1903 begann der Luftkrieg. Doch auch wenn im Ersten Weltkrieg zu allen anderen Schrecken nun auch noch der neue hinzukam, von Bomben aus der Luft getroffen zu werden, war es doch erst der Zweite Weltkrieg, bei dem die Luftherrschaft die entscheidende Rolle spielte.

Luftschiffe versprachen Ende der 20er Jahre eine völlig neue Form der Fortbewegung. Die R 100 flog in 78 Stunden von England nach Montreal. Doch mit der Katastrophe ihres Schwesterschiffes, der R 101, war das Schicksal dieser neuen Erfindung besiegelt. Es bestand immer das Risiko, daß das Schiff bei schlechtem Wetter nicht mehr steuerbar war und nach einem Zusammenstoß explodierte, und mit fünfeinhalb Millionen Kubikfuß Wasserstoff an Bord war eine Katastrophe dann unvermeidlich.

Tausend Meilen nördlich von Oslo gab dieser Pfosten in englischer Sprache (eine Reklame der Fluggesellschaft SAS, 1) Auskunft über Flugzeiten im Jahre 1951. Es war ein guter Fortschritt, seit Wilbur Wright 44 Jahre zuvor 124 Kilometer in zwei Stunden geflogen war und damit den Michelin-Pokal gewonnen hatte; noch einmal 44 Jahre später, und die Flugzeiten hatten sich noch drastischer verkürzt. 1990 brauchte der kürzeste Flug von Oslo nach New York nur noch fünf Stunden, und nach Paris waren es nur etwa zwei Stunden.

L'AVIATION a été l'une des inventions essentielles amenées par le monde moderne. C'est en 1913, une douzaine d'années après que les frères Wright ont réalisé leur première mission historique que les premiers combats aériens firent leur apparition. Si les contemporains de la Grande Guerre craignaient déjà les attaques aériennes, l'aviation ne devint décisive qu'au cours de la Seconde Guerre mondiale.

Le développement des dirigeables à la fin des années 20 visait à la création d'un important système de transport aérien. Le vol du R100, de la Grande-Bretagne à Montréal, dura soixante-dix-huit heures. La catastrophe qui frappa le dirigeable R101 mit un terme à cette expérience. En effet, on craignait en permanence que le mauvais temps n'entravât le contrôle des commandes, ce qui eût certainement entraîné une collision suivie d'une explosion. Avec plus d'un million et demi de mètres cube d'hydrogène à bord, la catastrophe aurait été inévitable.

Ce panneau de signalisation en langue anglaise, à plus de 1 500 kilomètres au nord d'Oslo (1), donne une estimation précise du temps de vol en 1955 (parrainage des Scandinavian Airlines). Il rappelle la victoire de Wilbur Wright, lequel avait gagné la Coupe Michelin, 44 ans plus tôt, en couvrant 124 kilomètres en deux heures. Une quarantaine d'années plus tard, les temps se sont même améliorés dans un rapport plus élevé. En 1990, le Oslo-New York n'a mis que cinq heures par la route la plus courte tandis que le voyage à Paris n'a nécessité que deux heures.

Traveltime by SAS to:

Rome 14 hrs. 15 min.

North Pole 6 hrs. 5 min.

Johannesburg 53 hrs. 55 min.

Tokyo via North Pole 32 hrs.

Fairbanks (Alaska) 14 hrs. 30 min.

Thule (Greenland) 6 hrs. 40 min.

Los Angeles Arctic routing 22 hrs.

Los Angeles via New York 36 hrs. 20 min.

Tokyo via India 70 hrs. 5 min.

New York 22 hrs. 55 min.

Santiago de Chile 74 hrs. 25 min.

Madrid 14 hrs.

London 8 hrs. 40 min.

Paris 12 hrs. 5 min.

1

2

3

THE R100 airship came of age in
November 1929. Before its maiden
voyage, waitresses set the silver service in a
dining-room worthy of a grand hotel (4).
After a successful launch, she was berthed
at the mooring tower at Cardington,
Bedfordshire, as the enthusiastic crowd
rushed towards her (1). The crash of the
R101 (shown here, 3, as literally the
skeleton of its former self), caused the
airship's demise as a popular option. In the
United States the German airship
Hindenburg landed safely after a 62-hour

4

flight from Frankfurt. Its end was similar to that of the R101, when 44 people died in the crash of which there were only eight survivors (2).

DAS Luftschiff R 100 lief 1929 vom Stapel. Vor dem Jungfernflug decken die Serviererinnen die Tafeln mit Silber, in einem Speisesaal, der einem Grand Hotel Ehre machen würde (4). Nach erfolgreich absolviertem Flug legt das Schiff in Cardington, Bedfordshire, an, und die Zuschauer stürmen begeistert hin (1). Nach

dem Absturz der R 101 (3) war das Luftschiff als populäres Transportmittel nicht mehr durchzusetzen. Das deutsche Luftschiff Hindenburg legte nach 62stündigem Atlantikflug sicher in den Vereinigten Staaten an, doch bei einem späteren Flug erlitt sie das gleiche Schicksal wie die R 101. 44 Menschen kamen bei dem Absturz um, nur acht überlebten (2).

NOVEMBRE 1929 : le dirigeable R100 va réaliser son premier voyage. Les serveuses disposent les couverts en argent

dans une salle à manger digne d'un grand hôtel (4). Après un lancement réussi, il est fixé à la tour d'amarrage de Cadington dans le Bedfordshire, et la foule enthousiaste s'y précipite (1). L'explosion du R101 (3, il ne reste ici que l'« ossature » du dirigeable) mit fin à la popularité de l'engin. Aux État-Unis, le dirigeable allemand Hindenburg arriva sain et sauf après un vol de soixante-deux heures depuis Francfort. Il connut, hélas, une fin semblable à celle du R101. 44 personnes trouvèrent la mort dans l'explosion et l'on ne découvrit que 8 survivants (2).

ON 12 April 1961, the Russian Yuri Gagarin (1) took his first space flight on board the Vostok I. The race to get the first man into space was terrific, given the intensity of Cold War competition as to which side had the more sophisticated technology. Gagarin orbited the earth in the 4.5 ton spacecraft for 108 minutes, reaching a height of 190 miles. He then fired braking rockets and the aircraft returned to earth by parachute. The USSR scored another 'first' when it put the first woman – Valentina Tereshkova – into orbit, travelling further than the longest-journeying US astronaut (2). The two of them joined hands in a Red Square salute – and a heroes' welcome back to earth – with Prime Minister Krushchev (3). An old, illiterate sheep-farmer, who looks as though he were born before the invention of the newspaper, has the cosmonauts' story read to him (4).

AM 12. April 1961 unternahm der Russe Juri Gagarin (1) mit der Wostok I den ersten bemannten Weltraumflug. Das Wettrennen darum, wer den ersten Menschen ins Weltall brachte, war bei der großen Rivalität der beiden Machtblöcke im Kalten Krieg ungeheuer gewesen, denn schließlich ging es darum zu zeigen, welche Seite die technisch überlegene war. Gagarin umrundete die Erde in dem viereinhalb Tonnen schweren Flugkörper 108 Minuten lang und erreichte dabei eine Höhe von 300 Kilometern. Dann zündete er die Bremsraketen, und die Raumkapsel kehrte an einem Fallschirm zur Erde zurück. Zum zweiten Mal gewann die Sowjetunion das Wettrennen, als sie die erste Frau in den Weltraum schickte — Walentina Tereschkowa, die weiter ins All hinausflog als der erfolgreichste amerikanische Astronaut (2). Der russische Premierminister Chruschtschow reicht den

1

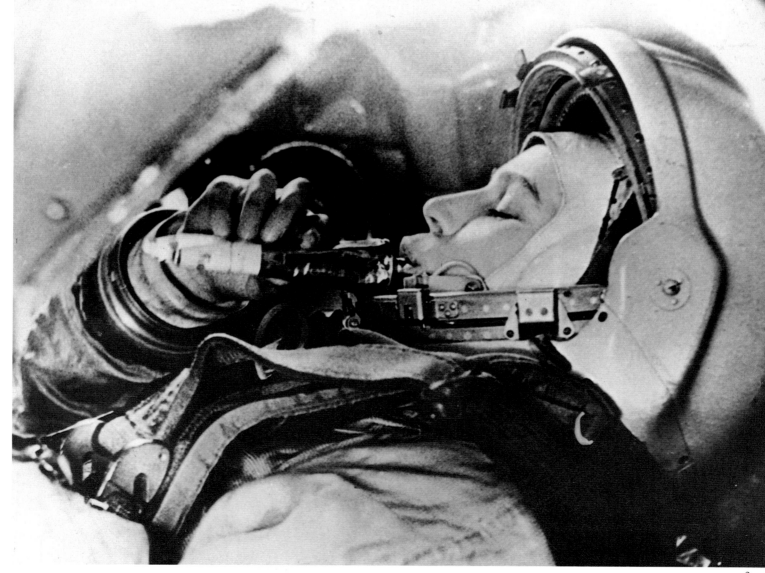

2

beiden beim Heldenempfang, der ihnen
bei ihrer Rückkehr auf dem Roten Platz
bereitet wurde, die Hand (3). Dieser
Schafhirte, der nicht lesen kann, läßt sich
vom Triumph der Kosmonauten vorlesen
(4).

L E 12 avril 1961, le Russe Youri
Gagarine (1) réalisa son premier vol
dans l'espace à bord du Vostock 1. La
course qu'occasionna l'envoi du premier
homme dans l'espace s'avéra fantastique.
C'était une façon de montrer de quel côté
se trouvait la technologie la plus
sophistiquée. Gagarine resta en vol orbital
pendant cent huit minutes à l'intérieur
d'un vaisseau spatial de 4 tonnes et demie à
une altitude de 327 kilomètres. Il mit
ensuite le feu aux fusées de freinage avant
d'atterrir en parachute. L'URSS releva un
nouveau défi avec Valentina Terechkova,
dont le voyage dura plus longtemps que
ceux des cosmonautes américains (2). À
leur retour, tous les deux sont salués
comme des héros sur la Place rouge. On les
voit ici donner la main au Premier ministre
Khrouchtchev (3). Un vieux berger illettré
se fait lire la saga des cosmonautes (4).

(Overleaf)

E ARTHRISE: the spectacular view of
our planet from space (1). Most of
Africa and part of Europe and Asia can be
seen in this image taken from the Apollo
11 spacecraft during its journey to the
moon (3). Cernan salutes the US flag when
the Apollo 17 lands on the moon in 1972
(2). The space module of the Apollo 12
craft is a powerful draw at the Japan World
Fair of 1970 (4).

(folgende Seite)

E RDAUFGANG: die Erde vom Weltall
aus gesehen (1). Teile Afrikas, Europas
und Asiens sind auf diesem Bild sichtbar,
das beim Mondflug der Raumkapsel
Apollo 11 entstand (3). Nach der
geglückten Mondlandung von Apollo 17
salutiert Astronaut Cernan vor der
amerikanischen Flagge (2). Die Mondfähre
der Apollo 12 sah man auf der
Weltausstellung in Japan, 1970 (4).

(Page suivante)

V OYAGE autour de la Terre :
spectaculaire, notre planète vue de
l'espace (1). Photo prise depuis Apollo 11
(3). Cernan salut le pavillon américain
quand Apollo 17 atterrit sur la Lune en
1972 (2). La capsule spatiale d'Apollo 12
est une grande attraction, en 1970, à la
Foire internationale du Japon (4).

3

4

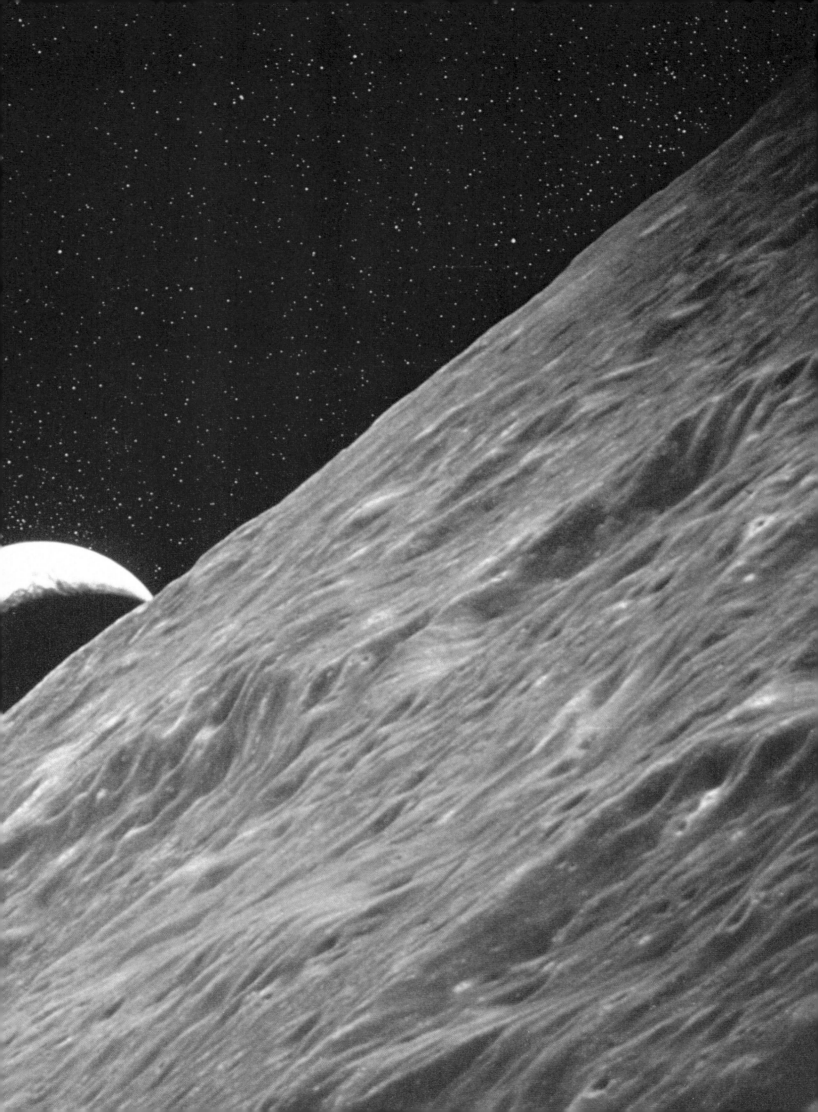

IN July 1969, Neil Armstrong, captain of the Apollo 11 mission, was the first man on the moon, observed by hundreds of millions of television viewers around the world. He described his descent from the Eagle lunar module as 'one small step for man, one giant leap for mankind'. He was accompanied by Edwin 'Buzz' Aldrin, whom he photographed descending from the module (4), and who can also be seen cautiously groping his way among the footprints in the moondust (3). The rocket launcher at Kennedy Space Center blasts off Apollo 11 in a characteristic 'pillar of flame' (1); as the module separates, it floats above the moon with the earth rising behind (2).

IM Juli 1969 betrat Neil Armstrong, Kapitän des Apollo-11-Fluges, als erster Mensch den Mond, unter den Augen von Millionen von Fernsehzuschauern in aller Welt. Er beschrieb seinen Ausstieg aus der Mondfähre *Eagle* mit den Worten: »Ein kleiner Schritt für einen Menschen, doch ein großer Sprung für die Menschheit.« Begleitet wurde er von Edwin »Buzz« Aldrin, den er photographierte, als dieser aus der Fähre klettert (4) und der auch zu sehen ist, wie er vorsichtig durch die Fußabdrücke im Mondstaub stakst (3). Von der Abschußrampe im Kennedy Space Center steigt Apollo 11 in der typischen »Feuersäule« auf (1); als die Mondfähre sich löst, schwebt sie über die Mondoberfläche, und im Hintergrund geht die Erde auf (2).

EN juillet 1969, Neil Armstrong, capitaine de la mission Apollo 11, devient le premier homme à marcher sur la Lune. Des centaines de millions de personnes de par le monde l'observent à la télévision. Il décrit, à la sortie de la capsule, son court passage sur la Lune comme « un petit pas pour un homme, mais un pas de géant pour l'humanité ». Il était accompagné d'Edwin « Buzz » Aldrin, qu'il photographia à sa descente du vaisseau spatial (4). On l'aperçoit ici foulant prudemment le sol entre les traces de pas dans la poussière lunaire (3). La fusée portant Apollo 11 fut lancée au Kennedy Space Center ; on voit ici la « colonne de flammes » caractéristique (1). La capsule séparée de la fusée flotte au-dessus de la Lune. À l'arrière-plan, on aperçoit la Terre « se lever » (2).

2

3

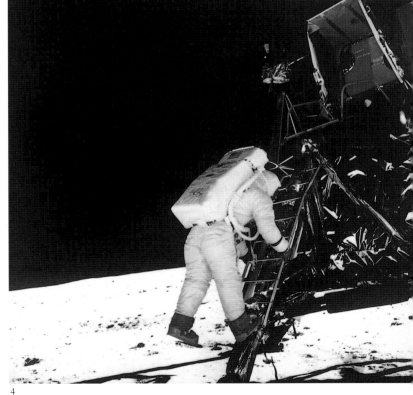

4

SPACE 335

THE US space shuttle *Challenger* exploded 72 seconds after take-off on 28 January 1986, to the horror of watching millions (2). Among the crew of seven who died was Christa McAuliffe, a schoolteacher selected as the first woman to fly in a new 'citizens in space' programme (1). The flight had already been postponed five times, three of them due to bad weather. Before blast-off, icicles had to be chipped from the shuttle by hand. These were the first US casualties in space, dealing a devastating blow to a programme already in serious difficulties from drastically over-running its budget.

AM 28. Januar 1986 explodierte die amerikanische Raumfähre *Challenger* 72 Sekunden nach dem Start, zum Entsetzen der Millionen, die das an ihren Fernsehgeräten miterlebten (2). Zu der siebenköpfigen Besatzung, die dabei umkam, gehörte auch die Lehrerin Christa McAuliffe, die als erste Frau des neuen Programms »Bürger fliegen in den Weltraum« ausgewählt worden war (1). Der Flug war bereits fünfmal verschoben worden, dreimal wegen schlechtem Wetter. Vor dem Start mußte die Fähre mit der Hand von Eiszapfen befreit werden. Es waren die ersten Todesopfer, die es bei US-Weltraumflügen gegeben hatte, und es war ein schwerer Schlag für ein Programm, das ohnehin wegen drastisch überzogenem Budget in großen Schwierigkeiten war.

LA navette spatiale américaine *Challenger* explosa 72 secondes après son lancement, le 28 janvier 1986, devant des millions de spectateurs horrifiés (2). Les sept personnes qui formaient l'équipage y trouvèrent la mort. Parmi les victimes, Christa McAuliffe, enseignante de son état, avait été sélectionnée pour être la première femme à voler dans le nouveau programme des « citoyens dans l'espace » (1). Le vol avait déjà été reporté cinq fois, dont trois à cause du mauvais temps. Avant la mise à feu, il avait fallu ôter à la main des glaçons fixés sur la navette. Cet accident, qui fit les premières victimes américaines de l'espace, porta un coup dévastateur à un programme qui connaissait déjà de sérieuses difficultés pour cause de dépassement spectaculaire du budget alloué.

1

2

1

Before the human guinea-pigs, the animal ones. In the 1950s animals were sent into space to see how they withstood flight conditions. Laika, the satellite dog in Sputnik III (1), achieved international fame – and indignation, when it was discovered that, mission accomplished, her food would be poisoned to prevent her dying slowly of starvation while still in orbit. In 1959, the US sent Sam (2), a 7-lb Rhesus monkey, 55 miles into space on a Project Mercury capsule. As late as 1970, NASA was performing an 'Orbiting Frog Otolith', placing two bullfrogs in a weightless environment for a period of days (3).

Vor den menschlichen Versuchskaninchen kamen die Tiere. In den 50er Jahren wurden Tiere in Raumkapseln ins All geschossen, um zu sehen, wie sie den Flug überstanden. Laika (1), die Hündin von Sputnik III, brachte es zu weltweiter Berühmtheit — und Empörung, als bekannt wurde, daß sie nach

ihrer Mission vergiftet würde, damit sie nicht in der Erdumlaufbahn verhungerte. 1959 schickten die Amerikaner den Rhesusaffen Sam an Bord einer Mercury-Kapsel in den Weltraum (2). Und noch 1970 gab es bei der NASA den »Erdumlauffrosch Otolith«: Zwei Ochsenfrösche wurden der Schwerelosigkeit ausgesetzt (3).

Les cobayes animaux ont précédé les cobayes humains. Au cours des années 50, on envoie des animaux dans l'espace afin d'observer leur comportement face aux conditions de vol. La chienne Laïka, dans Spoutnik III (1), connut le succès international. En 1959, à 89 kilomètres d'altitude, dans une capsule du projet Mercury, les États-Unis envoyèrent Sam dans l'espace (2), un singe-rhésus 7-lb. En 1970, la NASA procède au « *Orbiting Frog Otolith* » : deux crapauds-bœufs sont envoyés dans l'espace où ils resteront plusieurs jours en apesanteur (3).

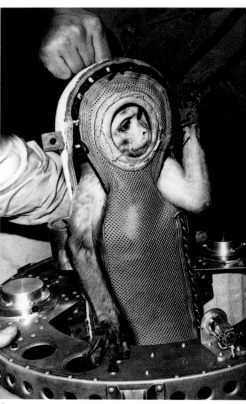

2

3

4

CHINA'S history over the last sixty years could be encapsulated in the costumes worn in these pictures. As Chairman Mao Tse-Tung addresses a meeting (1) calling for ever greater efforts against the Japanese enemy (2 – a propaganda poster in 1938), Nationalist Generalissimo Chiang Kai-Chek arrives at the 1939 meeting of the Kuomintang Nationalist Party, at which he was additionally named president of the Executive Council (4). While the Chairman's cotton kapok clothing matches that of the peasant, the Generalissimo obtains his garb from Paris outfitters. Meanwhile one of his soldiers, taken prisoner in Shantung, is given rough handling by the victorious Communists (3).

MAN könnte die ganze chinesische Geschichte der letzten sechzig Jahre aus den Kleidern ablesen, die auf diesen Bildern getragen werden. Der Parteivorsitzende Mao Tse-tung hält eine Rede (1), in der er verstärkte Anstrengungen gegen die japanischen Feinde fordert (2, ein Propagandaplakat aus dem Jahre 1938). Der Oberbefehlshaber der Nationalisten, Tschiang Kai-schek, erscheint zur Versammlung der nationalistischen Kuomintang-Partei im Jahre 1939, bei der er zusätzlich noch zum Präsidenten des Exekutivausschusses ernannt wurde (4). Der Vorsitzende Mao trägt den Baumwolldrillich der Bauern, der Oberbefehlshaber einen Pariser Maßanzug. Derweil fassen die siegreichen Kommunisten einen seiner Soldaten in Schantung nicht gerade mit Samthandschuhen an (3).

AU travers des costumes reproduits ici, on peut lire l'histoire de la Chine durant les 60 dernières années. Quand le président Mao prend la parole (1) pour demander de plus grands efforts dans la lutte contre l'ennemi japonais (2) — une affiche de propagande en 1938 ; le généralissime nationaliste Tchang Kaï-chek arrive en 1939 au meeting du Guomindang où il sera nommé président du conseil exécutif (4). Alors que les vêtements de coton du président ressemblent à ceux des paysans, le généralissime s'habille chez les couturiers français. Sur cette photographie, on peut voir l'un de ses soldats fait prisonnier à Shantung traité sans ménagements par les communistes victorieux (3).

THE Communist Youth Movement in Hanking (1) learn how to handle weapons. In 1966, Mao proclaimed a Cultural Revolution. Thousands of students, organized into Red Guards, moved around the country as here in 1967 (2), bearing banners of Mao and copies of his Little Red Schoolbook. From the same period is an example of the Red Guards' 'wall to wall' poster campaign (3).

MITGLIEDER der kommunistischen Jugendbewegung in Hangking lernen an der Waffe (1). 1966 rief Mao die Kultur-revolution aus. Tausende von Studenten, zu

Roten Garden organisiert, zogen mit Fahnen, Bildern Maos und der »Mao-Bibel« durchs Land (wie hier 1967, 2). Aus jener Zeit stammt auch das Bild von den Wandzeitungen, der Roten Garden (3).

LES membres du Mouvement de la jeunesse communiste à Hanking (1) apprennent à manier des armes. Mao proclame la Révolution culturelle. Des milliers d'étudiants organisés en Gardes rouges voyagent dans tout le pays, comme ici en 1967 (2). Un exemple de la campagne d'affichage « mur à mur » des Gardes rouges (3).

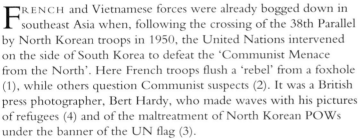

FRENCH and Vietnamese forces were already bogged down in southeast Asia when, following the crossing of the 38th Parallel by North Korean troops in 1950, the United Nations intervened on the side of South Korea to defeat the 'Communist Menace from the North'. Here French troops flush a 'rebel' from a foxhole (1), while others question Communist suspects (2). It was a British press photographer, Bert Hardy, who made waves with his pictures of refugees (4) and of the maltreatment of North Korean POWs under the banner of the UN flag (3).

DIE Fronten hatten sich in Südostasien bereits verhärtet, als nordkoreanische Truppen 1950 den 38. Breitengrad überschritten und die Vereinten Nationen auf seiten Südkoreas gegen die »kommunistische Bedrohung aus dem Norden« eingriffen. Hier holen französische Soldaten einen »Rebellen« aus einem Schützenloch (1), andere verhören verdächtige Kommunisten (2). Bert Hardy, ein britischer Pressephotograph, sorgte für Aufruhr, als er seine Bilder von Flüchtlingen (4) und von mißhandelten nordkoreanischen Kriegsgefangenen veröffentlichte (3).

LES forces françaises et vietnamiennes étaient déjà enlisées dans le Sud-Est asiatique quand les Nations unies intervinrent aux côtés de la Corée du Sud dans l'espoir d'écarter la « menace communiste du Nord ». Ici, les troupes françaises tirent un « rebelle » de son terrier (1), pendant que d'autres interrogent des suspects communistes (2). C'est un photographe de presse britannique, Bert Hardy, qui causa un grand trouble en publiant ces photos de réfugiés (4) et de prisonniers de guerre nord-coréens maltraités sous la bannière des Nations unies (3).

2

1

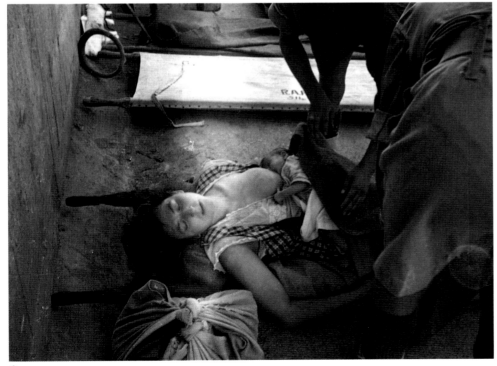

3

IN 1947 some hundreds of Jewish survivors were packed off to a detention camp in Cyprus (2, 3). And in 1948 the SS *United States* deliberately ran aground with 700 Jews on board, at Nahariya, near Haifa in Israel. The local population waded out to help bear the sick and old ashore (1).

Im Jahre 1947 erreichten einige Hundert jüdische Überlebende ein Lager auf Zypern (2, 3). Und 1948 setzte der Kapitän sein Schiff *SS United States*, mit 700 Juden an Bord, ein paar Meilen von dem Badeort Nahariya (nahe bei Haifa in Israel) absichtlich auf Grund; die Einheimischen kamen und holten die Alten und Kranken an Land (1).

EN 1947, des centaines de Juifs survivants sont envoyés dans un camp chypriote (2, 3). En 1948, le *SS United States*, avec 700 Juifs européens à son bord, arriva à Nahariya (près de Haïfa). La population locale vint aider à transporter les malades et les personnes âgées sur la terre ferme (1).

THESE Jewish Palestinian girls are celebrating the successful conclusion to a hard day's work signing up some of the 135,000 volunteering for National Service (1). The Hebrew posters over the doorway are part of the propaganda that resulted in the Israeli army being among the first to incorporate women as regular soldiers. Until 1948, Britain maintained its Palestinian mandate, searching both Jews and Arabs (2) for weapons and bombs on the streets of Jerusalem and imposing a blockade along the coast. To add to the confusion, the Irgun 'terrorist' organization (one of whose leaders, David Ben Gurion, became Israel's first Prime Minister) waged war against the then Israeli government in 1948. Their arms ship was ignited by government mortar bombs (3), destroying 600 tons of weapons.

DIESE jüdischen Mädchen in Palästina freuen sich über das Ende eines harten Arbeitstages, an dem sie einen Teil der 135.000 Freiwilligen für den Militärdienst eingeschrieben haben (1). Die hebräischen Plakate gehören zu einer Werbekampagne, in der auch Frauen zum Militärdienst berufen wurden — die israelische Armee war eine der ersten, die Frauen aufnahm. Bis 1948 war Palästina britisches Mandatsgebiet, und Juden wie Araber wurden nach Waffen und Bomben durchsucht (2); zudem gab es eine Seeblockade. Die Lage wurde noch verwirrender dadurch, daß die »Terroristen« der Gruppe Irgun Krieg gegen die offizielle israelische Regierung führten. Das Schiff, das ihnen Waffen bringen sollte, wurde von Minenwerfern der Regierungstruppen beschossen, und 600 Tonnen Waffen und Munition gingen in die Luft (3).

CES jeunes Juives installées en Palestine célèbrent l'heureuse issue d'une dure journée de travail : elles font partie des 135 000 volontaires au service national (1). Les affiches en langue hébraïque placées au-dessus de la porte aidèrent l'armée israélienne à intégrer des femmes en service régulier. Jusqu'en 1948, la Grande-Bretagne, imposant un blocus du littoral, maintint son mandat palestinien. Elle fouillait Juifs et Arabes dans les rues de Jérusalem (2) dans une hypothétique quête d'armes et de bombes. Pour ajouter à la confusion, l'Irgoun, que les Britanniques taxaient de terrorisme — l'un de ses chefs, David Ben Gourion, deviendra un Premier ministre israélien — livra une guerre farouche aux autorités. Le bateau qui abritait leurs armes fut incendié (3), détruisant pas moins de 600 tonnes d'armes.

2

3

THE British mandate ended at midnight 14/15 May 1948. Immediately Egyptian and Transjordan troops invaded Palestine. Arab Legion tanks started out several hours before the mandate expired (1). It took nearly twenty years, until 5 June 1967, for the Arab-Israeli conflict to erupt into a full-blown war. Israel, under the charismatic military leadership of General Moshe Dayan (4), emerged triumphant. On 8 June, Egypt admitted defeat (captured Egyptian troops, 2). A day later, Israel began an all-out offensive hours after Syria also accepted the ceasefire (3). Yasser Arafat (5), leader of the Palestine Liberation Organization, became the focus of mass opposition.

DAS britische Mandat endete am 15. Mai 1948. Sofort begannen ägyptische und transjordanische Truppen mit ihrer Invasion Palästinas. Die Panzer der arabischen Legion machten sich früh auf den Weg (1). Doch es dauerte fast zwanzig Jahre, bis am 5. Juni 1967 der israelisch-arabische Konflikt zu einem Krieg auswuchs. Die Israelis unter ihrem General

3

4

5

Moshe Dayan (4) waren siegreich. Am 8. Juni kapitulierten die Ägypter (ägyptische Kriegsgefangene, 2). Einen Tag darauf, nur Stunden nachdem auch Syrien den Waffenstillstand akzeptiert hatte (3), gingen die Israelis zum Großangriff über. Der Palästinenserführer Yassir Arafat (5) hatte viel Kritik einzustecken.

LE mandat britannique prit fin dans la nuit du 14 au 15 mai 1948. Les troupes égyptiennes et transjordaniennes envahirent immédiatement la Palestine. Les blindés de la Légion arabe avaient démarré plusieurs heures avant l'expiration du mandat (1). Il fallut près de vingt ans, jusqu'au 5 juin 1967, pour que la lutte israélo-arabe se mue en conflit généralisé. Israël l'emporta sous le commandement du général Moshe Dayan (4). Le 8 juin, l'Égypte reconnut sa défaite (2). Le lendemain, Israël entama une offensive générale, des heures après que la Syrie eût également accepté le cessez-le-feu (3). Yasser Arafat (5), le chef de l'Organisation de libération de la Palestine, devint l'objet d'une opposition massive.

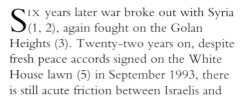

SIX years later war broke out with Syria (1, 2), again fought on the Golan Heights (3). Twenty-two years on, despite fresh peace accords signed on the White House lawn (5) in September 1993, there is still acute friction between Israelis and Palestinians, among whom the radical Hamas movement is initiating fresh direct action. Almost as the accord was signed, Palestinians adorned Jerusalem's Old City Walls with their flags and stoned Israeli police, who responded with violence (4).

SECHS Jahre darauf brach erneut Krieg mit Syrien aus (1, 2), der wiederum auf den Golan-Höhen ausgefochten wurde (3). Auch 22 Jahre später, trotz jüngster Friedensvereinbarungen, die im September 1993 auf dem Rasen des Weißen Hauses unterzeichnet wurden (5), halten die Konflikte zwischen Israelis und den

4

SIX ans plus tard, la guerre éclata avec la Syrie (1,2), et des combats se déroulèrent de nouveau sur les hauteurs du Golan (3). Vingt-deux ans plus tard, malgré les nouveaux accords de paix de septembre 1993 signés sur la pelouse de la Maison Blanche (5), il existe toujours de graves points de friction entre Israéliens et Palestiniens, tandis que le mouvement intégriste Hamas engage une nouvelle action directe. L'accord était presque signé quand des Palestiniens plantèrent leurs drapeaux sur les murs de la Vieille Ville de Jérusalem avant de lancer des pierres sur la police israélienne, dont la riposte fut violente (4).

5

Palästinensern an, deren radikale Hamas–Bewegung für neuen Zündstoff sorgt. Fast unmittelbar nach Unterzeichnung des Vertrages schmückten die Palästinenser die Wände der Jerusalemer Altstadt mit ihren Fahnen und warfen Steine auf israelische Polizisten, die zurückschossen (4).

In July 1969, shortly after the Protestants' annual Orange Day parades, violence erupted on the streets of Belfast and Londonderry (even the name was contentious, Catholics preferring to leave off the English prefix). Sympathies in the 'six counties' of Northern Ireland were sharply divided between the Protestant minority, who wanted to retain rule from Westminster, and the Roman Catholic majority, who wanted union with Eire (Ireland). While the former organized the paramilitary forces of the Ulster Freedom Fighters and the Ulster Volunteer Forces, the latter revived the military wing of the Irish Republican Army and spawned a radical new branch, the Irish National Liberation Army. In August 1969 British troops were sent in 'to keep the warring factions apart' and 'restore the peace' – the start of twenty-five further years of 'troubles'.

A cheap weapon of choice was the petrol bomb, often fired by youths (1). Street barricades were hastily thrown up from pallets and tyres (3). With youth unemployment, especially among Catholics, being the highest in the UK, many were drawn into the street fighting almost as a rite of passage to prove their manhood (2).

Im Juli 1969 kam es kurz nach den jährlichen protestantischen Umzügen zum Oraniertag zu Unruhen in Belfast und Londonderry. Die Meinungen in den »sechs Grafschaften« Nordirlands waren streng gespalten zwischen der protestantischen Minderheit, die weiterhin von Westminster aus regiert werden wollte, und der katholischen Mehrheit, die eine Vereinigung mit der Republik Irland forderte. Die Protestanten organisierten sich in den paramilitärischen Truppen der Ulster Freedom Fighters und Ulster Volunteer Forces, die Katholiken ließen den militärischen Flügel der Irisch-Republikanischen Armee wiederaufleben und gründeten einen radikalen neuen Zweig,

die Irisch-Nationale Befreiungsarmee. 1969 schickte London Truppen nach Nordirland, »um Konfrontationen zwischen den sich bekriegenden Parteien zu verhindern« und »den Frieden wiederherzustellen« — der Beginn von mittlerweile mehr als 25 Jahre währenden Unruhen.

Eine beliebte, weil billige Waffe waren Brandbomben, die oft von Jugendlichen geworfen wurden (1). Barrikaden wurden in aller Eile aus Paletten und Autoreifen errichtet (3). Die Jugendarbeitslosigkeit, gerade unter den Katholiken, war die höchste in Großbritannien, und für viele waren die Straßenkämpfe das einzige Mittel, mit dem sie ihre Männlichkeit beweisen konnten (2).

EN juillet 1969, juste après les parades annuelles des protestants pour le Orange Day, la violence éclata dans les rues de Belfast et de Londonderry (pour lequel le nom même donnait lieu à des discussions : les catholiques préférant ignorer le préfixe anglais). Les sympathies dans les « six comtés » d'Irlande du Nord étaient nettement tranchées entre la minorité protestante, qui désirait conserver la règle de Westminster, et la majorité catholique romaine qui désirait l'union avec l'Eire (Irlande du Sud). Alors que les premiers organisaient les forces paramilitaires de l'Ulster Freedom Fighters et les Ulster Volunteer Forces, les seconds faisaient renaître l'aile militaire de l'Armée

républicaine irlandaise et donnaient naissance à une nouvelle branche radicale, l'Armée de libération nationale irlandaise. En août 1969, le gouvernement britannique envoya des troupes dans le but de « séparer les factions guerrières » et de « rétablir la paix », ce qui n'eut pour autre résultat que de déclencher les « troubles » qui durent depuis vingt-cinq ans. Le cocktail Molotov, une arme bon marché, était souvent utilisé par les jeunes (1). Les barricades de rues étaient érigées à la hâte avec des caisses et des pneus (3). Les jeunes chômeurs, de plus en plus nombreux au Royaume-Uni, en particulier chez les catholiques, se mêlent aux combats de rue qui sont presque devenus un rite d'initiation à la virilité (2).

RIOT-SHIELDED British soldiers with a bleeding and unarmed protester (2). To many, the face of bigotry is that of the Reverend Ian Paisley, Ulster Unionist MP and a Protestant minister who sees the Pope as the anti-Christ. Here he is protesting away from home (1), at the celebration of a Catholic Mass at Canterbury Cathedral for the first time in 400 years in July 1970. Shortly before Christmas 1993, a mother carries her child past a PEACE sign (3). Perhaps this generation will be allowed to grow up using the streets as a thoroughfare rather than a battleground.

MIT Schilden geschützte britische Soldaten führen einen unbewaffneten, blutenden Demonstranten ab (2). Für viele die Bigotterie in Person: Reverend Ian Paisley, Parlamentsmitglied der Unionisten und protestantischer Pfarrer, für den der Papst der Antichrist ist. Hier (1) protestiert er einmal anderswo, vor der Kathedrale von Canterbury, wo im Juli 1970 zum ersten Mal seit 400 Jahren eine katholische Messe zelebriert wurde. Kurz vor Weihnachten 1993 trägt eine Mutter ihr Kind an einer Wand mit der Aufschrift PEACE vorbei (3). Vielleicht wird diese Generation die Straße wieder als Verbindungsweg von einem Ort zum anderen erleben, und nicht als Schlachtfeld.

LES soldats britanniques équipés d'une protection anti-émeute avec un manifestant blessé et sans armes (2). Le visage de la bigoterie est pour beaucoup symbolisé par celui du Révérend Ian Paisley, unioniste de l'Ulster et ministre protestant qui considère le pape comme un militant de l'Antéchrist. Ici, il manifeste loin de chez lui (1), en 1970, contre la célébration (la première depuis quatre siècles) d'une messe catholique à la cathédrale de Canterbury. Peu de temps avant Noël 1993, une mère portant son enfant passe devant un signe de la paix (3). Cette génération pourra-t-elle grandir et utiliser les rues comme des voies publiques et non comme des champs de bataille ?

1

2

3

2

3

am 15. August 1947 wurde Pandit Nehru
erster indischer Premierminister (5). Doch
die Auseinandersetzungen um die Teilung
des Landes in einen Moslemstaat Pakistan
im Norden und ein hauptsächlich von
Hindus bevölkertes Indien im Süden nahm
ein blutiges Ende: 25.000 Tote allein in
Neu-Delhi (3) und Kalkutta (1). Das
hinderte König Georg VI. nicht, dem
neuen indischen Parlament zu versichern:
»Indem Sie Ihre Unabhängigkeit durch
friedliche Verhandlungen errungen haben,
haben Sie freiheitsliebenden Völkern
überall auf der Welt ein Beispiel gegeben.«

4

5

IN April 1946 the British Cabinet
delegation to India held discussions with
the frail Hindu leader Mahatma Gandhi
(here assisted by his doctor and helper, 4).
The following year Lord Mountbatten (2,
with his wife Edwina), last Viceroy of
India, ended 150 years of British rule, and
on 15 August 1947 Pandit Nehru (5)
became first Indian Prime Minister.
However, the fighting over Partition into
the Moslem state of Pakistan to the north
and predominantly Hindu India to the
south provided a violent aftermath: 25,000
dead in New Delhi (3) and Calcutta (1)
alone. Nonetheless, King George VI

assured the new Constituent Assembly: 'In
thus achieving your independence by
agreement, you have set an example to the
freedom-loving people throughout the
world.'

IM April 1946 verhandelte eine
Delegation der britischen Regierung mit
dem Hinduführer Mahatma Gandhi (hier
von seiner Ärztin und einer Helferin
gestützt, 4) über das Schicksal Indiens. Im
folgenden Jahr erklärte der letzte
Vizekönig, Lord Mountbatten (2, mit
Gattin Edwina), die 150 Jahre britischer
Herrschaft über Indien für beendet, und

EN avril 1946, la délégation du cabinet
britannique en Inde entame des
discussions avec le frêle leader hindou
Mahatma Gandhi (soutenu ici par son
médecin et un assistant, 4). L'année
suivante, Lord Mountbatten (2, avec son
épouse Edwina), le dernier vice-roi de
l'Inde, met fin à un siècle et demi de
gouvernement britannique. Le 15 août
1947, le Pandit Nehru (5) devient Premier
ministre de l'ex-empire. Toutefois, le
conflit généré lors de la division en un État
musulman du Pakistan au nord et un État à
prédominance hindoue au sud sera très
violent : 25 000 morts rien qu'à New-
Delhi (3) et Calcutta (1). Néanmoins, le roi
George VI assure la nouvelle assemblée
constituante que : « En obtenant votre
indépendance par accord mutuel, vous
servirez d'exemple aux gens aimant la paix
de par le monde. »

1

2

3

4

BUDAPEST, 12 November 1956: uprising. In the brief moments of hope that their country might break free of the Russian occupation, these men are furiously dismantling a giant statue of Stalin (1) while others burn his portrait in a pyre of Soviet propaganda (3). Even humour enters into it, as the Russian tank has a sign hung on it with an order not to fire (2). Suspected members of the AVO (Secret Police) are subjected to summary reprisal (4). Girls as young as fifteen (5) were trained to carry guns against the Russian invasion.

AUFSTAND in Budapest, 12. November 1956. In der Hoffnung, daß ihr Land sich vom russischen Joch befreien könne, reißen diese Männer ein Standbild Stalins nieder (1), während andere sein Porträt verbrennen (3). Es war ein Aufstand mit Galgenhumor, wie dieses Schild beweist, das einen russischen Panzer auffordert, nicht zu schießen (2). Mit Mitgliedern der Geheimpolizei AVO wurde indes kurzer Prozeß gemacht (4). Selbst 15jährige Mädchen (5) übten den Umgang mit Waffen gegen die russische Invasion.

BUDAPEST, 12 novembre 1956 : le soulèvement. Lors d'une brève lueur d'espoir, ces hommes sont en train de démanteler avec fureur une statue gigantesque de Staline (1) pendant que d'autres brûlent son portrait (3). L'humour n'est d'ailleurs pas absent ; ici, le blindé russe porte une pancarte où l'on peut lire l'ordre de ne pas tirer (2). Ceux que l'on soupçonne d'appartenir à l'AVO (police secrète) sont exécutés (4). Des filles de quinze ans (5) s'entraînent à porter des armes pour lutter contre les envahisseurs soviétiques.

5

2

(Previous pages)

THE grey men taking the Red Square salute on the anniversary of the Revolution in November 1970 (1, Podgorny, Prime Minister Brezhnev, Kosygin, Suzin and others). A queue for Lenin's tomb on 25 February 1959 (2).

(vorige Seiten)

EINE graue Reihe grauer Männer nimmt auf dem Roten Platz die Parade zum Jahrestag der Revolution ab, November 1970 (1, Podgorny, Breschnjew, Kossygin, Suzin u. a.). Die Warteschlange am Lenin-Mausoleum, 25. Februar 1959 (2).

(Page précédentes)

NOVEMBRE 1970 : sur la Place rouge, une ligne de gris bureaucrates commémore la Révolution (1, Podgorny, le Premier ministre Brejnev, Kossyguine, Suzin etc.). 25 février 1959, devant le tombeau de Lénine (2).

3

L IFE in Russia, 1988, features food queues reminiscent of the starvation conditions that preceded the Revolution (1, 2). Not even the toughest Party line could legislate out the basic human need for a little romance. Here romantic and revolutionary fervour are combined for wedding couples at the Tomb of the Unknown Soldier (3).

D IE Lebensmittelknappheit in Rußland im Jahre 1988 unterschied sich nicht groß von den Hungerzeiten, die der Revolution vorangingen (1, 2). Nicht einmal der härtesten Politik gelang es, das menschliche Grundbedürfnis nach ein wenig Romantik zu vertreiben. Hier verbinden sich romantischer und revolutionärer Eifer bei einer Trauzeremonie am Grab des Unbekannten Soldaten (3).

1 988 : en Russie. Ces files indiennes caractéristiques pour obtenir de la nourriture évoquent la famine qui a précédé la Révolution (1, 2). Même la ligne la plus dure du Parti ne pouvait contrôler l'aspiration fondamentale de tout être humain au romanesque. Ici, c'est la ferveur révolutionnaire qui s'allie au romantisme chez ces couples qui ont choisi de se marier devant la tombe du Soldat inconnu (3).

1

2 3

4

5

PRAGUE, August 1968, otherwise known as the 'Prague Spring', introduced as a period of liberalization by Prime Minister Dubcek, crushed as the Russian tanks (nicknamed 'Goliaths') ploughed into the largely unarmed 'Davids' who sought to hold them back with attempts at reasoning and fraternization.

PRAG, August 1968, als der »Prager Frühling«, die Liberalisierungen des Premierministers Dubcek, von russischen Panzern niedergewalzt wird. Die »Goliaths« (wie man die Panzer nannte) überrollen die größtenteils unbewaffneten »Davids«, die sie mit Argumenten oder einfacher Herzlichkeit aufhalten wollten.

PRAGUE, août 1968. Le Printemps de Prague, annoncé comme une ère de libéralisation par le Premier ministre Dubcek, fut écrasé sous les chars soviétiques, malgré l'attitude d'une population tchèque désarmée, qui ne cherchait qu'à retenir les soviétiques, en leur faisant entendre raison et en fraternisant.

JEAN-PAUL Sartre did it. Simone de Beauvoir did it. In May 1968 it was hard to encounter anyone who *did not* have a part to play in *les événements* (1) or didn't at least claim they had, safely after the event. The Canadian writer Mavis Gallant kept a diary and observed that Sorbonne stone-throwing (4) brought forth the CRS with military responses of teargas (2) and baton charges (3): '… med. students kept out of it at the beginning, joined movement only as a reaction against the police… it wasn't safe for a doctor to help the wounded unless the doctor wore a helmet… wounded on stretchers beaten in a kind of frenzy. In Latin Quarter now, faces bruised, casts and bandages for what would seem to be ski accidents in another season, but these are fresh. Tendency of boys to behave like Old Soldiers: "I was on the barricades" like "I was in the Résistance"' (*Paris Notebooks* 1968/86).

JEAN-PAUL Sartre war dabei, Simone de Beauvoir war dabei. Im Mai 1968 war es schwer, jemanden zu finden, der *nicht* bei den *événements* dabeigewesen war (1). Die kanadische Schriftstellerin Mavis Gallant führte Tagebuch und beschreibt, wie sich die CRS von den Steinwürfen an der Sorbonne (4) zu martialischen Antworten mit Tränengas (2) und Schlagstöcken (3) hinreißen ließ: »Die Medizinstudenten hielten sich anfangs heraus und machten erst später aus Protest gegen die Polizei

1   4

mit… selbst auf die Verwundeten auf ihren Tragen schlugen sie noch in einer Art Rausch ein. Jetzt bin ich im Quartier Latin, zerschundene Gesichter, Bandagen und Gipsverbände, zu anderen Zeiten hätte man sie für die Opfer von Skiunfällen gehalten, doch die Verletzungen sind frisch. Die Jungs führen sich auf wie alte Kämpfer: ›Ich war auf den Barrikaden‹, genau wie die Alten einem ›Ich war bei der Résistance‹ erzählen«. (*Paris Notebooks*, 1968/86).

JEAN-PAUL Sartre y était. Simone de Beauvoir aussi. En mai 1968, il était fort difficile de rencontrer quelqu'un qui n'avait pas joué un rôle dans les événements, ou du moins qui le clamait très fort dès lors que tout danger semblait écarté (1). L'écrivain canadien Mavis Gallant, qui tenait son journal, observa les lanceurs de pavés de la Sorbonne (4) face aux CRS armés de gaz lacrymogènes (2) et de gourdins (3) : « Les étudiants en médecine restèrent dès le début à l'écart,

ne se joignant au mouvement que pour réagir contre la police (...) Il était risqué pour un médecin d'aider les blessés, sauf si le médecin portait un casque (...). Maintenant, au Quartier latin, des visages meurtris, des plâtres et des pansements pour ce qui ressemble à des accidents de ski survenus en une autre saison (…) Tendance des garçons à se conduire en vétérans : "J'ai fait les barricades", comme "J'étais dans la Résistance". » (*Paris Notebooks* 1968–1986)

THE early 1960s and a time of wire-laced walls (2), spotlights and sirens; Checkpoint Charlie and John Le Carré; of a miserably divided city. 'ATTENTION!: You are NOW leaving West Berlin' (1). Then, in 1989, the wall begins to come down: the first chink, seen from West (4) and East (5); with bulldozers moving in to make new crossing-points and 2.7 million East Germans given visas to go West (some of them on the Wall, 3).

DIE frühen 60er Jahre, eine Zeit der Wände mit Stacheldrähten (2), der Suchscheinwerfer und Sirenen, die Zeit von Checkpoint Charly und John Le Carré, die Zeit einer schaurig zweigeteilten Stadt. »ACHTUNG! Sie verlassen *jetzt* WEST-BERLIN« (1). Und dann, 1989, fällt die Mauer: die erste Kerbe, vom Westen aus gesehen (4), und vom Osten

1

2

3

(5); dann übernehmen die Bulldozer, um neue Übergänge zu schaffen, und 2,7 Millionen Ostdeutsche bekommen ein Visum für den Westen (ein paar von ihnen kann man hier auf der Mauer sehen, 3).

Le début des années 60, époque où les murs étaient entourés de barbelés (2), de projecteurs et de sirènes ; Check Point Charlie et John Le Carré ; temps difficiles pour une cité lamentablement divisée. « ATTENTION ! vous quittez MAINTENANT Berlin–Ouest » (1). Et puis, en 1989, le Mur a commencé à s'écrouler : la première brèche, vue de l'Ouest (4), et de l'Est (5) ; des bulldozers créent de nouveaux passages et 2,7 millions d'Allemands de l'Est, munis de visas, se rendent à l'Ouest (quelques-uns d'entre eux sur le Mur, 3).

4

5

Civil Protest

IN South Africa the introduction of apartheid in 1948 disbanded even the moderate Natives' Representative Council, leaving blacks no recourse but to work outside government dictates in order to pursue the mild but anti-segregationist policies of the Natives' Law Commission and to resist further forced deportations and cruel restrictions on their daily lives. In the United States, the foundation of the National Association for the Advancement of Coloured Peoples (NAACP) threw into relief both the aspirations and the limitations of campaigns for a better deal for those whose living conditions continued, particularly in the Southern states, to show little improvement on those of their forefathers, imported into slavery.

The sheer scope of the 'Protest Movement', as it came to be called, was tremendous. Pastors such as the Reverend Frank Chikane and Archbishop Desmond Tutu in South Africa, Martin Luther King in the United States, militant separatist Black Moslems (Malcolm X) and Black Panthers (Bobby Seale, Eldridge Cleaver, Stokeley Carmichael), all had mass followings, protesting against not only local issues but highlighting a system of injustice against which many – particularly among the young – could unite in defiance. Against them were ranged fringe extremists like the Ku Klux Klan and the Afrikaner Brotherhood (A.W.B.) who sought to revive neo-Nazi visions of racial purity based on spurious biblical texts.

The whole western protest movement could be claimed to hinge on the strikes and sit-ins that culminated in all that went by the shorthand of 'May 1968', a time of spontaneous uprising in Paris and London, Rome and Berlin, Colombia and Berkeley. Solidarity with national liberation movements around the world; opposition to the Vietnam War and US 'neo-imperialism'; concern over the relevance of much that was taught in institutes of higher education: the basic upsurge of civil rights movements worldwide was deeply idealistic, frequently religious in its motivation and romantic in its expression.

IN Südafrika wurde 1948 die Rassentrennung eingeführt und selbst der bescheidene Natives' Representative Council noch aufgelöst, so daß den Schwarzen nichts anderes übrigblieb, als sich außerhalb des Gesetzes zu stellen, wenn sie die gemäßigte, doch gegen die Apartheid gerichtete Politik der Natives' Law Commission unterstützen und sich weiterer Deportationen und unwürdigen Beschränkungen ihres täglichen Lebens widersetzen wollten. In den Vereinigten Staaten zeigte die Gründung der National Association for the Advancement of Colored Peoples (NAACP) sowohl die Hoffnungen wie auch die Grenzen von Kampagnen, die bessere Lebensbedingungen für jene schaffen wollten, die, besonders im Süden, kaum anders lebten als ihre Vorfahren, die Sklaven waren.

Die Bandbreite der »Protestbewegung« war ungeheuer. Geistliche wie Reverend Frank Chikane und Erzbischof Desmond Tutu in Südafrika, Martin Luther King in den Vereinigten Staaten, militant-separatistische Black Moslems (Malcolm X) und Black Panthers (Bobby Seale, Eldridge Cleaver, Stokeley Carmichael) hatten allesamt gewaltige Anhängerscharen und protestierten nicht nur regional begrenzt, sondern gegen das ganze ungerechte System, so daß sich viele im Protest zusammenschließen konnten. Ihnen gegenüber standen Extremisten wie der Ku-Klux-Klan oder die Afrikaner-Brüderschaft (AWB), die, gestützt auf verdrehte Bibelworte, nazihafte Vorstellungen von Rassenreinheit wiederaufleben ließen.

Angelpunkt der ganzen westlichen Protestbewegung waren die Streiks und Sit-ins, die in dem kulminierten, was man kurz »Mai '68« nennt, einer Zeit spontaner Aufstände in Paris und London, Rom und Berlin, Columbia und Berkeley. Solidarität mit nationalen Befreiungsbewegungen überall auf der Welt, Opposition gegen den Vietnamkrieg und den US-amerikanischen »Neoimperialismus«, die Frage nach dem Sinn von Universitäten: Die Grundstimmung der Bürgerrechtsbewegungen überall auf der Welt war außerordentlich idealistisch, vielfach religiös motiviert und romantisch in ihrer Art.

L'INTRODUCTION de l'apartheid en Afrique du Sud en 1948 entraîna la désagrégation du très modéré Conseil représentatif des indigènes. Dès lors, les Noirs n'eurent pas d'autre choix que celui d'agir en dehors du cadre imposé par les pouvoirs publics, d'une part pour suivre la Commission juridique des indigènes dans la voie antiségrégationniste toute modérée qui était la sienne, mais aussi pour résister à la multiplication des déportations forcées et aux vexations cruelles qu'ils subissaient dans leur vie quotidienne. Aux États-Unis, l'association nationale en faveur de la promotion des peuples de couleur (NAACP) suppléa aux limites des campagnes visant à améliorer le sort de ceux dont les conditions de vie, surtout dans les états du Sud, ne montraient guère d'amélioration par rapport à celles de leurs ancêtres amenés là en esclavage.

La portée du « Mouvement de protestation » comme on l'appela par la suite fut tout simplement immense. Il incluait des hommes d'église tels que le révérend Frank Chikane et l'archevêque Desmond Tutu en Afrique du Sud, ou encore Martin Luther King aux États-Unis, les militants séparatistes, Musulmans Noirs (les « Black Moslems » de Malcolm X) et Panthères Noires (« Black Panthers » – Bobby Seale, Eldridge Cleaver, Stokeley

Carmichael) ; ils comptaient tous de nombreux fidèles parce que leur protestation, qui allait bien au-delà de problèmes locaux prétextes, portait sur un système injuste que beaucoup – surtout parmi les jeunes – défiaient en s'unissant. Ils avaient à faire aux éléments extrémistes de tous bords, tels le Ku Klux Klan et la Fraternité afrikaner (AWB) qui cherchaient à raviver les mythes néonazis de la pureté de la race fondés sur de faux textes bibliques.

On a pu dire de l'ensemble du mouvement de protestation occidental qu'il se joua dans les grèves et les occupations de locaux qui culminèrent dans ce qu'on appela « Mai 68 », époque de soulèvements spontanés à Paris, Londres, Rome, Berlin, Columbia et Berkeley. Solidarité avec les mouvements de libération nationale de par le monde, opposition à la guerre du Viêt-nam et au « néo-impérialisme » des États-Unis, vaste remise en question de la pertinence du contenu des programmes des établissements d'enseignement supérieur : au fond, les mouvements en faveur des droits civils qui avaient surgi partout à travers le monde étaient profondément idéalistes, fréquemment religieux dans leurs motivations et romantiques dans leur expression.

THE Sharpeville massacre, provoked by
riots against the pass laws, took place
in 1960 (1). Shortly afterwards Nelson
Mandela, here photographed in discussion
with a teacher (2), earned a reputation as
the 'Black Pimpernel' for his
resourcefulness in evading arrest. The 1964
Treason Trials sentenced him and eight
others to life on Robben Island. Before his
deportation he told the Pretoria
courtroom: 'I do not deny that I planned

sabotage. We had either to accept
inferiority or fight against it by violence.'
In Johannesburg, in June 1976, three days
of uprising, leading to rioting and looting,
left over 100 dead and 1000 injured (3).
Blacks were outraged at this response to an
initially peaceful pupil-led protest,
provoked when Afrikaans was suddenly
made a compulsory subject on the school
curriculum.

IM Jahre 1960 kam es nach Aufständen
gegen die Paßgesetze zum Massaker von
Sharpeville (1). Später erwarb sich Nelson
Mandela, hier im Gespräch mit einem
Lehrer (2), seinen Ruf als »Schwarzer
Zorro«, weil er sich so geschickt immer
wieder der Verhaftung entzog. 1964 wegen
Hochverrats angeklagt, wurden er und acht
andere zu lebenslanger Haft auf Robben
Island verurteilt. Vor seiner Deportation
sagte er: »Ich leugne nicht, daß ich

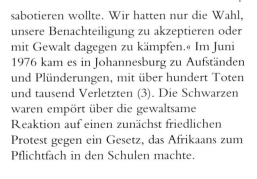

1

2

3

sabotieren wollte. Wir hatten nur die Wahl, unsere Benachteiligung zu akzeptieren oder mit Gewalt dagegen zu kämpfen.« Im Juni 1976 kam es in Johannesburg zu Aufständen und Plünderungen, mit über hundert Toten und tausend Verletzten (3). Die Schwarzen waren empört über die gewaltsame Reaktion auf einen zunächst friedlichen Protest gegen ein Gesetz, das Afrikaans zum Pflichtfach in den Schulen machte.

L E massacre de Sharpeville qui fit suite aux émeutes déclenchées par les lois entravant la libre circulation des Noirs eut lieu en 1960 (1). Nelson Mandela, que l'on voit ici photographié en discussion avec un enseignant (2), y acquit peu de temps après sa réputation de « Zorro Noir » tant il était habile à échapper aux arrestations. Jugé pour trahison en 1964, il fut condamné avec huit autres personnes à la prison à perpétuité sur Robben Island. Dans la salle

du tribunal à Prétoria il déclara : « Je ne nie pas l'intention de sabotage. Soit nous acceptions le statut d'infériorité soit nous le combattions par la violence. » À Johannesburg, en juin 1976, trois jours de soulèvements se traduisent par mille blessés et plus de cent morts (3). Les Noirs s'étaient sentis outragés par cette mesure prise en réponse à une protestation contre l'introduction soudaine de l'afrikaans obligatoire à l'école.

1

F OLLOWING the victory for the A.N.C.
on 27 April 1994, President Nelson
Mandela and Deputy President F. W. de
Klerk join hands (3). Members of the
extreme right-wing A.W.B. listen to their
leader, Eugene Terre Blanche (2), A woman
sits in the smoking ruins of her house (1).

N ach dem Wahlsieg der ANC am 27.
April 1994 heben Präsident Nelson
Mandela und F. W. de Klerk vor dem Union
Building gemeinsam die Hand (3). Derweil
lauschen Mitglieder der extrem rechtsgerich-
teten AWB ihrem Führer Eugene Terre
Blanche (2); eine Frau sitzt ratlos vor den
Ruinen ihres niedergebrannten Hauses (1).

À la suite de la victoire de l'ANC le 27
avril 1994, le président Nelson Mandela
et le vice-président F.W. de Klerk joignent
leurs bras levés (3). Ailleurs, les membres
d'extrême-droite de l'AWB écoutent leur
leader, Eugene Terre Blanche (2). Une
femme est assise au milieu de sa maison en
ruine (1).

2

3

MARCHES through the American Deep South – this one from Selma to Montgomery, Alabama, in March 1965 (1) – were a growing feature of the 1960s. Martin Luther King led 25,000 to the steps of the State Capitol to present their grievance to Governor George Wallace. Meanwhile, bombs were discovered in a black church, a funeral parlour and a leading black lawyer's home. Supporters of Adam Clayton Powell, a Harlem congressman denied his seat in 1967, shout black power slogans in protest on the steps of the House of Representatives (2). Malcolm X (3), who took the letter as his surname rather than that handed down by slavery – Little – was publicly shot dead in 1965 by a suspected Black Moslem.

MÄRSCHE im tiefen Süden Amerikas — wie hier 1965 von Selma nach Montgomery, Alabama (1) — gehörten zunehmend zum politischen Bild der 60er Jahre. Martin Luther King führte 25.000 Menschen zu den Stufen des Kapitols, wo sie ihre Sorgen Gouverneur George Wallace vortrugen. Derweil wurden Bomben in Häusern von Schwarzen

gefunden. Anhänger von Adam Clayton Powell, einem Abgeordneten aus Harlem, dem der Kongreß 1967 seinen Sitz verweigert hatte, rufen zum Protest Black-Power-Slogans auf den Stufen des Repräsentantenhauses (2). Malcolm X (3) wurde 1965 in aller Öffentlichkeit erschossen, vermutlich von einem Anhänger der Black Moslems.

2

3

La marche à travers le Sud profond américain – ici de Selma jusqu'à Montgomery, dans l'Alabama en mars 1965 (1) – est un phénomène des années 60. Martin Luther King conduisit vingt-cinq mille personnes au Capitole à Washington présenter leurs revendications au gouverneur George Wallace. Pendant ce temps on découvrait des bombes, notamment dans une

église noire. Des partisans de Adam Clayton Powell, un membre du Congrès qui défendait les intérêts de Harlem, hurlent des slogans pour le pouvoir des Noirs à la chambre des représentants (2). Malcolm X (3), qui préféra prendre ce nom plutôt que celui hérité de l'esclavage – Little – fut abattu par un homme suspecté d'appartenir aux Musulmans Noirs.

2

3

MARTIN Luther King addresses a crowd of a quarter of a million that included show business stars Marlon Brando, Burt Lancaster, Judy Garland and Bob Dylan (1, 2): 'I have a dream that one day this nation will rise up and live out the true meaning of its creed: "We hold these truths to be self-evident, that all men are created equal".' A year after President Lyndon Johnson signed the Civil Rights Act, he met with the six nuns leading the Civil Rights March from Selma, Alabama. The protest was in defiance of the police ban imposed after a gang of white supremacists attacked three liberal clergymen. One, the Rev. Reep, later died from his injuries. Pickets sitting down before the White House were bodily hauled away into police paddy wagons to be booked (3).

MARTIN Luther King spricht vor einer Viertelmillion Zuhörern, darunter die Stars Marlon Brando, Burt Lancaster, Judy Garland und Bob Dylan (1, 2): »Ich hatte einen Traum. Mir träumte, wie sich eines Tages diese Nation erheben wird und Wirklichkeit werden läßt, was sie sich auf die Fahnen geschrieben hat: »Folgende Wahrheit halten wir für selbstverständlich: daß alle Menschen gleich geboren sind.« Ein Jahr nachdem Präsident Lyndon Johnson das Bürgerrechtsgesetz unterzeichnet hatte, traf er sich mit sechs Nonnen, den Führerinnen eines Protestmarsches, der von Selma, Alabama, ausging. Diese Demonstration setzte sich über das polizeiliche Verbot hinweg, das nach einem Überfall weißer Extremisten auf drei liberale Geistliche erfolgt war. Einer von ihnen, Reverend Reep, starb später an den Folgen seiner Verletzungen. Streikposten, die sich vor dem Weißen Haus niedergelassen hatten, wurden fortgezerrt und zum Verhör gebracht (3).

MARTIN Luther King harangue une foule d'un quart de millions de personnes et parmi elles des vedettes du spectacle tels que Marlon Brando, Burt Lancaster, Judy Garland et Bob Dylan (1 et 2) : « Je rêve du jour où cette nation se lèvera pour vivre pleinement le sens véritable du credo qu'elle a fait sien : nous tenons pour évidentes ces vérités comme quoi tous les hommes ont été créés égaux. » Un an après avoir paraphé la loi sur les droits du citoyen, le président Lyndon Johnson rencontra les six religieuses qui conduisaient en mars la marche en faveur des droits civils partie de Selma dans l'Alabama. Il s'agissait d'une protestation contre les mesures d'interdiction décidées par la police après l'attaque commise sur trois religieux libéraux par une bande de militants convaincus de la supériorité blanche. Un des religieux, le révérend Reep, devait plus tard décéder des suites de ses blessures. Les manifestants qui ont installé des piquets devant la Maison blanche sont traînés à l'intérieur des cars de police (3).

1

IN summer 1979 the march for Gay Rights went right up Fifth Avenue to a rally in Central Park (1). Gays wanted to be able to come openly out of the closet and into women's clothes (if they felt like it) *and* be patriotic all-American boys (and proud of it). Over 40,000 marched in the 1983 Gay Pride Parade in New York City (2), on the anniversary of the founding of the Gay Alliance Association in Greenwich Village, formed after the police confronted gays in a bar there in 1969 and the Stonewall Riots erupted. The movement swiftly diversified so that gays became represented in a variety of occupations and, as here, their relatives too could come out in their support.

IM Sommer 1979 zog der Marsch für die Rechte der Homosexuellen mitten über die Fifth Avenue zu einer Versammlung im Central Park (1). Die Männer wollten sich offen zu ihren Neigungen bekennen können und auch in Frauenkleider schlüpfen (wenn sie dafür eine Vorliebe hatten); sie wollten trotzdem brave patriotische Jungs sein dürfen (und stolz darauf). Über 40.000 gingen 1983 für die Gay Pride Parade in New York auf die Straße (2), am Jahrestag der Gründung der Gay Alliance Association. Diese Vereinigung war 1969 in Greenwich Village gegründet worden, nachdem Polizisten gegen Männer in einer Bar vorgegangen waren und damit die sogenannten Stonewall Riots provoziert hatten. Die Bewegung verzweigte sich rasch, und Homosexuelle verschiedenster Couleur fanden dort ihr Sprachrohr. Auch die Angehörigen konnten, wie hier, mit auf die Straße gehen und demonstrieren.

EN été 1979, la marche en faveur des droits des homosexuels remonta toute la Cinquième avenue pour se terminer par un rassemblement à Central Park (1). Les homosexuels voulaient pouvoir sortir au grand jour et même s'habiller comme des femmes (si tel était leur bon plaisir) tout en étant « de bons Américains » (qui plus est fiers de l'être). Plus de quarante mille personnes prennent part à la parade des homosexuels en 1983 à New York (2) en commémoration de l'anniversaire de la fondation de l'association de l'alliance homosexuelle dans le quartier de Greenwich Village, née au lendemain de la bataille opposant forces de police et homosexuels dans un bar en 1969 et qui avait déclenché les émeutes de Stonewall. Le mouvement se diversifia bien vite de façon à représenter les homosexuels dans toute une variété d'emplois et afin que, comme ici, leurs parents puissent eux aussi manifester publiquement leur soutien.

Not every Boy Dreams of Being a Marine

GAY COMMUNITY CENTER
A PLACE OF OUR OWN

WashingtonD.C.

Miss America

2

2 3

4 5

B Y spring 1965 President Johnson was sending the Marines into Vietnam to protect the US military base at Da Nang from increasingly stringent Viet Cong guerrilla attacks. While a US soldier crouches at ease behind his automatic weapon and his skull trophy (1), a burnt-out tank lies abandoned by the road, a warning to the fleeing South Vietnamese refugees (2). A cyclist passes corpses in Hue, holding his nose to exclude the stench of death (5). By 1968 the Viet Cong Tet offensive had failed, but this was to be a classic instance of losing the battle to win the war. Not only was the US signally failing to win over the 'hearts and minds' of the South Vietnamese, but the Viet Cong were scoring one propaganda coup after another with pictures like these (2, 3, 4).

I M Frühjahr 1965 schickte Präsident Johnson die Marines nach Vietnam, wo sie die Militärbasis Da Nang vor den immer stärker werdenden Guerilla-Angriffen des Vietkong schützen sollten. Ein US-Soldat hat es sich mit seinem Gewehr und seinem Maskottchen bequem gemacht (1), und ein ausgebrannter Panzer liegt verlassen am Wegrand, eine Warnung für die vorbeizie-henden südvietnamesischen Flüchtlinge (2). Ein Radfahrer in Hué (5) hält sich die Nase zu, damit er die Leichen nicht riechen muß. 1968 war klar, daß die Tet-Offensive des Vietkong gescheitert war, doch war dies der klassische Fall einer Schlacht, die man verliert, um den Krieg zu gewinnen. Nicht genug, daß es den Amerikanern nicht gelang, »Verstand und Herz« der Südvietnamesen für sich zu gewinnen, errang der Vietkong mit Bildern wie diesen (2,3,4) einen Propagandasieg nach dem anderen.

D ÈS le printemps de 1965, le président Johnson envoyait les Marines au Viêt-nam assurer la protection de la base militaire américaine de Da Nang contre les attaques de la guérilla Viêt-cong de plus en plus virulentes. Tandis qu'un soldat américain s'accroupit derrière son arme automatique et le crâne qui est son trophée (1), un char d'assaut gît sur le côté de la route en guise d'avertissement aux réfugiés sud-vietnamiens qui fuient (2). Un cycliste dépasse des cadavres dans Hue, où règne l'odeur de la mort (5). Dès 1968 l'offensive Tet des Viêt-congs échouait, illustration du fait que perdre une bataille n'est pas perdre la guerre, bien au contraire. Non seulement les États-Unis se distinguèrent par leur incapacité à gagner les « cœurs et les esprits » des Sud-Vietnamiens, mais en plus la propagande des Viêt-congs marqua des points grâce à la diffusion d'images telles que celles-ci (2, 3 et 4).

2   3

IT was unusual for western photographers to get close enough to cover Viet Cong soldiers in action. Here the pictures are taken by a fellow Communist from eastern Europe (1). Casualties of course occurred on both sides, as the grief of this airlifted marine beside the body bag indicates (2). By April 1975 when Viet Cong encirclement forced the South Vietnamese president to flee and General Duong Van Minh to surrender Saigon, the war was over. It had taken 1.3 million Vietnamese and 56,000 US lives. There were also upwards of a million orphans, many of them badly maimed, like these two, ten-year-old Le Luy and six-year-old Cu Van Anh, who somehow managed to hold hands and walk together despite a shortage of limbs (3).

NUR selten kamen westliche Reporter nahe genug heran, um Aufnahmen des Vietkong im Feld zu machen. Dieses Bild (1) stammt von einem kommunistischen Waffenbruder, einem Photographen aus Osteuropa. Verluste gab es natürlich auf beiden Seiten, und diesem Marine, der mit einem Hubschrauber aus dem Einsatzgebiet geflogen wird, steht der Schmerz im Gesicht geschrieben (2). Im April 1975 war Saigon vom Vietkong eingekreist, der südvietnamesische Präsident floh, und General Duong Van Minh kapitulierte — der Krieg war beendet. 1,3 Millionen Vietnamesen und 56.000 Amerikaner waren umgekommen. Etwa eine Million Waisen blieben zurück, viele davon verstümmelt so wie diese beiden, der zehnjährige Le Luy und der sechsjährige Cu Van Anh, die sich trotz fehlender Gliedmaßen an den Händen fassen und zusammen spazierengehen (3).

IL n'était guère donné à des photographes occidentaux de pouvoir suffisamment s'approcher des soldats Viêt-congs en action pour les photographier. Ces photographies ont été prises par un camarade communiste d'Europe de l'Est (1). Il y avait bien sûr des victimes de part et d'autre ainsi que nous l'indique le chagrin qui se lit sur le visage de ce marin américain emporté dans les airs à côté du sac contenant un corps (2). Dès avril 1975 la guerre était terminée : le président sud-vietnamien avait été contraint à s'enfuir pour échapper à l'encerclement des Viêt-congs et le général Duong Van Minh avait présenté la capitulation de Saigon. Elle avait coûté la vie à 1,3 million de Vietnamiens et à 56 000 Américains. Elle laissait aussi plus d'un million d'orphelins, beaucoup d'entre eux effroyablement mutilés comme ceux-là, Le Luy âgé de dix ans et Cu Van Anh de six ans, qui parviennent malgré tout à marcher ensemble (3).

DEMONSTRATIONS against the Vietnam war took place in America: these (1, 2 and 3) were in Washington. The Pentagon blamed the press – singling out the iconic portrait of a little girl running naked down a road, burnt by napalm – for turning the tide of opinion and making it the most unpopular war in US history.

IN Amerika, hier in Washington (1, 2, 3), wurde gegen den Vietnamkrieg demonstriert. Das Pentagon machte die Presse dafür verantwortlich, daß dieser Krieg zum unpopulärsten in der Geschichte der Vereinigten Staaten wurde, indem sie Photos wie das eines kleines Mädchens verbreitete, das nackt und von Napalm verbrannt eine Straße hinunterläuft.

3

D<small>ES</small> manifestations hostiles à la guerre du Viêt-nam se
déroulèrent en Amérique : celles-ci (1, 2 et 3) se déroulent à
Washington. Le Pentagone en rejeta la faute sur la presse. Il
l'accusa d'avoir monté en épingle et vénéré tel un icône le portrait
d'une petite fille brûlée par le napalm courant toute nue sur la
route et provoqué un revirement de l'opinion publique, au point
que cette guerre devint la plus impopulaire de toute l'histoire des
États-Unis.

1

THE anti-war demonstrations – this one
(1) a candle-lit procession past the
White House – spread to Britain, and
erupted into violence when mounted
police and demonstrators fought outside
the American Embassy, Grosvenor Square,
London (2).

DIE Antikriegsdemonstrationen — hier
ein Kerzenzug am Weißen Haus (1)
— griffen auch nach England über, und
vor der amerikanischen Botschaft am
Londoner Grosvenor Square gingen
berittene Polizisten und Demonstranten
aufeinander los (2).

LES manifestations contre la guerre —
celle-ci (1) consiste en une procession
aux chandelles devant la Maison blanche
— gagnèrent la Grande-Bretagne où elles
donnèrent lieu à de violents accrochages
entre la police montée et les manifestants à
l'extérieur de l'ambassade américaine, à
Grosvenor Square à Londres (2).

2

Two visits to London ten years apart: Pope John Paul II paid the first papal visit to Britain in centuries when he toured England, Wales and Ireland in his 'popemobile' (2). Perhaps being Polish – the first non-Italian pope in 450 years – helped his keenness to travel. It was also the first occasion since the Reformation that a Pope and the Archbishop of Canterbury prayed together at Canterbury Cathedral, at the tomb of the martyred Thomas Becket. It was in March 1959 that the Dalai Lama, spiritual leader of Tibet, was forced to flee the holy city of Lhasa in the wake of Chinese repression of a nationalist independence movement. Chinese paratroopers were ordered to capture him alive (were he to be killed, the whole of Tibet would rise up) but he escaped, first to India and then to the West. Twenty-five years later, on a fortnight's stay in England (1), he was still urging Western governments to end cultural genocide in his homeland.

Zwei Besuche in London, und zehn Jahre liegen dazwischen: Papst Johannes Paul II. unternahm den ersten päpstlichen Besuch in Großbritannien seit Jahrhunderten und war mit dem »Papamobil« in England, Wales und Irland unterwegs (2). Vielleicht war er als Pole — der erste nicht-italienische Papst seit 450 Jahren — reiselustiger als seine Vorgänger. Es war auch das erste Mal seit der Reformation, daß ein Papst und ein Erzbischof von Canterbury gemeinsam in der dortigen Kathedrale am Grab des Märtyrers Thomas Becket beteten. Im März 1959 hatte der Dalai Lama, das geistliche Oberhaupt Tibets, aus der heiligen Stadt Lhasa flüchten müssen, als die Chinesen gegen tibetische Unabhängigkeitsbestrebungen vorgingen. Die chinesischen Fallschirmjäger hatten den Auftrag, ihn lebend zu fangen (wäre er getötet worden, hätte sich ganz Tibet erhoben), doch er entkam, zuerst nach Indien und dann in den Westen. 25 Jahre darauf kam er für zwei Wochen nach England (1), noch immer bei den Regierungen im Westen unterwegs, in der Hoffnung, daß sie etwas gegen den Völkermord in seiner Heimat unternehmen würden.

Deux visites à Londres à dix ans d'intervalle : la tournée du pape Jean-Paul II dans sa « papamobile » (2) en Angleterre, au pays de Galles et en Irlande était la première visite effectuée depuis des siècles par un pape en Grande-Bretagne. Le fait d'être Polonais — le premier pape non italien en quatre cent cinquante ans — est peut-être un facteur important quant à sa propension aux voyages. Cette visite offrait aussi au pape et à l'archevêque de Canterbury, depuis la Réforme, une occasion de prier ensemble dans la cathédrale de Canterbury et sur la tombe du martyr Thomas Becket. C'est en mars 1959 que le dalaï-lama, chef spirituel du Tibet, se vit contraint de fuir la cité sainte de Lhassa après que les Chinois eurent écrasé le mouvement nationaliste. Les parachutistes chinois avaient reçu l'ordre de le capturer vivant (sa mort aurait provoqué un soulèvement dans tout le Tibet) ; celui-ci, toutefois, réussit à s'échapper pour se réfugier d'abord en Inde puis en Occident. Vingt-cinq ans plus tard, profitant d'un séjour de deux semaines en Angleterre (1), il continuait d'inviter instamment les gouvernements occidentaux à mettre un terme au génocide culturel perpétré contre sa patrie.

1

(*Previous pages*)

A whirlpool of pilgrims in a 500-year-old ceremony: hundreds of thousands of pilgrims make their once-in-a-lifetime *Hajj* (journey to Mecca) and perform the *Tawaf* (sevenfold circling of the Ka'bah). This is the first house of God built on earth by Abraham and his son Ishmael, in the corner of which is embedded a black meteorite hurled by God at the disgraced Adam. Pilgrims are expected to kiss the stone or, at the very least if the crowds are too dense, point at it with the incantation: 'In the Name of God, God is Supreme'.

(*vorige Seiten*)

EIN Meer von Pilgern bei einer fünfhundert Jahre alten Zeremonie: Hunderttausende machen einmal im Leben ihre Hadsch (Wallfahrt nach Mekka) und vollziehen den Tawaf (siebenmaliges Umrunden der Kaaba). Dies ist das erste Gotteshaus auf Erden, errichtet von Abraham und seinem Sohn Ishmael, und in der Ecke eingeschlossen ist ein schwarzer Meteorit, den Gott dem gefallenen Adam nachschleuderte. Die Pilger sollen den Stein küssen, doch wenn der Andrang zu groß ist, genügt es, darauf zu zeigen und zu rufen: »Im Namen Allahs, Allah ist groß!«

(*pages précédentes*)

TOURBILLON de pèlerins au cours d'une cérémonie vieille de cinq cents ans : des dizaines de milliers de pèlerins effectuant leur *Hadj* (pèlerinage à La Mecque), que l'on doit faire une fois dans sa vie, exécutent le *Tawaf* (sept fois le tour de la *Ka'ba*). Voici la première maison de Dieu bâtie sur la terre par Abraham et son fils Ismaël. On y aperçoit, encastrée dans un coin, la météorite noire que le Seigneur projeta sur Adam tombé en disgrâce. Les pèlerins sont censés baiser la pierre ou, quand la foule se fait trop dense, se tourner vers le Seigneur en entonnant l'incantation : « Au nom de Dieu, Dieu est suprême. »

IT was with the Iranian Revolution of
1979 that a wave of politicized militancy
swept through the Moslem world (3).
Having forced their Shah into peripatetic
exile, the Iranians called on other Moslem
countries likewise to depose and replace
their 'westernized' rulers. Called
'fundamentalism' by non-Moslems, the
revolution was epitomized by the creation
of a theocratic Islamic state by Ayatollah
Khomeini (whose picture is carried
through Tehran, 1) and by these women
standing guard in Tehran (2) – women
issued with modern weapons but directed
to wear medieval clothing, with heavy
penalties for uncovering their arms or hair.

IN der Folge der iranischen Revolution
von 1979 ging eine Welle der
Politisierung und Militarisierung durch die
islamische Welt (3). Nachdem die Iraner
den Schah in ein klägliches Exil
gezwungen hatten, riefen sie ihre
moslemischen Brüder auf, ihnen
nachzueifern und ebenfalls ihre
»verwestlichten« Herrscher abzusetzen.
Sinnbilder dieser Revolution, die die
Ungläubigen »Fundamentalismus« nennen
und die einen theokratischen islamischen
Staat begründete, sind der Ayatolla
Khomeini (dessen Bild hier durch die

Straßen Teherans getragen wird, 1) und
diese Frauen, die in Teheran Wache halten
(2) — Frauen, die moderne Gewehre,
doch mittelalterliche Kleidung tragen, bei
schwerer Strafe, wenn sie Arme oder Haar
entblößen.

AVEC la révolution iranienne de 1979,
le monde musulman fut traversé par
une vague de militantisme politico-
religieux sans précédent (3). Après avoir
contraint leur Chah à errer en exil, les
Iraniens exhortèrent les autres pays
musulmans à déposer eux aussi leurs
« dirigeants occidentalisés ». Taxée de
« fondamentaliste » par les non-musulmans,
la révolution se traduisit par l'instauration
d'un état islamique théocratique avec
l'ayatollah Khomeyni à sa tête (dont le
portrait est arboré à travers les rues de
Téhéran, 1). Ces femmes qui montent la
garde à Téhéran (2), équipées d'armes
modernes, sont cependant enjointes de
s'habiller de façon médiévale au risque
d'encourir de lourdes peines en cas de
désobéissance.

O N 21 October 1966 (the last schoolday before the half-term holiday) Pantglas Junior School in Aberfan, South Wales, was buried beneath a giant slag-heap that engulfed it during heavy rains. During the miserable search through the sludge for bodies (1, 2), it turned out that nearly 200 people, from the school and 18 houses, had been entombed. Most were children, as can be seen by the diminutive coffins on the hillside above Aberfan (3). There were no survivors. The bad weather may have been 'natural' but the slag-heap, a relic of Wales's mining industry, was manmade, as was 'the disaster waiting to happen'. It was simply too near the village for safety.

A M 21. Oktober 1966 (dem letzten Schultag vor den Herbstferien) wurde die Pantglas Junior School in Aberfan, Südwales, unter einer gewaltigen Abraumhalde begraben, die bei schwerem Regen ins Rutschen gekommen war. An die 200 Menschen waren in der Schule und in 18 Häusern verschüttet, und verzweifelt wurde nach den Opfern gesucht (1, 2). Die meisten waren Kinder, wie man an den winzigen Särgen auf dem Hügel sehen kann (3). Es gab keine Überlebenden. Das schlechte Wetter mag »natürlich« gewesen sein, doch es war eine »Katastrophe, die nur darauf wartete, daß sie geschah«.

C E 21 octobre 1966 (le dernier jour d'école avant les vacances scolaires trimestrielles), l'école Pantglas Junior School à Aberfan, au pays de Galles, fut submergée par un terril qu'entraînèrent des pluies torrentielles. Les recherches entreprises pour retrouver les corps sous les tonnes de boue se déroulèrent dans des conditions épouvantables (1, 2) : environ 200 personnes de l'école et 18 habitants des maisons environnantes avaient été ensevelis. Il s'agissait pour la plupart d'enfants (3). Il n'y eut aucun survivant. Le mauvais temps était un phénomène inévitable, mais le terril était surtout beaucoup trop proche du village pour être inoffensif.

1

3

1

2

DESPITE the Clean Air Act of 1956, Manchester in the 1970s suffered from a yellowish fog caused by polluting emissions (3). The 1974 Nypro chemical plant disaster killed 28 outright and turned Flixborough into a ghost village (1). Twenty years later the oil tanker *Braer* ran aground after losing power in a storm (2).

OBWOHL es seit 1956 Gesetze gegen Luftverschmutzung gab, litt Manchester noch in den 70er Jahren unter gefährlichen Rauchschwaden aus den Schornsteinen (3). Das Unglück im Chemiewerk Nypro 1974 tötete 28 Menschen und machte aus Flixborough ein Geisterdorf (1). Zwanzig Jahre später lief der Öltanker *Braer* im Sturm auf Grund (2).

EN dépit de la loi sur l'air propre de 1956, Manchester étouffait encore dans un brouillard jaunâtre dans les années 70 (3). L'usine chimique de Nypro, en 1974, tua 28 personnes et transforma Flixborough en village fantôme (1). Le pétrolier *Braer* s'échoua vingt ans après sa panne (2).

3

1

IN December 1988, a Pan-American Boeing 747 jet suddenly exploded and crashed into the Scottish border town of Lockerbie. The plane came down in a fireball (1), torching a row of houses (2), killing all 259 passengers on board and at least 11 on the ground, making it Britain's worst-ever air disaster. The plane, on a flight to New York, broke up so rapidly that the crew were unable to send any message. It later became clear that a bomb had been the cause. Nothing whatever remained of some of the bodies, although debris was scattered widely (3).

IM Dezember 1988 explodierte eine Boeing 747 der Pan-American und stürzte in das Städtchen Lockerbie an der schottischen Grenze. Das Flugzeug ging in einem Feuerball nieder (1) und setzte eine Reihe von Häusern in Brand (2). Alle 259 Menschen an Bord kamen um, dazu mindestens elf am Boden. Das Flugzeug, das sich auf dem Weg nach New York befand, zerbarst so schlagartig, daß die Besatzung keinen Hilferuf mehr senden konnte. Untersuchungen ergaben, daß eine Bombe an Bord gewesen war. Die Trümmer lagen in weitem Umkreis verstreut (3).

EN décembre 1988, un Boeing 747 de la Pan Am explosa en vol avant de s'écraser sur la ville écossaise frontalière de Lockerbie. L'avion, véritable boule de feu (1), embrasa une rangée de maisons (2), causa la mort des 259 passagers avant d'écraser au moins 11 personnes au sol. L'avion se rompit si vite qu'il n'eut pas même le temps d'envoyer un message. L'enquête révéla par la suite qu'une bombe était à l'origine de l'accident. Il ne resta absolument rien de certains corps, malgré le fait que les débris fussent dispersés dans un rayon étendu (3).

2

3

SYDNEY, Australia, at the height of summer, January 1994. Flames from a massive forest fire look set to engulf the northern suburbs as hundreds of residents are evacuated (1). One Lindfield local hoses his roof down in the attempt to avoid losing his home (2), but the firestorms raged out of control statewide. Night is turned to day as flames illuminate the sky in what local police insist is either a careless or callous act of multiple arson.

SYDNEY, Australien, im Hochsommer, Januar 1994. Die Flammen eines gewaltigen Waldbrandes scheinen die nördlichen Vororte zu umschließen, und Hunderte von Einwohnern werden evakuiert (1). Im Stadtteil Lindfield bespritzt ein Bewohner sein Haus mit Wasser, in der Hoffnung, es dadurch zu retten, doch der Feuersturm geriet im ganzen Bundesland außer Kontrolle. Die Flammen machen die Nacht zum Tage.

SYDNEY, en Australie, au plus fort de l'été. Janvier 1994. Les flammes d'un gigantesque incendie de forêt semblent sur le point de dévorer les banlieues nord, dont les résidents sont évacués (1).Un habitant de Lindfield arrose en vain son toit (2). La nuit est transformée en jour par les flammes qui illuminent le ciel. La police locale répète à qui veut l'entendre que les incendies multiples sont causés par la négligence ou l'indifférence.

1

2

1

E VEN disasters can have their comical aspects. The 1993 floods in Faidhabad, Northern India, bring out children jumping from back to back of the buffaloes marooned in village floodwaters (1). Across Haryana. In the same month, but across the world in West Quincy, Illinois, a McDonald's billboard, still illuminated, pokes up from the Mississippi River after a levée burst (3). The Mayon volcano in the Philippines erupts in cascades of dust and lava (2). The Los Angeles earthquake of January 1994 created havoc through the city, with thousands (particularly the poorer people) still homeless eighteen months later. Here paramedic Dave Norman hoists rescue equipment in a tiny crevice of a collapsed parking lot (4).

S ELBST Katastrophen können ihre komischen Seiten haben. Bei den Überschwemmungen im nordindischen Faidhabad, 1993, springen Kinder von einem Büffelrücken zum anderen, denn die Tiere sitzen im Wasser fest (1). Im selben Monat, doch am anderen Ende der Welt, steht in West Quincy im amerikanischen Bundesstaat Illinois ein Reklameschild von McDonald's, noch immer beleuchtet, nach einem Dammbruch in den Fluten des Mississippi (3). Beim Ausbruch des Vulkans Mayon auf den Philippinen steigen Rauchwolken und Lava auf (2). Das Erdbeben in Los Angeles im Januar 1994 richtete in der ganzen Stadt Verwüstungen an, und Tausende (gerade in den ärmeren Vierteln) waren auch anderthalb Jahre später noch ohne Unterkunft. Hier läßt der Rettungssanitäter Dave Norman seine Ausrüstung durch einen winzigen Spalt in ein eingestürztes Parkhaus hinab (4).

2

3

4

LES catastrophes elles-mêmes comportent parfois certains aspects comiques. Les inondations de 1993 à Faidhabad, dans le nord de l'Inde, donnent aux enfants l'idée de bondir du dos d'un buffle abandonné à l'autre dans le village inondé (1). Le même mois, mais à l'autre bout du monde, plus exactement à West Quincy dans l'Illinois, l'enseigne du McDonald, qui est restée illluminée, surnage sur le Mississipi après l'affaissement d'une levée (3). Le volcan Mayon en éruption aux Philippines projette des cascades de poussière et de lave (2). Le tremblement de terre à Los Angeles en janvier 1994 sema la destruction dans la ville, laissant des milliers de gens (notamment les plus pauvres) dix-huit mois après, toujours sans foyer. On voit ici Dave Norman, membre des services paramédicaux, hisser du matériel de secours à l'intérieur d'une minuscule faille qui s'est creusée dans un lot de places de stationnement effondré (4).

2

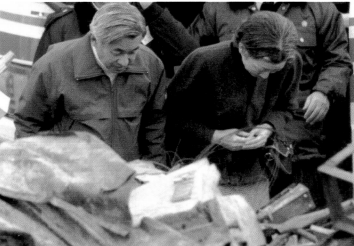

4

T HE city of Kobe, Japan, was the epicentre of an earthquake which killed over 7000 people in 1995 (1, 3). Cycles become the only functional means of transport (2). Emperor Akihito and Empress Michiko tour the disaster area (4).

D IE japanische Stadt Kobe lag im Zentrum eines Erdbebens, bei dem 1995 siebentausend Menschen umkamen (1, 3). Fahrräder waren die einzigen Transportmittel, mit denen man noch durchkam (2). Kaiser Akihito und Kaiserin Michiko besuchen das Katastrophengebiet (4).

L A cité de Kobe, au Japon, se trouvait sur l'épicentre du tremblement de terre qui tua plus de sept cent mille personnes en 1995 (1 et 2). Les bicyclettes sont devenues les seuls moyens de transport fonctionnels (2). L'empereur Akihito et l'impératrice Michiko se rendent sur les lieux sinistrés (4).

3

1

MOST of England's home matches were played at league club grounds until the 1950s, despite the availability of Wembley Stadium, which staged its first international in 1924 (England drawing 1-1 with Scotland). In fact until 1951, the only international matches played at Wembley were those between England and Scotland. White Hart Lane, the home of Tottenham Hotspur, hosted this match between England and France, England winning 4-1. Before the kick-off, the respective captains pose with three exotically dressed ladies (1).

DIE meisten Heimspiele der englischen Nationalmannschaft wurden bis in die 50er Jahre hinein auf den Plätzen der Fußballclubs gespielt, obwohl das Wembley Stadion zur Verfügung stand, wo das erste internationale Spiel 1924 stattgefunden hatte (England gegen Schottland, 1:1). Bis 1951 blieben die Spiele England gegen Schottland die einzigen internationalen, die in Wembley ausgetragen wurden. White Hart Lane, Heimat der Tottenham Hotspurs, war Schauplatz dieses Länderspiels England gegen Frankreich, das die Engländer 4:1 gewannen. Vor dem Anstoß lassen sich die Mannschaftskapitäne mit exotisch gewandeten Damen aufnehmen (1).

JUSQUE dans les années 50, malgré un stade de Wembley tout à fait disponible, la plupart des matchs joués à domicile par l'Angleterre se déroulaient sur les terrains des clubs de *League*. C'est en 1924 qu'on organisa à Wembley le premier match international (l'Angleterre ayant fait égalité 1 à 1 avec l'Écosse). De fait, jusqu'en 1951, les seuls matchs internationaux disputés à Wembley furent ceux qui mettaient en présence les équipes d'Angleterre et d'Écosse. White Hart Lane, la patrie de Tottenham Hotspur, accueille cette rencontre opposant l'Angleterre et la France, que la première remportera 4 à 1. Avant le coup d'envoi, les capitaines des équipes respectives se font photographier près de trois dames habillées de façon exotique (1).

2

ENGLAND (in dark shirts) score in the 3-1 victory over newly-crowned world champions West Germany at Wembley, December 1954 (2). Two of England's goalscorers are in the photograph; number 8 Roy Bentley (Chelsea) and, facing the camera, Ronnie Allen (West Bromwich Albion). Seven months earlier, England suffered a humiliating 7-1 defeat at the hands of Hungary in a pre-World Cup friendly played in Budapest. The 'Magical Magyars', as they were known, reached the final of the World Cup that year only to lose 3-2.

ENGLAND (im dunklen Trikot) erringt in Wembley einen 3:1-Sieg über den frischgekürten Weltmeister Westdeutschland, Dezember 1954 (2); zwei der englischen Torschützen sind zu sehen: Roy Bentley (Chelsey), Nummer 8, und, mit Blick in die Kamera, Ronnie Allen (West Bromwich Albion). Sieben Monate zuvor hatten die Engländer bei einem Freundschaftsspiel im Vorfeld der Weltmeisterschaft in Budapest eine beschämende 7:1-Niederlage einstecken müssen. Die »Magischen Magyaren«, wie sie genannt wurden, kamen ins Weltmeisterschafts-Endspiel jenes Jahres, doch sie verloren 3:2.

L'ANGLETERRE (en maillot sombre) marquant un but au cours de la rencontre à Wembley remportée 3 à 1 contre l'Allemagne de l'Ouest, alors tout récemment sacrée championne du monde en décembre 1954 (2). Deux buteurs de l'équipe anglaise photographiés : le maillot numéro 8 de Roy Bentley (Chelsea) et, faisant face à l'objectif, Ronnie Allen (West Bromwich Albion). Sept mois plus tôt, l'Angleterre avait subi une défaite humiliante, battue 7 à 1 par la Hongrie à Budapest à l'issue du match amical précédant la Coupe du monde. Les « Magyars magiques », comme on les nommait, parvinrent la même année jusqu'à la finale de la Coupe du monde qu'ils perdirent avec deux buts à trois.

ENGLISH football captain Bobby Moore being chaired after England's victory over West Germany in the 1966 World Cup Final, which had 50 per cent of the British population tuned in (1). Moore, a West Ham United player, won 108 caps in his career – more than any other professional. At the final of the Soccer World Championships in 1974, West Germany won 2-1 against Holland to become World Champions. Here team member Franz Beckenbauer is embraced by coach Helmut Schon at the end of the match (2). Brazilian player Zito celebrates scoring a second goal in his country's International against Czechoslovakia, played in Santiago, Chile, in 1962 (3). Brazil went on to win 3-1. Pele, the most famous Brazilian player of all time, displaying the trophy (4) after he helped Brazil win the 1970 World Cup in Mexico.

3

4

DER Kapitän der englischen Mannschaft, Bobby Moore, wird nach dem Sieg über Westdeutschland im Endspiel um den Weltmeisterschaftstitel 1966, ein Spiel, bei dem die Hälfte der britischen Bevölkerung an den Fernseh- und Radiogeräten saß, auf die Schultern gehoben (1). Moore, der für West Ham United spielte, wurde im Laufe seiner Karriere 108mal für die Nationalmannschaft aufgestellt — mehr als jeder andere Profifußballer. Im Endspiel des Jahres 1974 gewann Westdeutschland gegen Holland 2:1. Hier wird Franz Beckenbauer am Ende des Spiels von Trainer Helmut Schön umarmt (2). Der brasilianische Spieler Zito freut sich im Länderspiel gegen die Tschechoslowakei, 1962 in Santiago de Chile, über sein zweites Tor (3). Brasilien gewann 3:1. Der Brasilianer Pelé, der berühmteste Fußballspieler aller Zeiten (4), hebt stolz den Weltmeisterschaftspokal des Jahres 1970, den die Brasilianer in Mexiko gewannen.

LE capitaine de l'équipe anglaise de football, Bobby Moore, est porté en triomphe après la victoire de l'Angleterre sur l'Allemagne de l'Ouest à la finale de la Coupe du monde en 1966, qui fut suivie à la radio par 50 % de la population britannique (1). Moore remporta 108 trophées au cours de sa carrière — plus que tout autre joueur professionnel. À la finale du championnat du monde, en 1974, l'Allemagne de l'Ouest battit la Hollande 2 à 1 et devint ainsi championne du monde. On voit ici le joueur Franz Beckenbauer embrassé par l'entraîneur Helmut Schon à la fin du match (2). Le joueur brésilien Zito, fou de joie après son deuxième but au cours de la rencontre avec la Tchécoslovaquie. C'était à Santiago, au Chili, en 1962 (3). Le Brésil continua sur sa lancée en l'emportant 3 à 1. Pelé, le joueur brésilien le plus célèbre de tous les temps, (4), après la victoire du Brésil lors de la Coupe du monde de Mexico en 1970.

WEST Germany's centre forward Uwe Seeler is brought down by Uruguay's Manicera in the 1966 World Cup quarter-finals (1). Barcelona's captain Johan Cruyff, Holland's most gifted international, disputing his sending off before being escorted away by two policemen (2). George Best here seen in 1976 with Fulham at the twilight of his outstanding career (3). Argentina's Diego Maradona (4), valued in the 1970s at £3m, and possibly the greatest player ever, sabotaged his later career through drugs. Pelé celebrates with tears after Brazil's victory in the 1970 World Cup Final (5).

DER westdeutsche Mittelstürmer Uwe Seeler wird beim Weltmeisterschafts-Viertelfinale 1966 von Manicera aus Uruguay zu Fall gebracht (1). Hollands begabtester internationaler Spieler Johan Cruyff, der als Kapitän für Barcelona spielte, protestiert gegen seinen Platzverweis, doch zwei Polizisten eskortieren ihn vom Feld (2). George Best,

3

4

5

hier 1976 mit Fulham gegen Ende seiner
Karriere (3). Der Argentinier Diego
Maradona (4) war einer der größten
Fußballspieler überhaupt; später machte
ihm Kokainsucht schwer zu schaffen. Pelé
mit Freudentränen, als Brasilien 1970 den
Weltmeisterschaftstitel erringt (5).

S EELER, l'avant-centre allemand, est
envoyé au sol par Manicera, joueur
uruguayen, au cours des quarts de finale de
la Coupe du monde en 1966 (1). Le
capitaine de Barcelone, Johan Cruyff,
talentueux international hollandais,
conteste son expulsion du terrain avant de
s'exécuter, escorté par deux policiers (2).
George Best, qu'on voit ici en 1976 jouer
pour Fulham à l'époque mal connue de sa
remarquable carrière (3). L'Argentin Diego
Maradona (4), estimé à trois millions de
livres dans les années 70, sans doute le plus
formidable joueur de tous les temps, dont
la fin de carrière fut sabotée par la cocaïne.
Pelé pleure de joie lors de la Coupe du
monde en 1970 (5).

Suzanne Lenglen in play at the Wimbledon Lawn Tennis Championships, which she won in 1925 (1). Fred Perry, playing here in the men's semi-finals in 1936, won the men's singles for the third year running (2). In 1975, US player Arthur Ashe made tennis history to become the first black Wimbledon champion (3). Björn Borg's double-handed grip served to confuse the opposition as to whether he was coming in for a forehand or backhand shot. Here he is in action against Yugoslav Nicky Pilic in 1977 (4). He was unbeaten at Wimbledon between 1976 and 1980. Martina Navratilova (5) went on to win the Wimbledon women's singles nine times before retiring in 1994 after missing the much sought-after tenth record-breaking triumph.

Suzanne Lenglen in voller Aktion beim Tennisturnier in Wimbledon, das sie im Jahre 1925 gewann (1). Fred Perry, hier im Halbfinale der Männer 1936, gewann den Pokal drei Jahre in Folge (2). 1975 machte der Amerikaner Arthur Ashe Tennisgeschichte als erster schwarzer Wimbledonsieger (3). Björn Borgs doppelhändiger Griff verwirrte den Gegner, der nie wußte, ob er Vor- oder Rückhand spielen würde. Hier sieht man ihn 1977 im Match gegen den Jugoslawen Nicky Pilic (4). Zwischen 1976 und 1980 konnte ihn keiner in Wimbledon schlagen. Martina Nawratilowa (5) gewann das Frauen-Einzel neunmal; 1994 beendete sie ihre Karriere, nachdem ihr der zehnte Triumph, mit dem sie einen neuen Rekord aufgestellt hätte, nicht geglückt war.

Suzanne Lenglen, vainqueur au championnat de tennis à Wimbledon en 1925 (1). Fred Perry, qu'on voit ici disputer les demi-finales messieurs en 1936, remporta le simple messieurs pour la troisième année consécutive (2). En 1975, le joueur américain Arthur Ashe fut le premier champion Noir vainqueur à Wimbledon (3). Björn Borg, dont le jeu à deux mains désorientait ses adversaire. Le voici en action en 1977 contre le Yougoslave Nicky Pilic (4). Il resta invincible à Wimbledon de 1976 à 1980. Martina Navratilova (5) y remporta neuf fois le simple dames. Jusqu'à sa retraite, en 1994, elle ne parviendra pas à battre le record du monde en remportant la dixième victoire nécessaire.

1

2   3

4   5

2

Other star names of the 1980s
included Gabriela Sabatini of
Argentina (1), whose stunning looks caused
quite a stir, and Ivan Lendl, the Czech who
repeatedly returned without ever quite
winning (2). West German Boris Becker,
coached since early childhood by his father,
won in both 1985 and 1986 (3), while
American André Agassi became as famous
for his fashions (which included shaving his
chest and legs) as for his play (4).

Weitere Tennisstars der 80er Jahre in
Wimbledon waren die Argentinierin
Gabriela Sabatini (1), die auch als Schönheit
Aufsehen erregte, und der Tscheche Ivan
Lendl, der immer wieder dabei war und
doch nie gewann (2). Boris Becker, schon
als Kind von seinem Vater trainiert, siegte
1985 und 1986 (3). Der Amerikaner André
Agassi war für sein Modebewußtsein (er
rasierte sich Brust und Beine) ebenso
berühmt wie für sein Spiel (4).

1

3

Parmi les autres étoiles des années 80, on trouve l'Argentine Gabriela Sabatini (1), dont les tenues époustouflantes ne manquaient pas de susciter l'émoi, ainsi qu'Ivan Lendl, le Tchèque qui revenait toujours sans jamais vraiment parvenir à décrocher la victoire (2). L'Allemand Boris Becker, entraîné par son père depuis sa plus tendre enfance, fut vainqueur en 1985 et en 1986 (3), tandis que l'Américain André Agassi se rendait autant célèbre par ses fantaisies (comme celle de se raser la poitrine et les jambes) que par son jeu (4).

4

THE 1936 Olympic Games: those cheering wear logos as diverse as India and Brazil (1). The Olympic torch is run into the stadium beneath ranked banners of swastikas surmounted with eagles (2). Jesse Owens, US sprinter and long-jumper, is seen practising on board the SS *Manhattan* (3), on his way to represent his country – against Hitler's expressed wishes.

OLYMPISCHE Spiele 1936: begeisterte Zuschauer, darunter Inder und Brasilianer (1). Das olympische Feuer wird ins Stadion getragen, das vor adlergekrönten Hakenkreuzflaggen startt (2). Jesse Owens, Läufer und Weitspringer aus den USA, übt noch an Bord der *SS Manhattan*, um sein Land, gegen Hitlers ausdrücklichen Wunsch, zu vertreten (3).

LES Jeux olympiques de 1936 : ceux qui acclament portent des inscriptions aussi diverses que « Inde » et « Brésil » (1). La flamme olympique traverse une rangée de croix gammées et d'aigles (2). L'Américain Jesse Owens, sprinter et sauteur en longueur, s'entraînant à bord du *Manhattan* (3), pour aller représenter son pays, contre les vœux de Hitler.

IN Tokyo in 1991, Carl Lewis (USA) set a new men's 100m record (1). In 1992 Linford Christie (UK) won the silver at the Barcelona Olympics 100m (3, 4). In the 1993 World Championships, the US (gold) and British (silver) 100m teams celebrate (2).

IN Tokio stellte der Amerikaner Carl Lewis 1991 einen neuen 100-Meter-Rekord auf (1). 1992 gewann Linford Christie Silber im Hundertmeterlauf bei den Olympischen Spielen in Barcelona (3, 4). Bei der WM 1993 jubeln das amerikanische (Gold) und das britische 100-Meter-Team (Silber, 2).

À Tokyo, en 1991, Carl Lewis (États-Unis) a le nouveau record du 100 m (1). En 1992, Linford Christie (G.-B.) est second du 100 m aux JO de Barcelone (3, 4). Aux championnats du monde de 1993, américains (or) et britanniques (argent) du 100 m fêtent leur victoire (2).

RUSSIAN Olga Korbut, aged 20 here in 1975, rehearsing for the World Athletics Championships (1), following up her successes in the Olympic Games. Gwang-Suk Kim, of the People's Republic of (North) Korea, was another precocious 'wonder child', here seen performing on the asymmetric bars at the 1992 Barcelona Olympics (2).

DIE Russin Olga Korbut, hier 1975 mit zwanzig Jahren (1), trainiert nach ihrem großen Erfolg bei den Olympischen Spielen für die Leichtathletik-Weltmeisterschaft. Gwang-Suk Kim aus Nordkorea, ebenfalls ein »Wunderkind«, am Stufenbarren bei den Olympischen Spielen 1992 in Barcelona (2).

LA Russe Olga Korbut, alors âgée de vingt ans en 1975, se prépare ici aux championnats du monde d'athlétisme (1), après ses succès aux Jeux olympiques. Gwang-Suk kim, de la république populaire de Corée (du Nord), était un autre de ces « jeunes talents » précoces : on le voit ici aux barres asymétriques pendant les Jeux olympiques de Barcelone en 1992 (2).

2

CYCLING supremo Chris Broadman (UK), on his special streamlined machine and wearing a similarly aerodynamic helmet, wins the 'individual pursuit' category at the 1992 Barcelona Olympics.

DAS britische Radsportidol Chris Broadman auf seinem besonders windschnittigen Gefährt und mit einem ebenso aerodynamischen Helm auf dem Weg zum Sieg in der Kategorie »individuelle Verfolgungsfahrt« bei den Olympischen Spielen in Barcelona, 1992.

CHRIS Broadman (G.-B.), sur sa bicyclette aux lignes aérodynamiques, porte un casque également aérodynamique, et remporte la victoire dans la catégorie de la « poursuite individuelle » aux Jeux olympiques de Barcelone en 1992.

MR and Mrs Joe Louis take a stroll in 1936 (1). The following year he won the World Heavyweight Championship, holding it until 1949, the longest reign ever. In July 1951, Sugar Ray Robinson was caught by photographer Bert Hardy, practising at a gym in Paris shortly before his British match against Randolf Turpin (2). Robinson lost nine out of fifteen rounds and needed 14 stitches over his eye. This US heavyweight is the only champion ever to win under two names – first as Cassius Clay in 1964, then, after his conversion to Islam, as Muhammed Ali ten years later. He never missed an opportunity to say that he was the greatest champion of all time – and he probably was. He is pictured giving Sonny Liston 'a good whuppin' (his description) in their 1964 world title fight (3). Two years later, Muhammed Ali was pictured training at the Territorial Army Gymnasium, White City, London (4).

MR. Joe Louis und Gattin machen einen Spaziergang, 1936 (1). Im folgenden Jahr wurde Joe Louis Weltmeister im Schwergewicht und hielt diesen Titel bis 1949, länger als jeder andere. Der Photograph Bert Hardy hielt Sugar Ray Robinson im Juli 1951 beim Training in einer Pariser Sporthalle fest, kurz vor seinem Kampf gegen Randolf Turpin in England (2). Robinson verlor neun von fünfzehn Runden und mußte über dem Auge mit vierzehn Stichen genäht werden. Dieser amerikanische Schwergewichtler ist der einzige Champion, der unter zwei verschiedenen Namen den Titel gewann: zuerst 1964 als Cassius Clay, und dann, nach seiner Bekehrung zum Islam, zehn Jahre später als Muhammed Ali. Er ließ nie eine Gelegenheit aus zu verkünden, daß er der Größte aller Zeiten sei — und wahrscheinlich war er das tatsächlich. Im Kampf um den Weltmeisterschaftstitel 1964 sieht man ihn mit Sonny Liston, den

1

2

er (wie er das nannte) »ordentlich durchwalkt« (3). Die Aufnahme von Muhammed Ali beim Training entstand zwei Jahre später im Territorial Army Gymnasium, White City, London (4).

M et Mme Joe Louis se promenant dans les rues de la Nouvelle-Orléans en 1936 sous les applaudissements d'une foule admiratrice (1). Il remportait l'année suivante le championnat du monde des poids lourds pour conserver son titre jusqu'en 1949, un record en matière de longévité. En juillet 1951, Sugar Ray Robinson est surpris par le photographe Bert Hardy tandis qu'il s'entraîne dans une salle de gymnastique parisienne peu de temps avant le match qui doit l'opposer à Randolf Turpin (2). Robinson perdit neuf

rounds sur quinze et dut recevoir quatorze points de suture à l'arcade sourcilière. Ce poids lourd américain est le seul champion à avoir remporté la victoire sous deux noms : d'abord en tant que Cassius Clay en 1964, puis, dix ans plus tard, après sa conversion à l'Islam, sous celui de Mohammed Ali. Il ne perdait jamais une occasion de répéter qu'il était le plus grand champion de tous les temps, ce qui était probablement vrai. On le voit ici mettre « une bonne râclée » (selon son expression) à Sonny Liston lors du combat qu'ils livrèrent en 1964 pour le titre de champion du monde (3). Deux années plus tard, Mohammed Ali est photographié en plein entraînement au gymnase de la « Territorial Army », à White City, dans la capitale britannique (4).

THE racing driver Ayrton Senna was
such a hero in his native Brazil that
when he was killed on the racetrack in
May 1994, Brazil went into three days of
national mourning. Here he is engaged in
the Japanese (2) and the Australian (1)
Grand Prix races in 1993.

DER Rennfahrer Ayrton Senna war in
seinem Heimatland Brasilien ein
solcher Volksheld, daß drei Tage
Staatstrauer angeordnet wurden, als er im
Mai 1994 bei einem Unfall umkam. Hier
sieht man ihn 1993 bei den Rennen in
Japan (2) und Australien (1).

POUR Ayrton Senna, considéré comme
un héros par son peuple, le Brésil prit
officiellement le deuil trois jours durant
lors de sa disparition sur un circuit en mai
1994. On le voit ici disputant les Grands
Prix japonais (2) et australien (1) en 1993.

1 2

3

BRITISH racing driver Graham Hill relaxes at home in North London in 1962, watched by his wife Bette holding their daughter Bridget, and by tiny fellow competitor and son Damon (1). Over thirty years later, in 1993, the self-same son participates in the Italian Grand Prix (2). At the Monaco Grand Prix of 1992, Erik Comas leads Martin Brundle, Riccardo Patrese and Gerhard Berger (3), while in the same year Nigel Mansell and Michael Schumacher celebrate after the Mexican Grand Prix (4).

DER britische Rennfahrer Graham Hill ruht sich in seinem Haus im Londoner Norden aus, 1962, und seine Frau Bette mit Tochter Bridget im Arm sieht zu, wie Sohn Damon dem Vater Konkurrenz macht (1). Über dreißig Jahre später: derselbe Damon beim Großen Preis von Italien (2). In Monaco, 1992, liegt Eric Comas vor Martin Brundle, Riccardo Patrese und Gerhard Berger in Führung (3), und im selben Jahr feiern Nigel Mansell und Michael Schumacher nach dem Großen Preis von Mexiko (4).

LE coureur automobile britannique Graham Hill se détend chez lui en 1962, dans le nord de Londre, avec son épouse Bette, qui tient leur fille Bridget, et son tout petit concurrent de fils, Damon (1). Plus de trente ans plus tard, celui-ci participe au Grand Prix d'Italie (2). Grand Prix de Monaco en 1992 : Erik Comas mène ici devant Martin Brundle, Riccardo Patrese et Gerhard Berger (3). La même année, Nigel Mansell et Michael Schumacher fous de joie après le Grand Prix du Mexique (4).

4

Index